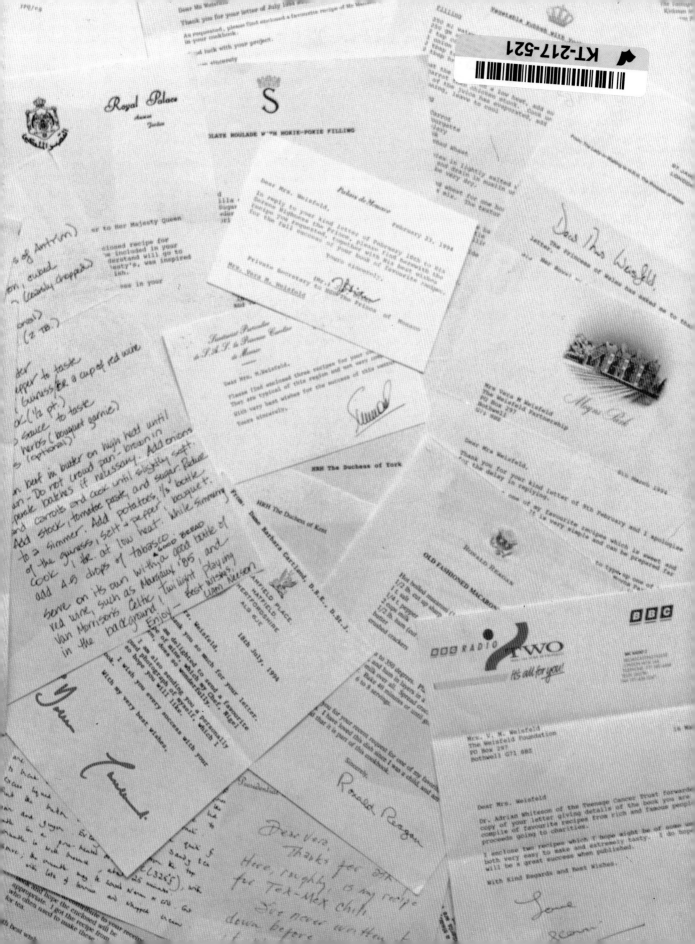

Recipes for Life

Celebrity Secrets from Around the World

Compiled by

Vera Weisfeld

Published by the Weisfeld Foundation
©Weisfeld Foundation, Glasgow, Scotland 1995.
The moral and intellectual rights of the author
are asserted.
ISBN 0 9527084 0 X

Cover: Gianni Versace
Layout: The Insider Publishing Group
Designer: John Gray
Graphic Reproduction: Mitchell Graphics, Glasgow
Photographs: The Sunday Mail Library
Printed and Bound by The British Printing Company
Edited by: Terry Houston and Eileen Crawford

THE WEISFELD FOUNDATION

WEISFELD FOUNDATION SPECIAL ACKNOWLEDGEMENT

Gerald and I sincerely thank all the kind and caring people who have contributed in any way to the compilation of this special book.
Without your help it would not have been possible.
It is our hope, that we continue to work together, through the sale of this book, to raise sufficient funds, to help people less fortunate than ourselves throughout the world.

May God Bless you all.

Vera

This book is dedicated to the memory of my parents, who raised
us with love and laughter,
and taught us to share life's blessings.

Contents

ROYAL PATRON OF THE
PRINCESS ROYAL TRUST FOR CARERS

Special Foreword

by

Her Royal Highness
ANNE
The Princess Royal

BUCKINGHAM PALACE

Following a near fatal air accident over Rio in 1990 Gerald and Vera Weisfeld decided to reassess their lives and sold their very successful business "What Everyone Wants" and dedicate their time to helping others. To do this they elected to stay in Scotland where they formed The Weisfeld Foundation. Over the past four years they have assisted numerous worthwhile causes including the Teenage Cancer Trust, The Special Olympics and latterly The Princess Royal Trust for Carers, who have benefitted enormously from their generosity.

This year Vera Weisfeld decided to seek the support of her many friends and acquaintances throughout the world to assist others less fortunate by the production of this book. She is to be congratulated on this effort and I wish her every success with this exciting new venture, the proceeds of which will all go to charity.

Anne

HIS HOLINESS
JOHN PAUL II

SECRETARIAT OF STATE

FIRST SECTION · GENERAL AFFAIRS

FROM THE VATICAN,

8 April 1994

Dear Mrs Weisfeld,

    I am directed to acknowledge the letter which you sent to the Holy Father. The sentiments which motivated your request are appreciated.

    With regard to your project, I have the honour to convey His Holiness's prayerful good wishes for your efforts on behalf of those in need.

                Yours sincerely,

                Monsignor L. Sandri
                Assessor

VERA WEISFELD   PORTRAIT: ANNE MACKINTOSH

Confessions of a Cook

LET ME BEGIN WITH A WEISFELD WARNING. This is not a conventional celebrities cookbook. It is a book about people who like good food - which isn't always one and the same thing. The man or woman who coined the phrase, "We are what we eat" knew a lot about life. When people drop their guards a little, and tell you what they really, really like to eat it's surprising just how much of their inner selves they reveal. In this book, the recipes are often dishes very public people like to prepare for themselves in their own private moments (indeed, quite a few of the recipes we received were hand-written). To my mind, that is much more interesting territory, altogether, than a standard cookery book. I hope you think so, too.

The vast majority of the recipes contributed have actually been tested for us and the remainder have been checked over by experts. But bear in mind, these are recipes largely the way individual people like to make them, and personal preferences can be variable. When you encounter, for example, Cliff Richard's favourite, a lot of eyebrows will shoot up in surprise. No, I'm not going to spoil it for you. Read the book.

As the emphasis is on people, *Recipes for Life* is categorised into its various sections by groupings of personalities, rather than by recipes. It means, of course, that every section contains a full range of dishes, progressing from soups and starters through snacks, vegetable and fish dishes, to pasta, poultry and meat dishes to desserts and cakes. There is also a Section devoted to contributions from my family and friends, as well as one covering dishes from many of the world's grand hotels. It's a "lucky dip" type of book which, hopefully, throws up something interesting or unexpected every time the reader picks it up.

It contains plenty of food for thought, too, for the serious host or hostess, frantically searching for new menu ideas. For them, the reference indices at the back should prove invaluable. One provides a full breakdown by food category, the other details the personality contributors and their favourite dishes, making it possible for anyone to devise their own special theme menus to suit any occasion. I have also included a number of suggested theme menus for special events and anniversaries. It would be quite a nice talking point, for example, to arrange a menu comprised entirely of Royalty's favourite dishes for a dinner to celebrate the Queen's official birthday; or a "political" menu to mark a function where there is to be a speech by a leading political figure.

In my own case, the big influence in my life, regarding good food and how to present it, was my mother. She was a quite extra-ordinary woman whose industriousness as a home maker rubbed off on all of us children. There were four of us - one boy and three girls - brought up by our parents in a small 'single-end' tenement flat in Coatbridge, a town in the industrial belt of Lanarkshire, Scotland. I was the middle child, and when I was six we moved to a bigger family home, still in the same town.

Like the neighbours we grew up with, we were a working class family. In those days, poverty, for larger families, was never too distant a prospect; as children we quickly learned to separate our needs from our wants. We may have had few worldly possessions, but we were rich beyond price in other directions - thanks, in large part, to our mother. As a girl in Co. Antrim, Northern Ireland, she had trained in service in the big houses of the landed gentry. When she and my father settled in Scotland, all those skills were lavished upon our home. She kept it sparkling like a new pin, and insisted we did, too.

Now I'll let you into a little secret. Although, by the standards of today, we were poor, we children probably ate better than Royalty. Mother cooked and baked to a mouth-watering standard which would match any professional chef in any of the top hotels. She regularly made for us the fine dishes she used to prepare in the big houses. Sundays were the best days. They were special family occasions. Out would come the good table linen and the napkins. Everything would be laid out just so. On a Sunday, in our house, as many as 20 of us, including relatives and mother's special friends, would sit down to a lunch rivalling anything in the land.

Sizzling roasts, fowl with delicious stuffing or accompanied by wonderful sauces were standard fare on those occasions. There might be pressed tongue, which mother would make, herself, after buying a whole ox-tongue from the butcher, and nearly always home-made pate made from the chicken livers. There would also be superb souffles and, from time to time, flambe puddings - a fiery spectacle which never failed to turn us children round-eyed with wonder. On Sunday evenings there would be another big spread for us all. Mother's baking would be laid out like a beautifully presented buffet. Apple and fruit tarts, German biscuits, the oh so difficult to make Florence cakes with their different layers of fruit, sponge and icing topping, all sitting on a very light pastry base - the list was seemingly endless. There would also be home-baked bread and scones, and home-made jams. Mrs Beeton would have met a real rival in our mum.

All this was just after the war, when food rationing for many commodities was still in force.For her doughs and mixtures, mother had to use powdered eggs, a pretty awful utility concoction invented by Government nutritionists which we children hated and would never eat. Fortunately for us, they were excellent for baking.

Another regular source of wonderment to us children were the exciting parcels which used to arrive from relatives in Ireland. Sometimes before high days and holidays, the postman would arrive with crinkly brown paper parcels, tied up with masses of string. There wasn't a great deal of mystery about their contents. Usually dangling from one end would be the neck and head of a plump chicken, turkey or even a goose . . . it certainly wouldn't be allowed these days by the postal authorities. The bird would then be plucked, cleaned and served up in great style. Guinea fowl, duck and quail would also make an occasional appearance on our table, thanks to those parcels from Ireland. Innocently, we children thought everyone ate like us, and had mothers who could turn their hand to anything, from baking to seamstressing.

Back then, when people didn't have much, sharing was a way of life; it certainly was in our community. Large families who had perhaps an unused ration of sugar would pass it on to neighbours who hadn't. Other commodities would also do the rounds, according to need. Mother was always a great sharer. Mind you, it would often come back to her. At the time there was no cream to be had, so every day neighbours and relatives used to save the creamy top of the milk for her when the deliveries came round. In due course, those offerings were transformed into whipped cream fillings for her pastries and cakes.

I have never forgotten those days. They were happy, happy times. In its way, this book is a memorial to my parents for all the good values they instilled in us as children by their example. I know they would approve, since every penny the Foundation receives from sales of *Recipes for Life* will be devoted to worthwhile causes.

Inevitably, in a book of this size, I haven't been able to include every single recipe we have received. Some proved to be duplicates of dishes already sent in; others have had to be omitted through sheer pressure on space. To those contributors, I extend our apologies, and our very sincere appreciation of their interest and help. At the Foundation we have been quite overwhelmed by the good will shown for this book.

It remains only for me to record the Foundation's gratitude to the hundreds of people who set aside busy schedules and devoted a slice of their time to look out and send us their favourite recipes. The messages of encouragement and support have been quite wonderful, and I can never thank everyone enough. Without them, this book simply would not have been possible.

Now let's sell a million!

Vera Weisfeld
The Weisfeld Foundation
Scotland

Bosnian children's faces tell the story: Someone cares.
Pictured are Gerald Weisfeld, Vera and son John.

The Weisfeld Foundation

THE SPANISH HAVE A WONDERFUL PROVERB ON LIFE: God writes straight in crooked lines. The year was 1990. In the thin atmosphere of the South American skies, high above the Brazilian capital of Rio de Janeiro, the DC10 passenger plane rocked violently as one of its engines exploded. Horrified passengers had barely time to register the fireball enveloping it before the aircraft plummeted like a stone towards the ground, as the pilot fought to regain control.

With flames streaming from the damaged engine, he averted disaster, manhandling the plane onto an even keel, then limped back to Rio to make an emergency landing. From start to finish, the drama took just 25 minutes - and several lifetimes for the terrified passengers.

On board were Gerald and Vera Weisfeld.

For them, it was a moment of truth which changed their lives. There and then, they vowed that if they survived they would sell off What Everyone Wants, their much loved multi-million pound retail stores empire, and devote their time to helping others. Safely on the ground, they were as good as their word. Within one month the business was sold.

What Everyone Wants had started out life as a single shop in Glasgow, Scotland, founded by Gerald whose business acumen perceived a potential gap in the market. When he was joined by Vera a few years later, they proved an unstoppable team. Gerald's financial expertise and farsighted shrewdness in reading the market, coupled with Vera's drive and energy in motivating staff and establishing stores which became a Mecca for the shopping public, saw them turn the organisation into a UK household name. When the What Everyone Wants chain was sold, the Weisfeld Foundation was created with a generous slice of the proceeds.

Thus the Weisfeld Foundation, in its present form, was born. It is fair to say, though, that the couple had long been headed in that direction. When at the helm of one of Britain's most successful retail chains, the couple had always firmly believed in putting back something into the communities which had so loyally supported them. In the early years, when they were a small company still making their way in the financial world, and profits were small, they gave in kind. At Christmas, Vera and the staff could be found parcelling up gifts for distribution to the less fortunate. "In our family we were taught to share," she says.

That viewpoint was one also shared by Gerald Weisfeld; he too, from the earliest days, insisted the company involve itself in charitable works. The giving grew along with the company. As it prospered, there were forays first into sponsorship of individual charitable projects, then into much larger donations to charities. Like everything the Weisfelds touched, it snowballed until eventually it became necessary for the couple to put their charitable work on a formal footing. They founded

Vera Weisfeld and Mother Theresa in Rome where they discussed the plight of the world's poor.

a special What Everyone Wants charitable Trust. In its final year, before being reformed as the Weisfeld Foundation, the Trust disbursed more than half a million pounds to charity, a quite staggering sum from a private organisation which funded all its charitable activities from its own resources.

The arrival of the Weisfeld Foundation meant stepping up a gear, and the couple devoting much more of their personal energies to the promotion and support of deserving causes. For one thing the Weisfelds knew beyond doubt, from years of experience with the Trust, was that there is no lack of pain, anguish, need and degradation of the human spirit in even the most affluent of societies.

The main thrust of the original company Trust's aims, as detailed in the dry as dust, impersonal language of the legal profession, is "the relief of poverty, the preservation of wildlife, the preservation and renewal of buildings of national and historic importance, the advancement of health and education, the assistance of disabled people, the encouragement of the Fine Arts and the advancement of religion."

That is but the bare bones of it. As a description of the aims and philosophy behind the present Weisfeld Foundation, it does it scant justice. First and foremost, the Weisfeld Foundation is about helping people to gain greater control over their own lives; it is also about raising the sum of human dignity, happiness and spiritual values in a world all too often deficient in those commodities.

It offers financial support on a number of levels. At a later stage this chapter will deal in specifics, outlining some of the charities the Foundation helps on a continuous basis; just as important, though, is the thinking behind that aid. There is a rationale to the Foundation's help, which falls into several broad categories.

First, there is aid to the innocents - principally young children and babies, who through no fault of their own are disadvantaged by medical conditions, deprivation, poverty or a multitude of social ills, such as addiction or violence within the home. Such children, the Foundation believes, need to be cared for and nurtured, and shown that they are loved, wanted and needed. From that encouragement flowers greater self esteem and an opportunity for them to fulfil their true potential as young men and women.

Then there are the excluded, notably the disabled, who are denied - very often simply by society's thoughtlessness - an opportunity to participate fully in mainstream living. For the disabled, although much is being done, the Foundation believes the barriers to them participating fully in today's society still remain all too numerous. Those barriers could be something as basic as the lack of a home dialysis machine, a regular home visit from a helper, or an access ramp for a wheelchair. Without such aids, many people remain condemned to an existence on the sidelines of life, as surely as if separated from it by a precipice. With those aids, their lives quite literally are transformed.

 Self worth, self help, and fulfilling personal potential . . . these are the watchwords of the Weisfeld Foundation. That ethos runs strongly through a very great deal of its work. It deals in down-to-earth, practical help, giving people the initial support and encouragement they need to triumph over dire circumstances before going on to take charge of their own lives, largely through their own efforts. Empowering people is a two-way traffic; they have to put in personal effort as well. In this life, no-one, as Vera is wont to remark, gets a free ride.

That self-help theme is to be seen yet again in one of the Foundation's most ambitious and imaginative long-term projects, the creation, in April, 1994, at Tel Aviv University, Israel, of the Vera and Gerald Weisfeld Extra-Ordinary Chair for the Economics of Peace and International Relations. That is its official title. A general public, in some ways much wiser than the academics, call it simply the Chair for Peace.

And rightly so. For that is its ultimate goal; to foster, in the first instance, peace and stability between the State of Israel and her neighbours through the medium of trade, then share that knowledge gained in the Middle East and elsewhere with others. Such studies have incalculable potential to help defuse the flashpoint areas of the world where cross-border tensions exist. From better understanding of the impact of international agreements come better future solutions. An educational research and study programme dear to the hearts of both Vera and Gerald Weisfeld - both serve on the University Trust's Board of Governors - their logic in funding the Chair for Peace is impeccable.

Political accommodations between nations, no matter how sophisticated and cleverly drawn, by their nature, tend to be somewhat artificial devices, often divorced from geographical or cultural imperatives. Trade is not. It is a natural activity, firmly grounded in the realities of life - because it is born of the people. Like a river, finding its own natural course, well established trade patterns have enduring qualities for peace which far surpass those emanating from politics. The Chair for Peace tacitly recognises this. Its stated aims are: "To conduct further research into the economic relations between nations and examine the causes and implications of economic bodies and agreements; to increase understanding of the economic and trade relations between Israel and other countries; and to further the prospects for regional economic co-operation between Israel and her neighbours." In sum, a truly awesome task; but what a grand and exciting vision it inspires.

In keeping with its belief that, as folk say in Scotland, "we're all Jock Thomson's bairns," (translation: we are all of us one family), the Foundation is also highly supportive of religious and spiritual values. It recognises that, without a spiritual dimension to life, we deny ourselves the richest part of our God-given existence. Vera Weisfeld is, herself, a Christian, whose Roman Catholic faith leads her naturally to support, through the Foundation, many different facets of Church life, ranging from charitable works to its Christian mission in many parts of the world. However, the Foundation respects all world religious faiths, and the power for good which lies within their different philosophies. It helps all charitable works on the basis of need not creed, and on whether they fall within the general aims of the Foundation. "My father taught us children that religion was the good you do in this world," says Vera. "Which religion a person followed was of lesser importance."

Lastly, there is the support the Foundation mobilises to respond rapidly to national and international disasters and emergencies. When 96 Liverpool football fans were crushed to death in the Hillsborough stadium disaster in England in April, 1989, wrecking the lives of scores of families, the Weisfelds were quick to respond with a major donation to its fund for the victims' dependants. More recently, on a trip to Rome, where the couple met with Mother Theresa, the chequebook again came out to help her work among the destitute and the dying on the streets of Calcutta in India.

For Children in Crisis, the Foundation orchestrated a massive appeal in Scotland for goods to deliver to the beleaguered population of Bosnia. Again, in that campaign, the strong streak of practicality which pervades so much of the Foundation's work asserted itself. It did more than just fill the trucks - one of which the Foundation donated - to go out in convoy with all manner of food, clothing, toys and medical supplies. The Weisfelds, accompanied by Vera's son, John, went out themselves on the trip to ensure the aid got through to the town of Tasovcici. They also wanted to see for themselves the true extent of the devastation wreaked upon the lives of innocent children and families in that merciless ethnic conflict. It is one of infinite complexity and, amid its shifting borders, has a seemingly limitless capacity to inflict horror, atrocity and death. It was a potentially hazardous trip - two Scottish aid workers have already died on mercy missions to the former Yugoslavia - but it passed off successfully and without incident, and the goods were distributed.

The Children in Crisis relief campaign is fairly typical of the hands on, sleeves up approach the Weisfeld Foundation adopts to worthy causes, particularly those on its own doorstep in Scotland. Vera Weisfeld can best be described as a lady in a hurry: she makes things happen, often at quite astounding speed. Her philosophy is a simple one: If the need is genuine and urgent, let's do it right now. In the county of Lanarkshire, not far from Glasgow, there stands a well-appointed refuge for battered women which is testament to that fact.

A few years back, as was her custom with many requests for help, Vera personally vetted the application (and woe betide anyone whose plea is other than genuine; she reads a person's character instinctively and unerringly). She attended a meeting of the woman's aid group which was seeking help. Carefully she listened to the women's stories, and the catalogues of violence, debt and drink or drug addiction which had forced them, as a last resort, to flee their homes and their partners. "Right, what do you need me to do?" she finally asked.

"We need a refuge. Somewhere we can go with the kids and know that we will be safe."

Vera nodded. Within 24 hours, a suitable property had been identified, surveyed, and an offer to purchase lodged with the estate agent handling the sale. A lot of women have reason to be glad of the speed with which that refuge became a reality.

Indeed, one of the great strengths of the Weisfeld Foundation is its lack of bureaucracy. It is blessed with the ability to respond quickly, and with a minimum of red tape, to requests it decides to act upon. In that respect, the Weisfelds are carrying on where the original Trust left off. But for the couple's intervention a few years ago, the Special Olympics staged in Glasgow almost certainly would have faced financial problems. With only weeks to go to the world's most important international sports event for the disabled, the organisers were at the end of their tether, having failed to attract major Scottish sponsorship. There was a very real danger of international teams pulling out, and the Special Olympics going ahead in much truncated form. Lack of major Scottish sponsorship was about to scythe through the event, creating exceptional difficulties for the host country organisers. In stepped the Weisfelds with a massive, six-figure sum and the Special Olympics were saved. The disabled athletes went on to captivate the hearts of all Scotland, which watched on television broadcasts many of the sporting events.

What that single donation did was much more than just save the Special Olympics. At a stroke, it advanced the cause of the disabled in Scotland by several years. It radically changed the perceptions of hundreds of thousands of Scots, who for the first time realised that here was a body of people

Have bus will travel . . . A Foundation vehicle gives youngsters and adults from a Glasgow housing scheme a chance to broaden horizons.

19

who had both the right and the inclination to stake their claim to a place in main-stream society. The Special Olympics proved to be the catalyst from which flowed many improvements. As is the way of the world, though, it is not enough, because we, the public, have short memories.

Vera and Gerald Weisfeld together make the decisions on all major bequests by the Foundation. If Vera has a favourite arena of involvement it would probably be safe to say that for her it is projects involving children. She is a major supporter of Cash for Kids, an annual campaign run by Radio Clyde, the UK's most popular commercial radio station outside of London. Every year for Christmas it throws its weight - and its airtime - behind a major drive to provide toys to children who otherwise would spend a pretty bleak festive season. It is one of the best supported charitable campaigns in the country. Vera is also President of KIND Scotland (Kids in need and distress). The Foundation supports the organisation's provision of a fully staffed residential centre, set in the quite magnificent Balbeg Country Estate near Straiton in Ayrshire. There children from deprived and distressed backgrounds are taken on probably the first real holiday of their young lives. For the first time they experience the wonders of Nature in a clean, happy, stable environment which fosters all manner of positive activities to expand their horizons and inspire personal development. Children are introduced to the benefits of good habits and healthy attitudes in an experience they remember all their lives. No-one who has ever read the children's letters to Vera and the Foundation, after a holiday at Balbeg, can fail to be moved by the simple joy that shines through them.

Other charities which benefit on a regular basis from Foundation support include the Princess Royal Trust for Carers which has set itself the goal of establishing a UK network of centres to which carers can come for advice, information and counselling to improve the lives of themselves and the people they look after. The Foundation also supports the Teenage Cancer Trust, whose Royal Patron is Her Royal Highness the Duchess of York. Both Vera and Gerald are also Patrons.

These days, because of her many commitments, Vera spends less time than previously was possible personally checking out projects or requests for support. That task devolves to her son, Michael, who also masterminds the often complex organisational and operational details involved in Foundation-supported campaigns. He might best be described as the Foundation's chief officer in the field. It can be a nerve-racking, at times gut-wrenching business. More than once, Michael's work has taken him into rough, tough city areas where, to reach the family or organisation involved, he has had to park his car several streets away from his destination, lest it be vandalised or robbed.

Inevitably, many of the stories he hears are heart-rending. One of the most harrowing and emotionally charged assignments he faced was visiting a voluntary organisation set up to help the families of murdered children. Looking at photographs of the bright young faces of child victims - many of whose cases he remembered from newspaper reports - left an indelible impression. The organisation got its financial aid, but not before being required to match it, pound for pound, from other sources.

That is often a Foundation stipulation.

The bulk of its work is related to the purely voluntary field. Being non-professional organisations, they are not always as experienced as others in finding their way round the funding circuit. By offering to match cash they raise, the Foundation gives them the extra leverage they need to gain grants from other bodies, such as local authorities. It also meets the criterion of self-help which the

Courage personified, a completely paralysed Motor Neurone victim shares a joke with Vera.

Foundation considers so important. From time to time, too, the Foundation will use its considerable behind the scenes influence to back publicity campaigns for organisations it believes should be brought to the public's notice.

Surprisingly, giving away money can sometimes be quite difficult - when the goal is effective help which will result in long-term benefit to an organisation. One such instance was a request for a Foundation mini-bus for a children's voluntary group within a sprawling housing estate, riddled with social deprivation, on the outskirts of Glasgow. Having established that the transport would hugely benefit the group's activities, and that there were volunteer drivers for it, the Foundation had no difficulty in providing a suitable vehicle. Obtaining insurance for it was another matter. The housing scheme was an insurance blackspot.

Michael knew the Foundation could have paid any heavy excess premium for the first year of use (the Foundation's policy, when providing groups with transport, is to pay the running costs for one year; thereafter, the organisation takes over that responsibility). But he also knew that it would saddle the organisation with crippling costs when the premiums came to be renewed. Another

A spontaneous kiss of gratitude from a Bosnian woman on the mercy trip.

solution had to be found. Eventually, a neighbourhood business agreed to garage the bus in secure premises - making it possible for the group to get less punitive insurance.

The story has a lighter side. One day, while driving his Porsche sports car, Michael found himself behind the new Foundation bus, packed with children, heading off on an outing. Spotting his "flash" car, the youngsters peering out of the back windows were quick to give him a cheeky version of the Churchillian salute - little knowing of the hours of head-scratching its driver had put in to get them the bus. Naturally, the episode had Michael laughing his head off. "It gives me a lift every time I see a Foundation bus on the road," he says.

As the person who vets the letters requesting help from the Foundation, Michael is well placed to notice trends. Currently, the Foundation has seen a large increase in the number of requests it gets from individuals. While these are all carefully considered, the Foundation's main work lies in helping the voluntary group sector.

It would be impossible to list all the organisations and individuals the Weisfelds have helped through the Trust and latterly, the Foundation, down the years. What is provided here is a snapshot of its work, and the rationale behind its giving. It should also be said that the Foundation does not fall into the trap of viewing areas of need through statistics. As a famous British Prime Minister once said of unemployment trends, when a man loses his job he is not a statistic, he is a disaster of one. For the Foundation, the worth of the individual is paramount. That factor is a major component of nearly every facet of its work, making it a Foundation worthy of everyone's support.

GERALD WEISFELD   PORTRAIT: ANNE MACKINTOSH

"My husband Gerald is the visionary of the partnership and
without him there would have been no successful business
or the Weisfeld Foundation"

HRH Princess Diana

Royalty

W HEN WE THINK OF ROYALTY AND THE NOBILITY, and the great State and Court occasions, we think of sumptuous spreads, and banqueting tables groaning under the weight of wonderful dishes. In olden days, swan, stork, and even gulls and seals would make an appearance on the table on special feast days. From pretty vague recollections of history lessons, the most enduring impression we have is of King Henry VIII style characters with huge appetites, sitting down to course after course. Certainly, there has been no lack of such figures down the centuries. Probably the most robust trencherman of them all was France's Louis XVI who would partake of a giant meal comprising of chicken, lamb, cutlets, eggs and ham, washed down by one and a half bottles of wine - then ride to the hunt. Sitting down to meals comprising ten dishes in the first course, followed by six in the second was not uncommon.

Compared to that, today's Royalty is modest, indeed, in its eating habits. One suspects that, given the large number of functions they are required to attend, in their off duty moments they like to get their feet up and enjoy much simpler fare. Actually, history shows that being a member of today's Royal household is a much less hazardous affair than it used to be. In Tudor times, when Sir Walter Raleigh first brought back the potato, the court kitchens, unfamiliar with the new vegetable, used to throw away the potato and serve the leaves, which are mildly poisonous.

Poisoning - either accidental or deliberate - was an ever present fear at court meals. Royalty's drinking vessels used to be lined with crystals which were supposed to change colour in the presence of poison. Charles II used to keep his personal cutlery and salt in a special locked box for precisely the same reason. Such precautions can't have been a very wonderful aid to the digestion! However, we have nothing to fear in this section; the recipes are delicious.

Our own Royalty splits into two very distinct camps on food favourites. Princess Diana loves the delicate flavours of Watercress Soup, while Prince Andrew likes the light, but extremely tasty, Smoked Trout Souffle. At the other end of the scale, the Duchess of York displays an exceptionally sweet tooth, with her love of Chocolate Roulade with Hokie-Pokie filling, while the Duchess of Kent confesses to a liking for Not So Humble Apple Crumble. Abroad, Prince Rainier opts for light Spinach Rissoles.

Among the other British contributors, from Lord Ivar Mountbatten to Lady Bute, there is a complete absence of the supposed liking by the Establishment for British "stodge." Light fish, seafood and chicken dishes predominate. Indeed, there's only one recipe, Steak and Kidney Pie from the late Lord White of Hull, who sadly died while the book was in production, which could be called truly traditional. Will this change civilisation as we know it? Very probably - and for the better.

PRINCE ANDREW

Watercress Soup

2 oz/50 g butter
2 oz/50 g plain flour
2 pints/1.2 litres chicken stock
12 oz/350 g watercress
1 pint/575 ml single cream
Watercress leaves to garnish
  (optional)

Serves: 4 to 6

METHOD

Melt the butter in a pan, add the flour and cook for a couple of minutes on a low heat, stirring gently. Slowly add the warmed chicken stock until you have a creamy consistency. Wash the watercress thoroughly and add to the pan. Cook over a low heat until the stalks are soft, stirring occasionally. This will take about 20 minutes. Remove from the heat and allow to cool, then liquidize the soup in a blender or food processor and pour it through a fine sieve. Chill, and then stir in the cream, reserving a little to garnish each portion. A few leaves of watercress, blanched, can provide additional garnish if wanted.

PRINCE ANDREW

His Royal Highness The Duke of York

Smoked Trout Souffle

METHOD

Lightly butter a $2^1/_2$ pint/1.5 litre souffle dish. Melt the butter in a pan, add the flour and cook for 1 minute. Gradually add the milk, stirring all the time until the sauce has thickened. Remove from the heat and beat in the egg yolks, smoked trout, horseradish, herbs, and salt and pepper to taste.

In a clean, dry bowl, whisk the egg whites until they form stiff peaks. Beat a spoonful of the egg whites into the sauce and then gently fold in the rest. Pour into the souffle dish and bake in an oven preheated to 180C/350F/ Gas Mark 4 for 20 minutes, or until golden brown and puffed on top. Serve immediately.

$1^1/_2$ oz/40 g butter
$1^1/_2$ oz/40 g plain flour
$^3/_4$ pint/425 ml milk
6 eggs, separated
1 packet of smoked trout
  (about 5 oz/150 g), finely flaked
2 tsp horseradish sauce (optional)
1 tbsp finely chopped fresh dill
1 tbsp finely chopped fresh tarragon
Salt and freshly ground black pepper

Serves: 6

HRH The Duchess of York   Portrait: Anne Mackintosh

Chocolate Roulade
with Hokie-Pokie Filling

SARAH

Her Royal Highness The Duchess of York

6 eggs, separated
$\frac{1}{4}$ tsp vanilla extract
8 oz/225 g cocoa powder
Double cream, to decorate (optional)
Icing sugar, for dusting

For the filling
$\frac{1}{2}$ pint/275 ml double cream
4 Crunchie bars

"Break the Crunchie bars into small pieces with the end of a rolling pin."

Serves: 6 to 8

METHOD

Line a large Swiss roll tin with greaseproof paper. Whisk the egg yolks, vanilla extract and sugar in a bowl until pale and thick, then gently fold in the sifted cocoa powder with a metal spoon.

In a separate bowl, whisk the egg whites until they stand in firm peaks. Roughly stir a quarter of the egg whites into the egg yolk mixture to lighten it, then pour this mixture into the remaining egg whites and fold in gentlywith a metal spoon. Pour into the prepared tin and spread evenly. Bake in an oven preheated to 180C/350F/Gas Mark 4 for 20 minutes, or until well risen and springy to the touch. Turn out on to a sheet of greaseproof paper dusted with a little icing sugar and carefully peel off the lining paper. Roll up loosely with the backing paper and leave to cool.

Meanwhile, prepare the filling. Whip the double cream until it forms soft peaks. Break the Crunchie bars into small pieces with the end of a rolling pin and fold into the cream. Unroll the roulade base, spread the filling over it and carefully re-roll. Transfer to a serving plate. Decorate if wished by whipping the double cream until stiff and piping it over the roulade, then dust with icing sugar.

Not-so-humble Apple Crumble

10 oz/275 g sweet shortcrust pastry

3 1b/1.25 kg apples

Zest of 1¹/₂ oranges

A generous pinch of ground cinnamon

3 cloves

Caster sugar, to taste

2¹/₂ oz/65 g unsalted butter

3¹/₂ oz/100 g plain flour

2¹/₂ oz/65 g brown sugar

1¹/₂ tsp very finely chopped fresh ginger root

"This is delicious served either hot or cold, with fresh raspberries or blackberries and whipped cream."

Serves: 6 to 8

METHOD

Roll out the pastry to just under 1/6 inch/4 mm thick and use to line a 10 inch/25 cm flan tin or ovenproof dish. Place in the refrigerator for 15 minutes and then bake in an oven preheated to 180C/350F/Gas Mark 4 for 15 to 20 minutes.

Peel and core the apples, then cut them into even wedges, about 6 per apple. Place the apple wedges in a large saucepan and add the orange zest, cinnamon and cloves. Cover with a lid and cook over a gentle heat until the apples are soft. Stir the apples from time to time to prevent them colouring, but try not to break them up. Stir in sugar to taste, then drain off the excess liquid and leave to cool. Pack the apples quite firmly into the pastry case.

Rub the butter into the flour until it has a sandy texture, then mix in the brown sugar and ginger. Spread evenly over the apples. Place the dish in an oven preheated to 160C/325F Gas Mark 3 (with the fan on if you have a fan oven) and bake until the crumble is well browned (about 25 minutes).

Barba Giuan (Rissoles)

8 oz/225 g plain flour
Salt and freshly ground black pepper
3$\frac{1}{2}$ oz/100 g butter,
   cut into small pieces
2 - 3 tbsp water
5 oz/150 g Swiss chards or spinach,
   finely chopped
1 onion, finely chopped
$\frac{1}{2}$ oz/15 g butter
1 egg
2 oz/50 g parmesan cheese,
   freshly grated
1 egg yolk, beaten
Oil for frying

Makes about 22

*"Shallow-fry the rissoles
in oil and serve hot,
accompanied
by tomato sauce."*

METHOD

Put the flour in a bowl with a pinch of salt and rub in the butter until the mixture resembles fine breadcrumbs. Stir in 2 to 3 tablespoons of water until it forms a firm dough. Cover and chill.

Cook the Swiss chard or spinach in boiling salted water until just tender, then drain thoroughly and leave to cool.

Fry the onion in the butter until golden, then mix it with the chard or spinach, egg, cheese and seasoning.Roll out the pastry thinly on a lightly floured surface and cut it into 3 inch/5 cm rounds. Put a teaspoonful of the filling on to one half of each round, brush the edges of the pastry with the egg yolk, then fold over to make a turnover. Press the edges together well to seal.

QUEEN NOOR OF JORDAN WITH HER HUSBAND KING HUSSEIN

Vegetable Kubbeh with Yoghurt Mint Dip

For the filling

1 onion, finely chopped

1 tbsp olive oil

8 oz/225 g green lentils, soaked for 3
*   hours and then drained*

2 tbsp carrot, very finely chopped

8 fl oz/225 ml water or chicken stock

2 tsp chopped fresh coriander leaves

2 tbsp finely chopped,
*   skinned and deseeded tomato*

Salt and freshly ground black pepper

Oil for deep frying

Makes about 24

For the dip

1 cucumber, peeled and grated,
*   with excess juice squeezed out*

8 fl oz/225 ml yoghurt

Juice of $\frac{1}{2}$ lemon

1 garlic clove, finely chopped

1 tbsp fresh mint, finely chopped

For the coating

8 oz/225 g carrots, chopped

8 oz/225 g courgettes, chopped

8 oz/225 g celery, chopped

8 oz/225 g leeks, chopped

1 lb/450 g cracked wheat

METHOD

To make the filling, sweat the onion in the oil over a low heat, then add the lentils, carrot and water or stock. Cook until the lentils are soft and most of the liquid has evaporated, then add the coriander and tomato, season to taste and leave to cool.

To make the coating, boil the vegetables in lightly salted water until very well done. Mince finely in a food processor and drain through muslin until all excess liquid has gone. The mixture must be very dry. Soak the cracked wheat in water to cover for 1 hour, squeeze out the excess water, then add to the vegetable mixture. The consistency should be moist but workable. Roll the mixture into walnut-sized balls and press a finger into each ball to make a well in the centre. Put a little of the filling in this well, then mould into a pear shape, ensuring that the filling is totally enclosed. Deep-fry in hot oil until golden brown, drain well on kitchen paper and serve with the dip.

To make the dip, mix together all the ingredients.

Pissaladiere

³/₄ oz/20 g fresh yeast
1 1b/450 g strong plain flour
4 fl oz/110 ml olive oil
A large pinch of salt
About ¹/₄ pint/150 ml milk

For the sauce
4 tbsp olive oil
4 large onions, thinly sliced
3 tbsp tomato puree or 4 tomatoes, skinned,
  seeded and finely chopped
Salt and freshly ground black pepper
2 garlic cloves, finely chopped
12 anchovy fillets, cut in half lengthways
2 oz/50 g stoned black olives

> *"Please find enclosed a recipe*
> *for your cookbook. It is*
> *typical of this region and not*
> *very complicated."*

Serves: 6 to 8

METHOD

Mix the yeast with 4 tablespoons of lukewarm water in a small bowl and leave to stand for 10 minutes, until frothy. Put the flour in a large bowl and make a well in the centre. Pour in the olive oil and the yeast mixture, then add the salt. Mix together, adding enough milk to make a fairly soft dough. Knead for about 10 minutes, until the dough is smooth and elastic, then place it in a bowl, cover and leave in a warm place for about 45 minutes or until the dough is almost doubled in size.

Knock down the dough and roll it out to ¹/₂ inch/1 cm thick. Place it on an oiled baking sheet and spread the onion mixture sauce (*below*) over the top, then sprinkle with the chopped garlic and arrange the anchovy fillets over the surface in a lattice pattern. Put the olives in the spaces between the anchovies. Leave to rise for 15 minutes, then bake in an oven preheated to 200C/400F/Gas Mark 6 for about 25 to 35 minutes, or until the dough is lightly browned. Serve warm.

To make the sauce, heat the oil in a large pan, add the onions and cook gently for about 30 minutes, until soft andgolden. Stir in the tomato puree or fresh tomatoes and season to taste.

Circassian Chicken PRINCE SADRUDDIN AGA KHAN

1 medium-sized chicken
2-3 cups chicken stock
8 oz/225 g white bread slices,
  cut into pieces
12 oz/350 g walnuts,
  chopped finely
1 cup milk or cream
1 tsp salt
$^1/_2$ tsp cayenne pepper
Some walnut oil,
  for decorating
Some cayenne pepper,
  for decorating

Serves: 4

METHOD

Carefully wash the chicken in cold water, then place it in a pan of boiling water, bring back to the boil, then reduce the heat and simmer gently until cooked through. Remove the chicken and leave to cool. Reserve the chicken stock.

Using 2 to 3 cups of the chicken stock, soak the bread in a bowl for 10 minutes, then drain off any excess stock before putting the bread in a liquidizer, together with the walnuts and the milk or cream. Season with salt and the cayenne pepper, then blend until quite smooth.

Remove the skin and chop the chicken into small pieces, add the walnut mixture and place in a serving dish. Decorate with trails of walnut oil and cayenne pepper. Serve cold with rice or vegetables.

Titled Gentry

LORD IVAR MOUNTBATTEN — Artichoke Hearts in Creamy Mustard Sauce

"This is the easiest of starters to prepare and one which all our guests ask how to make. When I tell them, they are amazed at the simplicity of such a delicious dish."

2 cans of artichoke hearts
$^1/_2$ pint/275 ml double cream
2 - 3 tsp grainy mustard
4 oz/110 g Cheddar cheese, grated

Serves: 4

METHOD

Drain the artichokes and place them in an ovenproof dish. Mix the cream with the mustard and half the cheese. Pour this mixture over the artichokes and sprinkle the remaining cheese on the top. Bake in an oven preheated to 180C/350F/Gas Mark 4 for approximately 25 minutes, until the cheese is bubbling, and then serve.

Carrot Souffle

2-3 1b/900 g - 1.25 kg carrots,
    chopped
1 tsp honey
2$^{1}/_{2}$ tbsp soft brown sugar
$^{1}/_{2}$ tsp grated nutmeg
2 egg yolks
1$^{1}/_{2}$ oz/40 g Gruyere cheese,
    grated (optional)
Salt and freshly ground black pepper
4 egg whites
A handful of cornflakes, crushed,
    for sprinkling
$^{1}/_{2}$ oz/15 g butter, melted

METHOD

Boil the carrots in salted water until tender, then drain. Puree them with the honey, 1$^{1}/_{2}$ tablespoons of the sugar, nutmeg, egg yolks and cheese. Season to taste. Beat the egg whites until stiff, then fold in the carrot mixture. Butter a souffle dish and pour in the mixture. Sprinkle with the remaining sugar and bake in an oven preheated to 190C/375F/Gas Mark 5 for 30 to 35 minutes, until well risen. Combine the cornflakes and melted butter and sprinkle this mixture on top of the souffle 10 minutes before the end of the cooking time.

Serves: 4

Sweet and Sour Pickled Salmon

JANET MOUNTBATTEN
Marchioness Milford Haven

METHOD

Cut the fish into 1 inch/2.5 cm pieces, removing any fine bones with tweezers. Put all the ingredients except the salmon in a large saucepan and bring to the boil, then reduce the heat. Add the fish to the pan and simmer only until it changes to a paler colour (1 to 2 minutes should be adequate). Do not let it boil. Remove the pieces of fish with a slotted spoon, place them in a large heatproof jar and pour over the cooking liquid. Cover, leave to cool and then store in the fridge for 3 days before serving.

Serve cold on a bed of lettuce, garnished with onion rings.

2 1b/900 g salmon fillet,
    skinned
$^{3}/_{4}$ pint/425 ml water
8 fl oz/225 ml cider vinegar
3 - 4 oz/75 - 110 g granulated
    sugar, to taste
2 large bay leaves,
    broken in half
5 cloves
15 peppercorns
1 tsp salt
3 small onions, sliced into rings
Fresh dill (optional)

"This attractive starter is very easy to prepare and will keep happily in the fridge for up to 3 weeks in a pickling jar. When in season, salmon trout can be used instead of salmon."

Serves: 6

Avocado Ring with Prawns

Lady Bute

"Small cubes of cooked fish or chicken may be substituted for the prawns."

1 tbsp gelatine

$^1/_2$ pint/275 ml chicken stock

3 avocados

Juice of $^1/_2$ lemon

$^1/_2$ pint/275 ml mayonnaise

$^1/_4$ pint/125 ml double cream

Salt and freshly ground
  black pepper

8 oz/225 g peeled prawns

Serves: 6 to 8

METHOD

Put the gelatine in a bowl with 4 tablespoons of cold water and set aside for a few minutes until it becomes spongy. Heat the chicken stock in a pan, add the gelatine and stir until dissolved. Do not allow it to boil or the gelatine will become stringy.

Peel, half and stone the avocado, setting aside one of the halves for garnish. Mash the avocados with the lemon juice and then mix in half the mayonnaise, the cream, and salt and pepper to taste. Stir in the gelatine mixture and pour into a 3 pint/1.75 litre ring mould. Chill until set.

Mix the prawns with the rest of the mayonnaise. Turn out the avocado ring and fill the centre with the prawns. Garnish with the reserved avocado, cut into slices or cubes.

LADY JAKOBOVITS

Wife of Baron Jakobovits, former Chief Rabbi of the United Hebrew Congregations of the British Commonwealth of Nations, London

Smoked Salmon and Mango

3 - 4 slices fresh mango
1- 2 slices smoked salmon
2 slices kiwi fruit
Lemon juice
Fresh mint leaves

METHOD

Arrange the mango slices on a serving plate and cover with the smoked salmon. Decorate with the kiwi fruit and then sprinkle with lemon juice. Garnish with fresh mint leaves and serve.

Serves: 1

GERALD CAVENDISH GROSVENOR, THE DUKE OF WESTMINSTER

The Duke of Westminster

Chicken with Apricots and Mushroom Stuffing

2 chicken breasts (see Method below)

2 oz/50 g onions, finely chopped

1 chicken liver, finely chopped

3 oz/75 g flat mushrooms, finely chopped

12 oz/350 g butter

1 egg white

Salt and freshly ground black pepper

Worcestershire sauce

3 - 4 oz/75 - 110 g white breadcrumbs

6 - 8 dried apricots

A sprig of fresh tarragon, chopped

For the mushroom and brandy sauce

$^1/_2$ oz/15 g butter

3 flat mushrooms, finely chopped

$^1/_2$ onion, finely chopped

8 fl oz/225 ml chicken stock

4 tbsp brandy

$^1/_4$ pint/150 ml double cream

Serves: 2

METHOD

Remove the breasts from a good-sized chicken, leaving them attached together by the skin in the middle. This will provide a cavity down the centre for stuffing. Fry the onions, liver and mushrooms in 2 oz/50 g of butter over a medium heat for 5 minutes, then mince or process to a paste.

Add the egg white, seasoning, a shake of Worcestershire sauce and the breadcrumbs and process again to a thick paste. Place the dried apricots down the centre cavity of the chicken breasts, overlapping them slightly. Spread a layer of the mushroom paste about $^1/_2$ inch/1 cm thick over the apricots (you may not need all of it) and sprinkle the tarragon on top.

Fold the breasts together to form a long roll and tie several times along its length with string. Place in a roasting bag with the remaining butter and tie the bag with string. Put the bag in a roasting tray and cook in an oven preheated to 180C/350F/Gas Mark 4 for 1 hour, ensuring that the chicken is immersed in the melted butter at all times. Remove from the oven and allow to rest for 15 minutes, still immersed in the butter.

To make the mushroom and brandy sauce, heat the butter in a small frying pan and saute the mushrooms and onion for 5 minutes, until softened. Add the brandy and boil rapidly for about 3 minutes, until syrupy, then add the chicken stock and bring to the boil. Simmer for about 15 minutes, until reduced by a third, then stir in the cream and season to taste. Remove the chicken from the butter and placed it on a warm serving plate. Take off the string, cut the chicken into slices $^1/_2$ inch/1 cm thick and serve with the sauce.

LORD WHITE OF HULL

PORTRAIT: ANNE MACKINTOSH

Steak and Kidney Pie

1 beef kidney, cut into 1 inch/2.5 cm pieces

$2^1/_2$ lb/1.1 kg stewing beef,
  cut into 1 inch/2.5 cm pieces.

$^1/_4$ cup all-purpose flour

3 tbsp olive oil

1 large onion, chopped

$^1/_2$ cup of dry red wine or beer

$^1/_2$ cup of water

2 beef stock cubes

2 tsp Worcestershire sauce

$^1/_4$ tsp freshly ground black pepper

pastry for 9 inch/23 cm pie crust

1 egg yolk

Serves: 4

> *"This was one of Lord White's favourite meals. His other much-loved dish was extremely simple, beans on toast."*

METHOD

Wash the kidney thoroughly and with a sharp knife remove the membrane and white parts, before dicing. On waxed paper, coat the kidney and beef chunks with flour. Heat the oil in a large saucepan over a medium-high heat, then cook the meat, several pieces at a time, until well browned. Remove the pieces as they are browned and add more oil, if needed. Reduce the heat to medium, add the onion to the pan juices and cook until tender, about 3 minutes, stirring occasionally. Stir in the wine, stock cubes, Worcestershire sauce and pepper, until the stock cubes are dissolved. Add the meat and bring to the boil, then reduce the heat to low and simmer for 2 hours or until the meat is tender. Spoon everything into a 4 pint/2.25 litre round shallow casserole dish.

To prepare the pastry, roll it out to make a circle 1 inch/2.5 cm larger than the casserole dish. Fit this loosely over the dish and trim the pastry overhang to about 1 inch/2.5 cm, then flute the edge with the prongs of a fork. Beat the egg yolk with 1 teaspoon of water, then brush the pastry with this mixture. Make slits in the top of the pie crust with the point of a knife. Place the pie in an oven preheated to 200C/400F/Gas Mark 6 for 40 minutes, until browned and bubbly. Cover loosely with foil if the crust browns too quickly.

Almond Meringue with Strawberries

"If you assemble your meringue several hours in advance of the party, it will be easier to cut. Use a knife with a serrated blade for the task."

For the meringue

4 large egg whites

8 oz/225 g caster sugar

3 oz/75 g flaked almonds, toasted

For the filling

$^3/_4$ pint/425 ml double cream, whipped

8 oz/225 g strawberries, chopped

Serves: 6 to 8

METHOD

For the filling, whip up the double cream until it is quite stiff. Set aside 8 of the best whole strawberries for decoration, and chop the rest.

Toast the flaked almonds under the grill until light brown, then set aside. For the meringue, put a piece of baking parchment onto a baking tray, and mark out two circles on it (drawing round a medium size plate with a pencil).

In a large, clean bowl whisk up the egg whites until they form stiff peaks. Then, whisking continuously, add the sugar a spoonful at a time until all of it has been used up. Sprinkle the cooled almonds through the meringue mixture, then using a large metal spoon divide it evenly between the marked circles. Smooth the mixture evenly into two rounds, at the same time working the almonds through the mixture.

Bake in a low oven 110C/225F/Gas Mark $^1/_4$ for $2^1/_2$ to 3 hours. When they are cooked the meringue rounds should lift fairly easily off the parchment when cool. If they appear very soft or marshmallow-like underneath, bake them a little longer.

To assemble, put one meringue half on a blob of cream to anchor it to a serving plate. Cover with the chopped strawberries and cream - saving about a third of the cream for decorating the top meringue. Place the top half on the filling, then pipe rosettes of cream round the edges. Put a strawberry on each rosette.

JOHN MAJOR, PRIME MINISTER OF THE UNITED KINGDOM   PORTRAIT: ANNE MACKINTOSH

Church & State

NO-ONE KNOWS WHEN THE PRACTICE OF BREAKING BREAD with our neighbours began. It is probably as old as time, itself, stretching back far beyond the dawn of recorded history. The changing of the seasons, the bringing in of the harvest and religious festivals have always been marked by special meals. Between communities and nations, the unwritten laws of hospitality have played an important role in promoting friendship and understanding between peoples. It is difficult to quarrel with someone when you have shared a meal with them in the intimacy of their home. Food is a wonderful way of cementing bonds of sharing and caring.

In great affairs of state, in business and trade, dining together is an invaluable diplomatic tool. Over the dinner table, we get the chance to see facets of people's characters and personalities which might not otherwise surface in formal office surroundings. Meals are great ice-breakers; they put people at ease, and the less formal the occasion the better. By that, I don't mean we should ignore presentation. A nicely prepared meal, well presented and served, with the correct table cutlery and accompaniments and good table decorations adds to the sense of occasion; just that fairly intimate gatherings tend to work better than the large-scale, formal banquet.

Not that banquets don't have their place in the scheme of things. They can be memorable, glittering occasions, with the ladies dressed in all their finery and the men in dinner suits. Under the chandeliers, or surrounded by tapestries and murals in some great hall, the best of them are something to tell your grandchildren about.

The instinct to celebrate major events in our lives and our societies with special meals is universal, from the camaraderie of the Mess Hall (as one offering in this Section shows) to the street parties up and down the land marking Coronations and momentous anniversaries in our history such as VE Day. Street parties are the modern day equivalent of the great feasts held in the Middle Ages. If you had attended the open air feast for the enthronement of Archbishop Nevill of York back in 1465, you would have been dining on 1000 sheep, 2000 pigs, 2000 geese, 4000 rabbits, a dozen porpoises and seals and huge quantities of fish and game. To be fair, they didn't consume it all at once; the feasting went on for days.

How important are modern communal jamborees? Very. They bind our society together in good fellowship. And they remain in the mind forever.

JOHN MAJOR, MP

Prime Minister of the United Kingdom

Onion Soup

"This is good topped with large toasted slices of French bread which have been covered with grated Gruyere cheese and grilled until golden."

8 medium onions, thinly sliced

2 oz/50 g butter

1 tbsp olive oil

1 tsp mustard, to taste

Salt and freshly ground black pepper

3 cans of consomme soup

8 fl oz/225 ml white wine

Serves: 4 to 6

METHOD

In a pan, fry the onions in the butter and olive oil until golden. Add the mustard, salt and pepper, then stir in the consomme and simmer for 1 hour. Stir in the white wine a few minutes before the end and serve hot.

Cullen Skink

ALEX SALMOND, MP

Leader of the Scottish National Party

$1^1/_2$ lb/675 g potatoes,
  boiled and mashed

1 medium smoked haddock
(about 12 - 14 oz/350 - 400 g)

$^3/_4$ pint/425 ml water

1 onion, chopped

1 pint/575 ml milk

Salt and freshly ground black pepper

1 oz/25 g butter

Serves: 4 to 6

METHOD

Boil up the potatoes in salted water, for mashing. Skin the smoked haddock and place it in another pan with the water. Bring to the boil, add the onion and simmer for a few minutes until the haddock is cooked. Take the fish out of the liquid and flake the flesh, removing all bones. Strain the cooking liquid into a clean pan, add the milk and bring to a simmer. Add salt to taste and simmer for a few minutes, then stir in enough mashed potato to thicken the soup to the consistency you prefer. Add the butter, cut into small pieces, and return the flaked fish to the pan. Add pepper to taste, heat through, then serve.

ALEX SALMOND, MP

MALCOLM RIFKIND, MP   PORTRAIT: ANNE MACKINTOSH

Layered Pancakes with Smoked Salmon

MALCOLM RIFKIND, MP

Secretary of State for Foreign and Commonwealth Affairs

2 oz/50 g plain flour

Pinch of salt

$^1/_2$ egg, beaten

4 fl oz/110 ml milk

$^1/_2$ oz/15 g butter, melted,
  plus extra for frying

For the filling

8 oz/225 g low-fat cream cheese

1 tbsp horseradish sauce

A little milk (optional)

12 oz/350 g smoked salmon,
  thinly sliced

Chopped fresh chives, to garnish

Serves: 6 to 8

METHOD

For the pancake batter, mix all the ingredients together in a blender or food processor and leave to stand in the fridge for at least 30 minutes. Heat a very little butter in a 6 inch/15 cm frying pan and pour in about 2 to 3 tablespoons of batter, tilting the pan to coat it evenly. Cook for 1 to 2 minutes, then turn and cook the other side. Cook the remaining batter in the same way - it should make 6 to 8 pancakes. For the filling, mix the cream cheese with the horseradish sauce in a bowl, adding a little milk if it is too thick. Spread 5 to 6 pancakes with this mixture. Layer with the smoked salmon, then place a plain pancake on top and press down firmly. Spread the remaining filling over the sides and cover with chopped chives. Slice like a cake and serve as a starter with a green salad.

JAMES MOLYNEAUX, MP

Former Leader of the Unionist Party, Northern Ireland

Savoury Omelette

1 tbsp plain flour

4 fl oz/110 ml milk

4 eggs, beaten

$^1/_2$ onion, finely chopped

1 tbsp chopped fresh parsley

Salt and freshly ground black pepper

1 oz/25 g butter

Serves: 2

METHOD

Mix the flour and milk to a smooth paste, then stir in the eggs, onion, parsley and seasoning. Melt the butter in a frying pan, pour in the mixture and cook gently until brown underneath. Cut in pieces and turn to cook the other side.

In Memory of the Late

John Smith, QC, MP

Labour Party Leader

Poached Salmon

Prepare the fish, filleting, or placing whole in a large fish kettle. Cover
with boiling water and allow to boil for 3 minutes. Remove the kettle
and leave the fish in the water overnight. The next day it should be a
perfectly cooked cold salmon.

TONY BENN, LABOUR MP

The Cup that Cheers

"Take one pint/575 ml of pure water and boil it in a kettle with North Sea gas. Add one tea bag from the Commonwealth, some milk, and sugar from the Third World and stir until the tea assumes a satisfying deep brown colour. Then remove the tea bag and take every hour, or more often if necessary."

PADDY ASHDOWN, MP

Tuna Fish Pie

PADDY ASHDOWN, MP

Leader of the Liberal Democratic Party

1 1/2lb/675 g potatoes

2 oz/50 g margarine

1tbsp plain flour

Salt and freshly ground pepper

7 fl oz/200 ml milk

2 oz/50 g mature Cheddar cheese, grated

7 oz/200 g can of line-caught tuna fish, drained
  (with the sign that it isn't netted)

1 tbs fresh parsley, finely chopped

3 eggs, hardboiled and roughly chopped

2 tomatoes, sliced (optional)

Serves: 2

METHOD

Cook the potatoes in boiling salted water until tender, then drain and mash them. Melt the margarine in a pan and stir in the flour, salt and pepper. Gradually add the milk and simmer until the sauce has thickened. Stir in the cheese until melted, then carefully add the tuna, parsley and hard-boiled eggs. Fold them in gently to avoid mashing the mixture. Pour it into a greased ovenproof dish. Arrange the slices of tomato on top, and cover with the mashed potato. Place in an oven preheated to 190C/ 375F/Gas Mark 5 for 20 to 30 minutes, or until golden brown. Serve with any vegetable.

"This is one of my family's favourite supper dishes."

SIR MICHAEL HIRST

Chairman of the Conservative Party, Scotland

Sole au Whisky

METHOD

Melt half the butter in a non-stick frying pan. Gently fry 4 sole fillets in a single layer for 2 to 3 minutes on each side. Remove and keep warm. Repeat with the remaining fish fillets. Melt the remaining butter in the pan, add the fennel and garlic and fry gently for 5 to 10 minutes, until softened. Increase the heat, add the whisky and stir until reduced slightly, then lower the heat and stir in the prawns and tomatoes. Simmer gently for 5 minutes, then stir in the cream and heat through. Taste and add seasoning as required. Pour the sauce over the fish and serve.

2 oz/50 g butter

8 Dover or lemon sole fillets

1 small fennel bulb, thinly sliced

1 garlic clove,
  crushed with $\frac{1}{2}$ tsp salt

4 tbsp whisky

4 oz/110 g peeled prawns

2 large tomatoes, skinned,
  deseeded and chopped

$\frac{1}{4}$ pint/150 ml double cream

Salt and freshly ground black pepper

Serves: 4

53

MAJOR GENERAL P.A.J. CORDINGLEY, DSO

Gulf Breakfast

"When I and 12,000 Desert Rats deployed to the Gulf in September, 1990, we were condemned to six months of eating composite rations. These tinned meals, containing an average of 3,500 calories a day, after a time became monotonous, there being only seven variations. Breakfast was cold meat, skinless sausages and baked beans (you could, of course, have the evening stew early if you became desperate). As the waiting for battle continued and as we moved nearer the enemy, we chose to eat twice a day, once after first light and once before sunset. Our military cooks did everything possible to improve the meals' taste but, of course, there was not a shop for 400 miles. They worked miracles and how they found eggs I do not know.

In my headquarters we always ate as a group, perhaps forty of us. The friendship which sprang up, as a result, was heart-warming and hugely beneficial to us all. We could discuss the coming war and give comfort to each other. Somehow it seemed more important in the morning, often after a long night's work, than it was at the end of the day. And with this friendship went breakfast, a fried egg on fried toast with spam or luncheon meat in batter and two skinless fried sausages, all hidden under a mound of baked beans. It sounds revolting and must have caused Desert Storm sickness, but to this day it reminds me of a dramatic, but happy, harmonious and memorable period in our lives."

Kim's Pasta

DOUGLAS HURD, MP

Former Secretary of State for Foreign and Commonwealth Affairs

"During the April, 1992, election campaign quick suppers were a must between daytime canvassing and evening meetings in the constituency. My daughter-in-law introduced us to this way of enlivening pasta. It has become very popular in the Hurd household and bears her name."

1 lb/450 g fresh or dried spaghetti

A little olive oil

$^1/_2$ pint/275 ml double cream

8 oz/225 g smoked salmon
  trimmings, cut into strips

3 tbsp chopped fresh parsley

Freshly ground black pepper

Lemon juice, to taste

Serves: 4

METHOD

Cook the spaghetti in a large pan of boiling salted water with a little olive oil, until al dente (if the pasta is fresh, it takes only about 2 to 3 minutes to cook and is much nicer). Drain the pasta in a colander and put the cream, smoked salmon, parsley, black pepper and a dash of lemon juice into the saucepan. Swirl it around over a low heat for about a minute, then put the spaghetti back into the saucepan and swirl it around again. Transfer to a large platter and serve immediately.

Major General P. A. J. Cordingley

PORTRAIT: ANNE MACKINTOSH

55

LADY THATCHER   PORTRAIT: ANNE MACKINTOSH

MARGARET THATCHER, OM

The Lady Thatcher
Former Prime Minister of the United Kingdom

Pasta with Pork and Basil

3 tbsp Parmesan cheese, freshly grated
4 tbsp fresh basil, freshly grated
1 garlic clove, crushed
Salt and freshly ground black pepper
4 pork steaks, fat removed
2 tbsp olive oil
1 oz/25 g butter
6 oz/175 g mushrooms, thickly sliced
$^1/_2$ oz/15 g plain flour
4 tbsp dry white wine
$^1/_2$ pint/275 ml chicken stock
$^1/_4$ pint/150 ml double cream
1 heaped tsp Dijon mustard
2 tbsp fresh chives, chopped
1 tbsp fresh parsley, chopped
10 oz/275 g fusilli or other pasta shapes

Serves: 4

"An undressed green salad makes a good accompaniment to this dish. Pork or beef meatballs can be substituted for the pork steaks."

METHOD

In a bowl, mix together 1 tablespoon of the grated Parmesan cheese, 2 tablespoons of the basil, the garlic and salt and pepper, then transfer this mixture to a large plate. Press the pork steaks into it on both sides to coat well.

Heat the oil in a frying pan and fry the pork steaks over a moderate heat for about 5 minutes per side, until cooked right through. Transfer the steaks to a dish, cover and keep warm. Melt the butter in the pan and fry the mushrooms for 2 to 3 minutes. Sprinkle in the flour and cook, stirring, until the fat is absorbed, then stir in the white wine. Gradually add the stock, stirring constantly, until the mixture boils and thickens. Add the cream, mustard, remaining Parmesan cheese and the parsley and chives and adjust the seasoning.

Bring a large pan of salted water to the boil and cook the pasta in it for about 8 minutes or until al dente. Drain and put it in a warmed serving dish. Arrange the pork on top, adding any juices from the meat to the sauce. Pour the sauce over, sprinkle with the remaining 2 tbs chopped basil and serve.

TONY BLAIR, MP

Leader of the Labour Party

Pasta with Sun-dried Tomatoes

1 lb/450 g fresh tagliatelle,
  fettucini or other long ribbon pasta

1 - 2 tbsp olive oil, to taste

2 - 3 garlic cloves, chopped

$^1/_2$ small jar of sun-dried tomatoes,
  cut into strips

2 tbsp capers, chopped

6 - 8 black olives, chopped

2 tbsp fresh parsley, chopped

Serves: 4

METHOD

Cook the pasta in a large pan of boiling salted water, with a drop of olive oil to prevent it sticking. This takes only a few minutes for fresh pasta, about 8 to 10 minutes for dried pasta. Meanwhile, prepare the sauce. Heat the oil in a frying pan, add the garlic and cook for a few minutes to flavour the oil. Add all the other ingredients and stir to coat them with the oil. Drain the pasta, then return it to the pan. Tip the contents of the frying pan over the pasta and toss well. Serve with a green salad.

Stewed Oxtail

BETTY BOOTHROYD, MP

Speaker, House of Commons

"Oxtail takes a long time to cook, so it is as well to cook it partially the day before. Another advantage is that it can be set in a bowl overnight, so the grease will solidify, and by morning this can be skimmed off easily. This makes the stew less rich and much more digestible."

1 oxtail, divided at the joints

1 large onion, sliced

3 carrots, diced

3 - 4 young turnips, diced

3 cloves (optional)

1 blade of mace (optional)

$^1/_4$ tsp allspice (optional)

1 bouquet garni (optional)

Salt and freshly ground black pepper

1 tbsp lemon juice

Serves: 4

METHOD

Place the oxtail in a saucepan and cover with water. Boil for 15 minutes, then drain through a fine sieve to remove the scum. Replace the meat in the pan and add the vegetables, seasoning, spices and herbs, if using. Cover with fresh water and simmer until tender, approximately $2^1/_2$ hours. Add the lemon juice and serve on a hot dish with croutons or toast fingers.

Tony Blair, MP

MICHAEL HESELTINE, MP   Steak and Kidney Pie

Deputy Prime Minister

Oil or dripping for frying
1¹/₂ lb/675 g stewing steak,
  cut into cubes
8 oz/225 g kidney, cut into pieces
  and core removed
1 medium onion, sliced
2 heaped tbsp plain flour
2 tbsp tomato puree
1 pint/575 ml beef or chicken stock
¹/₄ pint/150 ml red wine
8 oz/225 g mushrooms, sliced
2 tbsp fresh parsley, chopped
A large pinch of dried basil
Salt and freshly ground black pepper
12 oz/350 g puff pastry
Beaten egg, to glaze

Serves: 6

METHOD

Heat some oil or dripping in a deep, heavy casserole dish and briskly fry the steak cubes and kidney pieces until the meat is sealed on all sides. Add the onion and fry until softened. Sprinkle in the flour and cook, stirring, for 1 to 2 minutes until it has absorbed the fat, then stir in the tomato puree, followed by the stock, wine, mushrooms and herbs. Bring to the boil and simmer for 1 hour, or until the meat is tender but not overcooked. Adjust the seasoning and transfer the mixture to a large pie dish.

Roll out the pastry. Put a strip of pastry round the edge of the dish, brush with water and then cover with the remaining pastry. Trim the edges, then flake them with a knife and decorate the top with leaves made from the pastry trimmings. Brush all over with beaten egg and cook in an oven preheated to 200C/400F/Gas Mark 6 for 30 to 35 minutes, until well browned.

Meat Roll

President, Scottish National Party

1 lb/450 g lean steak, minced

8 oz/225 g ham, minced

1 egg, beaten

4 oz/110 g fresh breadcrumbs

Salt and freshly ground black pepper

1 tsp mustard

Serves: 4

METHOD

Mix all the ingredients thoroughly in a large bowl, then pack them into a stone cylinder jar, or a 2 lb/900 g loaf tin and cover with foil. Stand the jar or tin in a deep roasting tin and pour in boiling water to come three-quarters of the way up the container. Bake in an oven preheated to 180C/350F/Gas Mark 4 for $1\frac{1}{2}$ hours, then turn out on to a dish. Serve hot or cold. Don't let the water level get too low while in the oven.

"This meat roll is delicious with sliced beetroot. Some people like to add HP sauce to the mixture."

KENNETH CLARKE, MP

Chancellor of the Exchequer

Creme Brulee

4 large egg yolks

1 pint/575 ml double cream

Caster sugar, for sprinkling

Serves: 6

METHOD

Whisk the egg yolks in a large bowl. Bring the cream to the boil in a saucepan, then pour it over the egg yolks, whisking constantly. Return the mixture to the pan and stir over a very gentle heat until it thickens enough to coat the back of a spoon. Do not let it boil. Pour into a shallow 10 inch/25 cm long ovenproof dish and leave to cool, then refrigerate overnight. Sprinkle caster sugar over the top of the cream in an even layer about $^1/_8$ inch/3mm thick. Place the dish under a very hot grill until the sugar has melted and caramelized. Remove and allow to cool, then chill again in the refrigerator before serving.

Creme Brulee

MICHAEL HOWARD, MP

Home Secretary

4 large egg yolks

1 pint/575 ml double cream

Scant tsp vanilla essence

1 dsp caster sugar

4 oz/110 g caster sugar

(for the topping)

Serves: 6

METHOD

Heat the cream with the vanilla essence in a large, heavy-bottomed saucepan. In a separate bowl, lightly beat the egg yolks with the dsp of sugar, then pour in the scalding cream. Mix gently, return to the saucepan and heat over a very low flame, stirring continuously, until the mixture starts to coat the sides of the pan and has a thicker consistency. It will become even thicker when cold.

Pour into ramekins or a shallow, heatproof dish and allow to cool. Chill in the refrigerator for several hours, or even better, overnight. Cover the chilled cream with a generous, even layer of caster sugar, ensuring no cream is showing through from underneath. Place the dish very near the top of a grill preheated to maximum temperature - and watch it like a hawk. When the sugar topping begins to turn rich brown in patches whip it out and, when cool, chill it again. Serve cold.

"The top will be like sheet ice but will crack when attacked with a spoon."

Kenneth Clarke, MP

PETER LILLEY, MP

Secretary of State for Social Security

Old English Treacle Tart

1 lb/450 g shortcrust pastry
14 fl oz/400 ml golden syrup
2 oz/50 g fresh breadcrumbs
$1/_2$ tsp ground ginger
grated zest and juice of $1/_2$ lemon
grated zest and juice of $1/_2$ orange
2 tbsp soft brown sugar
2 tbsp double cream
1 apple, peeled, cored and grated
1 tsp butter
1 large egg yolk, beaten

Serves: 6

METHOD

Roll out the pastry on a lightly floured work surface, and then line a deep 8 inch/20 cm tart tin with it, reserving the pastry trimmings. Bake blind in an oven preheated to 190C/375F/Gas Mark 5 for 10 to 15 minutes. Remove from the oven and reduce the temperature to 180C/350F/Gas Mark 4.

Melt the syrup in a saucepan and stir in the breadcrumbs, ginger, lemon and orange zest and juice, sugar, cream, apple and butter. Mix thoroughly and pour the mixture into the pastry case. Re-roll the pastry trimmings to an oval 8 inches/20 cm long. Cut it into strips about $1/_2$ inch/1 cm wide and arrange them on top of the tart, weaving them under and over each other to make a lattice. Brush the lattice with the beaten egg yolk, then bake for 20 to 25 minutes or until the pastry is golden brown. Leave the tart to cool and then serve with whipped cream.

Lemon Souffle Pudding

SIR LEON BRITTAN, MEP

"This is a light, hot, tangy pudding which can be made quickly in a food processor."

4 eggs, separated
Grated zest and juice
* of 2 large lemons*
8 oz/225 g caster sugar
1 oz/25 g butter
2 oz/50 g plain flour
16 fl oz/450 ml milk

Serves: 4 to 6

METHOD

Put the egg yolks, lemon zest and juice, sugar, butter and flour into a food processor and process until they are thoroughly blended. With the machine switched on, add the milk through the feed tube until combined. In a bowl, beat the egg whites until they form stiff peaks, then fold them into the mixture with a metal spoon. Pour into a greased $2^1/_2$ pint/1.4 litre ovenproof dish. Stand this dish in a roasting tin and pour hot water into the tin to come half way up the sides of the dish. Bake in an oven preheated to 180C/350F/Gas Mark 4 for 35 minutes, until golden brown.

Apple Fruit Cake

EDWINA CURRIE, MP

4 oz/110 g plain flour
$^1/_4$ tsp bicarbonate of soda
1 tsp mixed spice
$^1/_2$ tsp ground coriander
4 oz/110 g wholemeal flour
4 oz/110 g margarine
6 oz/175 g soft brown sugar
2 eggs
5 oz/150 g currants
5 oz/150 g raisins
2 oz/50 g chopped mixed peel (optional)
Grated zest of 1 lemon
8 oz/225 g cooking apples,
  peeled and coarsely grated

Serves: 4 to 6

METHOD

Grease and line a deep 8 inch/20 cm round cake tin. Sift the plain flour, soda and spices into a bowl and mix in the wholemeal flour. In a separate bowl, cream the fat and sugar until light and fluffy. Beat in the eggs, one at a time, following each with a spoonful of the flour mixture. Fold in the remaining flour mixture, then the dried fruit, mixed peel, if using, lemon zest and grated apples. Spoon the mixture into the prepared tin, level the top and bake just below the centre of an oven preheated to 180C/350F/Gas Mark 4 for about $1^1/_4$ hours. Leave to cool in the tin for about 10 minutes before turning the cake out on to a wire rack to cool completely.

MICHAEL PORTILLO, MP

Minister of State for Defence

Rich Bread and Butter Pudding

8 small slices of bread, buttered
$^1/_2$ oz/15 g candied lemon
  or orange peel
2 oz /50g currants
$^1/_2$ pint/275 ml milk
2 $^1/_4$ fl oz/60 ml double cream
2 oz/50 g caster sugar
Zest of $^1/_2$ lemon, grated
3 eggs, whisked
Fresh nutmeg, grated, to garnish

Serves: 4

METHOD

Use a 2 pint/1.2 litre enamel baking dish, well buttered. Cut each slice of buttered bread in half, leaving on the crusts. Arrange a layer of bread over the base of the dish. Sprinkle over the candied peel and half the currants. Cover with a second layer of bread, and the remainder of the fruit.

In a bowl, measure out the milk. Add the double cream, and mix. Stir in the sugar and the lemon zest. In another small bowl, whisk the eggs on their own, then add to the milk mixture and stir. Pour the mixture over the bread. Sprinkle the nutmeg on top and bake in an oven preheated to 180C/350F/Gas Mark 4 for 30 to 40 minutes. Serve warm.

Ian Lang, MP

President, Board of Trade

4 oz/110 g butter, softened
2 eggs
6 oz/175 g self-raising flour
6 oz/175 g caster sugar
grated zest of 1 lemon

For the icing
4 oz/110 g granulated sugar
Juice of 1 lemon

Serves: 4 to 6

Lemon Ice Cake

METHOD

Grease a 7 inch/18 cm cake tin and line the base with greaseproof paper. Put all the ingredients for the cake into a bowl and beat until smooth. This can be done in a food processor. Transfer the mixture to the prepared tin and bake in an oven preheated to 180C/350F/Gas Mark 4 for 50 minutes, or until firm and well risen. For the icing, mix together the sugar and lemon juice and spoon it over the cake as soon as it comes out of the oven. Leave in the tin until completely cold, before removing.

"This cake freezes well."

PORTRAIT: ANNE MACKINTOSH

SIR DOUGLAS HARDIE

Former Director, Confederation of British Industry

Scripture Cake

"This recipe was supplied by my wife who obtained it from her mother, a church organist for many years. It is, of course, necessary to interpret the Biblical references in a baking context!"

1)	$1^1/_2$ cupfuls	Judges V, 25
2)	2 cupfuls	Jeremiah VI, 20
3)	5 of	Jeremiah XVII, 11
4)	2 tbsp	1 Samuel XIV, 25
5)	2 cupfuls	1 Samuel XXX, 12
6)	2 cupfuls	Nahum III, 12
7)	1 cupful	Numbers XVII, 8
8)	$4^1/_2$ cupfuls	1 Kings IV, 23
9)	2 tsp	Amos IV, 5
10)	A pinch of	Leviticus II, 13
11)	2 tsp	2 Chronicles IX, 9
12)	$^1/_2$ cupful	Judges IV, 19

Follow Solomon's advice for making a good boy (Proverbs XXIII,14) and you will have a good cake. In case you require it, a 'crib' of the ingredients appears near the end of the Business Section.

Macaroons

JAMES CALLAGHAN

Lord Callaghan of Cardiff, KG
Former Labour Prime Minister

METHOD

Beat all the ingredients together very thoroughly until a smooth dough is formed. This can be done in a food processor. Break off small pieces of dough, roll them into balls and place them well apart on a baking tray lined with oiled greaseproof paper. Bake in an oven preheated to 220C/425F/Gas Mark 7 for 6 to 7 minutes, until they are golden but spongy to the touch. Cool on a wire rack before peeling off the paper.

4 oz/110 g ground almonds
$^1/_4$ tsp almond essence
3 oz/75 g icing sugar
1 egg white

**Makes about
18 macaroons**

THE MOST REVD. GEORGE L. CAREY

Archbishop of Canterbury

Chocolate Meringue Cake

For the cake

4 egg whites

8 oz/225 g caster sugar

For the chocolate buttercream

*6 oz/175 g good quality plain
  chocolate*

3 egg whites

6 oz/175 icing sugar

*10 oz/275 g unsalted butter,
  softened*

4 oz/110 g flaked almonds

Icing sugar, to decorate

METHOD   Serves: 6 to 8

Line 2 large or 4 small baking trays with Bakewell paper. To prepare the meringue bases, in a bowl whisk the 4 egg whites until stiff but not dry. Add 2 tablespoons of the sugar and keep whisking until very stiff and shiny. Fold in the remaining sugar. Divide the mixture into 4 and spread thinly on the Bakewell paper into circles about 7 inches/18 cm in diameter. Bake in an oven preheated to 130C/250F/Gas Mark $\frac{1}{2}$ for about $1\frac{1}{2}$ hours, until crisp and dry. Peel off the paper and leave to cool on a wire rack.

For the buttercream, melt the chocolate in a soup plate set over a pan of hot water. Whisk the 3 egg whites and sugar together in a bowl set over a pan of simmering water until the mixture is stiff, smooth and shiny. In a separate bowl, beat the butter until light and creamy, then gradually beat in the egg mixture. Fold in the melted chocolate. Sandwich the meringue discs together with the filling and then spread the top and sides with the remaining cream. Completely cover the sides with the toasted almonds.

———— Sayings to Keep You Sane ————

In everyone's life there are periods when you wonder if things are ever going to get better, or if you are ever going to win through to the light at the end of the tunnel. I've had my fair share of the bad times, as well as the good. It is simply not possible to raise two young children on your own while being the family's sole breadwinner without coming close to the end of your tether. In times of stress, I developed my own ways of coping with life's ups and downs. For example, when the children were young, there was my "Indian war dance" when I would go whooping and dancing round the living room, stamping my feet, tearing up paper and letting off steam. It's amazing how therapeutic it proved. It certainly seemed to work for me. I brought up two boys without ever raising a voice or lowering a hand to them.

A lot of the time, though, I relied on the wise sayings I picked up from people like my mother to gain a better perspective on a problem or situation. In fact, my friends often refer to them as "Vera-isms." Here's just a couple to be going on with. "Never forget the bowl you were baked in," reminding us always to remember where we came from. Another great one was, "Learn to separate your needs from your wants."

There is great wisdom in simplicity. Such sayings have a habit of getting your feet back firmly on the ground . . . until you need the next one!

Vera Weisfeld

International Statesmen

Cream of Vegetable Soup

2 medium onions, finely chopped

2 tbsp olive oil

2 or 3 courgettes, diced

2 or 3 carrots, diced

8 oz/225 g pumpkin flesh, chopped

1 or 2 tbsp chopped fresh celery,
  parsley and dill leaves

$1/_2$ chicken stock cube

Salt and freshly ground black pepper

2 or 3 tsp rolled oats

1 large turkey wing or 2 chicken wings

Serves: 4

In Memory of

YITZHAK RABIN

Prime Minister of Israel

A man with a clear vision for peace

METHOD

Fry the onions in the oil until light golden brown, then add all the other vegetables and cook gently for a couple of minutes. Cover the vegetables with water. Add the herbs, chicken stock cube and seasoning and bring to the boil, then add the oats and turkey or chicken wings. Cook for about 30 minutes (or for 15 minutes in a pressure cooker). Cool slightly, then discard the poultry skin and bones and most of the herbs. Puree the soup in a blender, return to the pan and reheat gently.

PAUL KEATING

Prime Minister of Australia

6 boneless, skinless chicken breasts

2 oz/50 g plain flour,
  seasoned with salt and pepper

4 oz/110 g butter

3 fl oz/75 ml lemon juice

Zest of 1 lemon

Salt

Freshly ground black pepper

Serves: 6

Lemon Chicken

"Serve with a selection of steamed fresh vegetables."

METHOD

Dredge the chicken breasts with the seasoned flour, then place them in a buttered ovenproof dish. Melt the butter in a pan and stir in the lemon juice and zest and seasoning. Bring the mixture almost to the boil, stirring well, then pour it over the chicken. Bake in an oven preheated to 200C/400F/Gas Mark 6 for 20 minutes, then turn the chicken breasts and cook for a further 20 minutes.

DR JOHN HEWSON

Leader of Opposition, Australia

Steak, Chips and Salad

"Simply the best."

Take one piece of fillet steak, place it on a grill and cook to medium. Season with crushed black peppercorns while cooking, then remove from the grill and transfer to a hot plate. Garnish with a teaspoon of hot English mustard and serve with a fresh garden salad, lots of freshly ground black pepper and French fries.

Serves: 1

Ginger Ice Cream Cake

CHRIS PATTEN

Governor of Hong Kong

METHOD

To make the meringue, whisk the egg whites until stiff. Gradually add the sugar, whisking thoroughly between each addition. Fold in the vinegar. Pipe three 8 inch/20 cm circles of meringue on to baking sheets lined with Bakewell paper and place them in an oven preheated to 140C/275F/Gas Mark 1 for 1½ hours, or until dry. Remove them from the oven, cool on a wire rack, then peel off the Bakewell paper.

For the meringue

4 egg whites

8 oz/225 g caster sugar

½ tsp vinegar

For the filling

¾ pint/425 ml double cream

1¾ pints/1 litre ice cream

6 oz/175 g preserved stem ginger,

 finely chopped

Serves: 10 to 12

For the filling, whip the cream into soft peaks. Soften the ice cream so that it can be easily scooped. Place one meringue circle on a serving dish, spread it with a quarter of the whipped cream and sprinkle with half the chopped ginger. Spoon half the ice cream over the ginger in an even layer, then cover with a second meringue circle. Spread with a quarter of the cream, sprinkle with the rest of the ginger and cover with the remaining ice cream. Place the third meringue circle on top. Cover the top and the sides with the remaining cream, piping it around the top edges of the cake to give a good finish. Place in a freezer. Remove from the freezer 15 minutes before serving.

"This is a real favourite at Government House and is served at all sorts of occasions, from family birthdays to state dinners."

RONALD REAGAN

US Politics

PINNING DOWN POLITICIANS TO A DECISION can be a difficult business, but one thing always gets their vote - good food. Virtually every State Governor in the USA is represented in this American political section, as well as several former Presidents and First Ladies. The result is a wide selection of - to the European palate - unusual and adventurous American dishes which go a long way to disproving the claim so often made that the USA's taste in food is rather bland. There's hardly a tomato ketchup bottle in sight!

A number of the recipes are for popular local State dishes. Within the main courses, the ones I found most intriguing were for some of the chicken dishes, in particular raspberry chicken. The combination of the fruit's tartness with light corn syrup and the more delicate tastes of chicken, which, at any time, takes flavours wonderfully from short marinades or when cooked with sauces, is an inspired choice. Don't ignore the barbecue dishes, either. The secret to their success lies in the barbecue sauces, which is a whole folklore in its own right. The recipes for them are often handed down in families from generation to generation - the ingredients a jealously guarded secret.

The famous American sweet tooth is also well to the fore. This section contains a large number of desserts, from Mississipi Mud Cake to many apple dishes, and of course, cookies. And don't miss the sub-section on world politics, in which Chris Patten, the United Kingdom's Governor of Hong Kong, confesses all on his secret passion . . . Ginger Ice Cream Cake.

One cautionary note. Make sure you have all the ingredients for some of these dishes before you start. Not all the herbs and spices are standard to non-American kitchens. You may have to do a little sleuthing to acquire them or their equivalent. Some of the recipes have had to be altered slightly because certain ingredients aren't available here. However, these days, in addition to delicatessens and ethnic specialist shops, good major supermarkets carry a surprisingly large range of non-European and North American ingredients.

E. BENJAMIN NELSON

Governor of the State of Nebraska, USA

Chip Dip

"Good luck with your project. I hope this recipe is of help to you."

$1/_2$ can of chilli sauce
8 oz/225 g cream cheese, softened
4 fl oz/110 ml mayonnaise
2 oz/50 g chopped onion
2 tsp horseradish
1 can of shrimps, drained and rinsed

METHOD

Blend the chilli sauce into the cream cheese. Mix in the rest of the ingredients, then add the shrimps carefully. Chill until ready to serve.

Serves: 4

Squash Souffle

JOHN G. ROWLAND

Governor of the State of Connecticut

"Serve this as an accompaniment to roast turkey or chicken."

12 oz/350 g butternut squash, peeled,
  deseeded and cut into cubes
$1/_2$ pint/275 ml double cream
3 eggs
2 oz/50 g butter, melted
1 oz/25 g granulated sugar
1 oz/25 g plain flour
A pinch each of salt and ground cinnamon

METHOD

Cook the butternut squash in boiling salted water until very tender, then drain and leave to cool. Put the squash, cream, eggs and melted butter in a blender or food processor and blend to a puree. Add the sugar, flour, salt and cinnamon and process until well combined. Pour the mixture into a greased 2 pint/1.2 litre casserole dish and bake in an oven preheated to 180C/350F/Gas Mark 4 for 45 to 60 minutes, covering the top with aluminium foil for the last 15 minutes if it browns too quickly. Serve immediately.

Serves: 6

Broccoli and Cheese Quiche

TOMMY G. THOMPSON

Governor of the State of Wisconsin, USA

METHOD

Arrange the broccoli and cheese in the pastry case. Beat together the eggs, cream and seasoning in a bowl, then pour this mixture over the cheese and broccoli. Bake in an oven preheated to 180C/350F/Gas Mark 4 for 35 to 40 minutes, or until the top is golden brown and a knife inserted 1 inch/2.5 cm from the edge comes out clean.

8 oz/225 g broccoli, chopped
6 oz/175 g Cheddar cheese, grated
Prebaked 10 inch/25 cm pastry case
4 eggs
12 fl oz/350 ml single or double cream
$1/4$ tsp salt
A pinch of pepper
A pinch of nutmeg

Serves: 8

MICHAEL O. LEAVITT

Governor of the State of Utah

Golden Cheese and Ham Bake

5 slices of soft bread, cut into $1/2$ inch/1 cm cubes
12 oz/350 g Cheddar cheese, grated
8 oz/225 g ham, chopped
6 eggs, lightly beaten
$1/2$ tsp mustard powder
$3/4$ pint/425 ml milk
$1/2$ tsp salt
A pinch of cayenne pepper
A dash of Worcestershire sauce
1 small onion, finely chopped

Serves: 4

METHOD

Put the bread in a casserole dish and sprinkle over the cheese and ham. Beat together all the remaining ingredients and pour the mixture over the bread and cheese. Cover with foil and refrigerate for 8 hours or overnight. Remove the foil and bake in an oven preheated to 180C/350F/Gas Mark 4 for 45 minutes.

BILL WELD

Governor of the State of Massachusetts

Eggs a la Bill

2 eggs
2 tbsp milk
salt
Freshly ground black pepper
2 tbsp orange juice
$^1/_2$ oz/15 g butter or margarine

Serves: 1

METHOD

Put all the ingredients except the butter or margarine in a bowl and mix well. Melt the butter in a frying pan and pour in the egg mixture. With a wooden fork, scramble the eggs over a low heat. Serve with two slices of toast, and sausages or bacon.

"A fast and filling breakfast."

Kentucky Hot Brown

BRERETON C. JONES

Governor of the State of Kentucky

"Always serve piping hot."

METHOD

Place a slice of toast in each of 6 individual heatproof dishes, cover with the chicken slices and top with the remaining toast. Melt $2^1/_2$ oz/65 g of the butter in a pan and stir in the flour. Gradually add the milk, stirring constantly, until thick and smooth. Blend in the egg yolks, then the cheese and the remaining butter. Season to taste. Divide this sauce between the baking dishes, then criss-cross 2 rashers of bacon over each one. Sprinkle a little Parmesan cheese over them and place under a hot grill until golden brown.

12 slices of white bread, toasted
12-18 slices of cooked chicken
  or chicken breast roll
3 oz/75 g butter
1 oz/25 g plain flour
$1^1/_4$ pints/750 ml milk
2 egg yolks, beaten
$1^1/_2$ oz/40 g Parmesan cheese, freshly grated,
  plus extra for sprinkling
Salt and freshly ground black pepper
12 rashers of bacon, cooked and drained

Serves: 6

Mount Diablo Dip

STEPHEN MERRILL

Governor of the State of New Hampshire

3 to 4 ripe avocados

$^1/_2$ tsp chilli powder

1 tsp paprika

$^1/_2$ tsp cayenne pepper

$^3/_4$ pint/425 ml soured cream

1 green pepper, finely chopped

2 ripe tomatoes, chopped

5 spring onions, chopped

4 oz/110 g pitted black olives, sliced

8 oz/225 g Cheddar cheese, grated

1 large bag of tortilla chips

Serves: 4 to 6

METHOD

Peel, stone and mash the avocados and put them in a large shallow heatproof dish. Mix the spices with the soured cream and spread on top of the avocados. Layer the green pepper, tomatoes, spring onions and olives on top of the cream. Cover with the cheese and place under a hot grill until the cheese is bubbling.

"Tastes great when served with tortilla chips."

BOB MILLER

Governor of the State of Nevada

Silver State Potatoes

METHOD

Boil and grate the potatoes. Combine all the other ingredients in a pan except the potatoes. Simmer over a low heat until the cheese melts, then stir in the potatoes and place in a lightly greased baking dish. For the topping, mix the crushed cornflakes with the melted butter. Sprinkle on top of the potato mixture and bake in an oven preheated to 350F/180C/Gas Mark 4 for 40 to 45 minutes, until golden brown. This dish freezes and reheats extremely well.

Serves: 4

16 fl oz/450 ml soured cream

1 tbsp salt

4 tbsp milk

2 oz/50 g butter

10 oz/275 g can of cream
* of chicken soup*

2 oz/50 g Cheddar cheese, grated

1 small onion, chopped

1 lb/900 g kg potatoes, peeled,
* boiled and grated*

For the topping

$1^1/_2$ oz/40 g cornflakes, crushed

1 oz/25 g butter, melted

WALTER J. HICKEL

Governor of the State of Alaska

Salmonburgers

"A very tasty dish."

1 lb/450 g fresh or canned salmon, cooked
2 medium potatoes, grated
2 eggs
1 medium onion, minced
Salt and freshly ground black pepper, to taste

METHOD

Mix together all the ingredients to make a soft batter, then fry as hamburgers, in a little butter or oil, allowing sufficient time to cook the potato.

Serves: 2

Seafood Gumbo a la Edwin Edwards

EDWIN W. EDWARDS

Governor of the State of Louisiana

METHOD

Heat the oil in a pan, add the flour and cook over a moderate heat, stirring constantly, for about 15 minutes to make a dark roux. Add the onions, garlic and green pepper and fry until limp. Add the sausage and cook for a few minutes, then add the water, stirring well. Bring to the boil and cook over a medium heat for $1^1/_2$ to 2 hours. Stir in the prawns and crabmeat and cook for a few minutes. Season with salt, pepper, cayenne and file powder to taste. Sprinkle with the parsley and serve with rice.

NOTE: *To make gumbo, you need file powder, a special Cajun spice mix available in some delicatessens. If you can't obtain it, you can make up your own by mixing together 1 teaspoon each of garlic powder, salt and ground white pepper, $^1/_2$ teaspoon each of dried oregano and thyme and $1^1/_2$ teaspoons of paprika.*

2 tbsp oil
2 tbsp plain flour
2 large onions, chopped
2 garlic cloves, chopped
$^1/_2$ green pepper, chopped
1 lb/450 g Andouille sausage or
  other well flavoured sausage,
   cut into slices 1 - 2 inches/2.5 - 5 cm thick
3 pints/1.5 litres water
$2^1/_2$ lb/1.1 kg small prawns, shelled
8 oz/250 g crabmeat
Salt and freshly ground black pepper
Cayenne pepper, to taste
File powder, to taste
3 - 4 sprigs of fresh parsley, chopped

Serves: 4 to 6 *

*We have cut back on the original recipe quantities to serve a smaller number of people.

78

Shrimp Boil

MIKE LOWRY

Governor of the State of Washington

3 pints/1.5 litres water

3 bay leaves

A few peppercorns

1 tsp mustard seed

$^1/_2$ tsp dried basil or 3 fresh basil leaves, chopped

2 whole cloves

A pinch of cumin seeds

1 tsp dried red pepper flakes

A pinch of celery seeds

A pinch of fennel seeds

A pinch of caraway seeds

$^1/_2$ tsp dried marjoram

$^1/_2$ tsp dried thyme

1 small onion, chopped

2 celery sticks, chopped

2 garlic cloves, finely chopped

$^1/_2$ lemon, coarsely chopped

2 tsp sea salt

2 tsp cayenne pepper

2 tsp Worcestershire sauce

4 fl oz/110 ml dry white wine

1 lb/450 g peeled prawns

For the Cajun sauce dipping

$1^1/_2$ tbsp wine vinegar

2 tbsp Creole or Dijon mustard

$^1/_2$ tsp horseradish sauce

$^1/_2$ tsp paprika

2 tbsp salt

Freshly ground black pepper

6 tbsp olive oil

1 celery stick, very finely chopped

2 green onions, very finely chopped

2 tbsp fresh parsley, chopped

> *"This seafood dish
> is a big favourite
> of mine."*

METHOD

Bring the water to the boil in a large pan and add all the ingredients except the prawns. Simmer for 30 minutes. Add the prawns and cook for a further 5 minutes. Serve with the cajun sauce.

SAUCE

For the Cajun sauce, combine the vinegar with the mustard, horseradish, paprika, salt and pepper. Gradually add the olive oil, whisking vigorously, then stir in the celery, onions and parsley.

NOTE. *Quantities have been reduced from the original recipe*

Serves: 4

Rhode Island Clam Chowder

LINCOLN ALMOND
Governor of the State of Rhode Island and Providence Plantations

1 small onion, finely diced

1 stalk of celery, diced

2 tbs butter, melted

12 canned clams, chopped
 (liquid reserved)

8 fl oz/225 ml clam juice

1 1/4 pint/725 ml chicken stock

2 medium potatoes, coarsely diced

2 oz/50 g butter, melted

2 oz/50 g flour

8 fl oz/225 ml milk

5 fl oz/150 ml double cream

A dash of thyme

A dash of salt

A dash of white pepper

METHOD

In a large saucepan, saute the onion and celery in butter until transparent. Add the liquid from the clams, the clam juice, stock and potatoes. Simmer until the potatoes are tender. In a separate pan, over a low heat, add the butter and stir in the flour until the mixture is smooth. Do not brown. Transfer the flour mixture to the main stock, and stir in gently. Add the clams, milk and cream and stir gently, over a medium heat. When the sauce starts to thicken, season to taste. Continue to stir until it is the consistency you want, then serve.

"Take care to use a medium heat."

Serves: 4

GASTON CAPERTON
Governor of the State of West Virginia

Poached Salmon with Courgettes

4 salmon steaks, $^1/_2$ inch/1 cm thick

$^1/_4$ pint/150 ml dry white wine

$^1/_4$ pint/150 ml water or fish stock

1 lb/450 g courgettes, cut into matchsticks

Salt and freshly ground black pepper

2 tsp chopped fresh basil

Sprigs of basil, to garnish

METHOD

Place the salmon in a large saucepan and add the wine and water or stock. Bring to a gentle simmer, then cover and poach for 4 to 5 minutes, turning the steaks after three minutes. Steam the courgettes in a vegetable steamer for 2 to 3 minutes, then transfer to a bowl, season and toss gently with the chopped basil. Transfer to serving plates and top with the poached salmon. Garnish with sprigs of basil.

Serves: 4

RONALD REAGAN

Former President of the United States of America

Old-fashioned Macaroni and Cheese

8 oz/225 g macaroni

8 oz/225 g sharp Cheddar cheese,
  sliced or grated

1 tsp salt

$^1/_4$ tsp freshly ground black pepper

8 oz/225 g ham, cut into chunks

$^3/_4$ pint/425 ml milk

Crushed crackers or other savoury biscuits

A knob of butter

Serves: 4

METHOD

Cook the macaroni in a large pan of boiling salted water until just tender, then drain well. Place the macaroni, cheese, salt, pepper and ham in layers in a buttered casserole dish and pour the milk over the mixture. Sprinkle the cracker crumbs over the top and dot it with butter. Bake in an oven preheated to 180C/350F/Gas Mark 4 for 40 minutes or until golden brown. Serve hot.

"Thank you for your request for one of my favourite recipes. I have loved this dish since I was a child, and am pleased that it is part of this cookbook."

Wild Rice Casserole

ARNE H. CARLSON

Governor of the State of Minnesota

METHOD

4 oz/110 g butter

6 oz/175 g wild rice

2 oz/50 g flaked almonds

8 oz/225 g small button mushrooms

2 tbsp chopped fresh chives or spring onions

16 fl oz/450 ml chicken stock

Serves: 4

Wash the rice in several changes of cold water, discarding any chaff, then drain thoroughly. Melt the butter in a heavy frying pan and add all the ingredients except the chicken stock. Stirring constantly, cook until the rice turns yellow. Place the contents in a casserole dish and stir in the chicken stock. Cover tightly and bake in an oven preheated to 160C/325F/Gas Mark 3 for 1 hour.

"Luxurious wild rice was the staple food of the Indians in the northern lake country of Minnesota and Canada. One of the world's rare flavours, it costs little to serve. An ounce (25g) of dry rice cooks up to a generous serving that lends an aristocratic touch to any meal. It is often served at the Minnesota Governor's residence."

Chicken with Barbecue Sauce

---

*"This is one of our favourite recipes. Any leftover sauce
can be kept in the fridge or frozen."*

---

3 lb/1.25 kg chicken, quartered

1 large garlic clove, crushed

1 tsp salt

$^1/_2$ tsp freshly ground black pepper

1 tbsp oil

3 tbsp lemon juice

Serves: 4

For the barbecue sauce

4 tbsp cider vinegar

$^3/_4$ pint/425ml water

6 oz/175 g granulated sugar

4 oz/110 g butter or margarine

5 tbsp Dijon mustard

2 onions, coarsely chopped

$^1/_2$ tsp each of salt and
  freshly ground black pepper

4 fl oz/110 ml Worcestershire sauce

1 pint/575 ml tomato ketchup

6 - 8 tbsp lemon juice

Cayenne pepper, to taste

METHOD

Put the chicken pieces, garlic, seasoning, oil and lemon juice in a strong plastic bag, seal and then shake to coat well. Refrigerate for 24 hours, turning the bag frequently. Remove the chicken pieces from the bag, place it on a barbecue (or under a hot grill), skin-side up, and cook until well browned, basting it with the marinade from the bag. Turn and cook the other side. About 20 minutes before the chicken is fully cooked, start to baste it with the barbecue sauce. The chicken can also be cooked in an oven preheated to 200C/400F/Gas Mark 6.

To make the barbecue sauce, put the vinegar, water, sugar, butter or margarine, mustard, onions, salt and pepper into a large pan and bring to the boil. Reduce the heat and cook slowly for about 20 minutes, until the onion is tender. Add the Worcestershire sauce, tomato ketchup, lemon juice and cayenne and simmer gently for 45 minutes. Taste for further seasoning

THOMAS R. CARPER

Governor of the State of Delaware

1 chicken, skinned and cut into serving pieces
Salt and freshly ground black pepper
3 oz/75 g butter
4 celery sticks, chopped
6 oz/175 g olives, sliced
1 small red pepper, sliced
4 oz/110 g mushrooms, chopped
1 garlic clove, crushed
1 tbsp plain flour
8 fl oz/225 ml sherry
$1/_4$ pint/150 ml chicken stock

Chicken New Orleans

METHOD

Season the chicken pieces with salt and pepper, then heat the butter in a frying pan and cook the chicken until browned on all sides. Remove it from the pan. Put the celery, olives, red pepper, mushrooms and garlic in the pan and fry until softened. Stir in the flour and cook for 3 minutes, then stir in the sherry and stock. Return the chicken to the pan, cover and simmer for about 20 minutes, until the chicken is tender. Serve with rice.

Serves: 4

"Delaware is noted for its poultry industry and some of the First Family's favourite dishes are made with chicken."

Chicken in Orange Sauce

METHOD

Sprinkle the chicken breasts with salt, then heat the butter in a pan, add the chicken and cook until browned all over. Remove the chicken from the pan and set aside. Add the flour, cinnamon, cloves and $1^1/_2$ teaspoons of salt to the juice in the pan and stir to make a smooth paste. Add the orange juice and Tabasco and cook, stirring constantly, until the mixture thickens and comes to the boil. Add the chicken, almonds and raisins, then cover and simmer over a low heat for 45 minutes or until the chicken is tender. Add the mandarin oranges for the last 5 minutes of cooking time. Serve with rice.

Serves: 4

JOHN A. KITZHABER

Governor of the State of Oregon

4 boneless chicken breasts
salt
2 oz/50 g butter
2 tbsp plain flour
$1/_8$ tsp cinnamon
2 cloves
12 fl oz/350 ml orange juice
$1/_4$ tsp Tabasco sauce
2 oz/50 g almonds, chopped
3 oz/75 g raisins
10 oz/275 g can of mandarin oranges, drained

"Annabel Kitzhaber, the Governor's mother, has assured me this is his favourite meal."

DON SUNDQUIST

Governor of the State of Tennessee

Poppy Seed Chicken Casserole

4 boneless chicken breasts,
  cooked until tender
2 cans cream of chicken soup
4 fl oz/110 ml soured cream
36 Ritz crackers, crushed
1 tbsp poppy seeds

For the topping
36 Ritz crackers, crushed
2 tbsp poppy seeds
3 oz/75 g margarine

Serves: 4

METHOD

Cut the chicken into small pieces, and fry in a pan with a little margarine. When cooked to tenderness, place in a 9 x 13 inch/23 x 33 cm ovenproof dish. Add the soup, soured cream, most of the crackers and the poppy seeds. For the topping, sprinkle the remaining cracker crumbs over the casserole, followed by some more poppy seeds. Melt the margarine and drizzle it over the mixture and bake in an over preheated to 160C/325F/Gas Mark 3 for 30 minutes.

Raspberry Chicken

CHRISTINE TODD WHITMAN

Governor of the State of New Jersey

"Test for tenderness before removing from the oven."

12 oz/350 g raspberries
3 fl oz/75 g light corn syrup
2 tbsp lemon juice
1 tbsp corn starch
$\frac{1}{2}$ tsp salt
A dash of freshly ground black pepper
3 chicken breasts, boned, skinned and halved

Serves: 4 to 6

METHOD

Place 8 oz/225 g of the raspberries, the corn syrup and the lemon juice in a blender and blend on high until smooth. In a small pan, stir together the corn starch, salt and pepper. Gradually stir in the raspberry mixture until smooth, then, stirring constantly, bring to a boil over a medium heat and boil for 1 minute. Arrange the chicken and the remaining raspberries in a greased 10 x 6 x 2 inch/ 25 x 15 x 5 cm baking dish. Spoon the sauce over the chicken. Bake in an oven preheated to 200C/ 400F/Gas Mark 6 for 25 to 35 minutes or until the chicken is tender.

Marinated Chicken Breasts

DAVID WALTERS
Governor of the State of Oklahoma

12 fl oz/350 ml pineapple juice
4 oz/110 g sugar
2 fl oz/50 ml soy sauce
1 tsp garlic powder
1 glass of sherry, dry
1 tsp ginger, powdered
4 tbs red wine vinegar
6 boned chicken breasts

For the rice
1 lb/450 g Basmati rice
4 oz/110 g mushrooms, finely chopped
Salt, to taste
1 bay leaf

Serves: 6

METHOD
In a large bowl, mix together all the ingredients, except the chicken. Reserve one cup of the marinade and pour the remainder over the the chicken breasts. Marinate for at least 12 hours, or overnight, from time to time spooning the liquid over the meat. The following day, cook over a charcoal grill, turning regularly until cooked through and nicely browned.

For the rice, after washing in several changes of water, drain thoroughly, and transfer to a pan. Pour in the marinade, stir once to ensure the grains are well coated, and leave to absorb for 30 minutes. Add the chopped mushrooms and bay leaf, then pour in enough water to cover, season and stir once. Bring to the boil, then simmer until the liquid is absorbed. Drain and beat the rice with a fork to make it light and fluffy.

PETE WILSON
Governor of the State of California

4 skinless part-boned chicken breasts
3 tbsp Dijon mustard
$^1/_4$ pint/150 ml Paul Newman
  Italian salad dressing
Juice of $^1/_2$ lemon

Serves: 4

Barbecued Chicken

METHOD
Slash the chicken breasts diagonally about $^1/_2$ inch/1 cm deep, then coat with the mustard. Arrange them in a shallow dish, pour over the salad dressing and lemon juice and leave to marinate for up to 4 hours. Remove the chicken from the marinade and cook on a barbecue (or under a hot grill) until tender, turning the pieces over halfway through and brushing occasionally with any leftover marinade.

"This is a simple and delicious way to prepare chicken."

GARY E. JOHNSON

Governor of the State of New Mexico

Green Chilli Chicken Burritos

8 oz/225 g boneless chicken, shredded

8 fl oz/225 ml water

1 tbsp ground cumin

$^1/_2$ tbsp freshly chopped chilli peppers

$^1/_2$ small onion, finely diced

1 garlic clove, finely diced

1 x 4 oz/110 g can of green chilli
  (New Mexico's State Vegetable!)

10 flour tortillas

1 lb/450 g can of Old El Paso refried beans

Cheddar cheese, grated for topping, to taste

METHOD

Put the water in a pot and heat together the chicken, cumin, chilli peppers, onion and garlic. Bring to a boil and reduce slightly. When the mixture thickens and the shredded chicken is tender, add the green chillies and mix well. Roll up the mixture with some beans in the tortillas. Place on a greased baking tray and cover with cheese. Bake in an oven preheated to 190C/375F/Gas Mark 5 until the cheese turns brown.

Serves: 3 to 4

Turkey Sopa

FIFE SYMINGTON

Governor of the State of Arizona, USA

METHOD

Melt the butter or margarine in a pan, add the onion and cook until tender. Add the chillies, taco sauce, soups and turkey or chicken. Place layers of tortillas on the bottom of a 2 inch/5 cm deep casserole dish, then add alternate layers of the soup mixture, tortillas and cheese for three layers, making sure the top layer is cheese. Bake in an oven preheated to 180C/350/Gas Mark 4 for 1 hour until thoroughly heated and the cheese is melted.

1 1/2 oz/ 40 g butter or margarine

1 medium onion, chopped

1 can green chillies, diced

1 jar Old El Paso hot taco sauce

1 can cream of mushroom soup

1 can cream of chicken soup

1 can consomme

1 lb/450 g thick cut cooked turkey
  or chicken roll, cubed

12 corn tortillas, cut into strips

2 lb/900 g Cheddar cheese, grated

"This recipe has a uniquely south-west taste."

Serves: 8 to 10

Cabbage Rolls

WILLIAM J. JANKLOW

Governor of South Dakota

12 cabbage leaves

1 lb/450 g beef, minced

1 medium onion, chopped

4 oz/110 g quick-cooking rice

1 tsp salt

1 tsp paprika

A pinch of freshly ground black pepper

1 x 15 oz/425 g can of tomato puree

Serves:4 to 6

METHOD

Place the cabbage leaves in a saucepan and cook. Combine the minced beef, onion, rice, salt and paprika with one-quarter of the tomato puree, and mix well.Place 3 to 4 tbs of the beef mixture on each cabbage leaf, roll to enclose the meat and secure with toothpicks. Place the rolls seam-side down in a deep casserole dish and pour over the remaining tomato puree. Bake in a preheated oven, 180C/350F/Gas Mark 4 for 50 to 60 minutes until a fork passes easily through the cabbage leaves.

GEORGE V. VOINOVICH

Governor of the State of Ohio

Pork Chops with Apples

METHOD

Season the pork chops and grill for 10 minutes on each side until golden. Meanwhile, combine the apple juice, ketchup, soy sauce, sugar, cornflour and ginger in a saucepan and cook over a medium heat until the mixture thickens. Add any juices from the pork chops. Put the chops into an overproof dish, place 1 apple ring on each chop, then pour over the sauce and bake in an oven preheated to 180C/350F/Gas Mark 4 for 20 minutes, basting several times.

8 loin pork chops

Salt and freshly ground black pepper

4 fl oz/110 ml apple juice

3 tbsp tomato ketchup

8 tbsp light soy sauce

2 oz/50 g soft brown sugar

2 tbsp cornflour

$1\frac{1}{2}$ tsp chopped fresh ginger root

2 Granny Smith apples, peeled,
  cored and cut into 8 rings

Serves: 4

"Great when served with rice and broccoli!"

Lamb Shanks

VICKI REYNOLDS

Mayor, City of Beverly Hills, California

METHOD

Season the meat. Heat the oil in a large heavy frying pan and cook the lamb for about 10 minutes, until browned. Remove from the pan and set aside. Drain off most of the fat from the pan, add the garlic, onion, carrots and celery to the pan and saute until softened, about 10 minutes. Pour in the wine and cook for 2 minutes, then scrape the pan with a wooden spoon to loosen the browned bits. Transfer the mixture to a large stock pot and add the tomatoes, breaking them into bite-sized pieces. Add the lamb and all the remaining ingredients and bring to the boil, then reduce the heat and simmer, skimming as necessary, for about 1 hour until the meat is very tender. Remove the lid and boil hard for 5 to 10 minutes to reduce the liquid slightly. Up to this point, this dish can be prepared in advance, then refrigerated until required. Skim the fat off the top before reheating. When serving, use tongs to remove the lamb steaks from the pot because the tender meat will fall apart easily. Put one shank on each plate, then season the bean mixture to taste and spoon it over the meat.

4 lamb leg steaks
Salt
Freshly ground black pepper
2 tbsp olive oil
1 large garlic clove, crushed
1 large onion, diced
2 medium carrots, diced
2 celery sticks, diced
1 glass of dry red wine
13 oz/375 g can of tomatoes
14 oz/400 g can of black-
  eyed beans, drained
1 1/2 pints/850 ml chicken stock
2 sprigs of rosemary
1 bay leaf

Serves: 4

SENATOR PHIL GRAMM

Texas

Award-Winning Chilli

1 lb/450 g beef, minced
1 lb/450 g beef, cut into 1/2 inch/1 cm cubes
1 small onion, finely chopped
2 x 8 oz/225 g cans of tomato puree
2 x 8 oz/225 g cans of water
4 tbsp chilli powder
1- 2 tsp salt
2 tsp paprika (optional)
1 tbsp ground cumin (optional)
1/2 - 1 tsp red pepper (optional)
2 garlic cloves, minced
2 - 3 tbsp plain flour

METHOD

In a heavy saucepan, brown the meat, then transfer to a large casserole dish. Mix together all the ingredients except for the flour in a preheated oven, 180C/350F/Gas Mark 4 for 2 hours. Add the flour, then cook for another 15 minutes.

Serves: 6 to 8

Advice to my Son - for Tim

The trick is, to live your days
as if each one may be your last
(for they go fast, and young men lose their lives
in strange and unimaginable ways)
but at the same time, plan long range
(for they go slow; if you survive
the shattered windshield and the bursting shell
you will arrive
at our approximation here below
of heaven or hell).

To be specific, between the peony and the rose
plant squash and spinach, turnips and tomatoes;
beauty is nectar
and nectar, in a desert, saves -
but the stomach craves stronger sustenance
than the honeyed vine.
Therefore, marry a pretty girl
after seeing her mother;
speak truth to one man,
work with another;
and always serve bread with your wine.

But son,
always serve wine

"Advice to My Son," from LIQUID PAPER: NEW AND SELECTED POEMS by Peter Meinke, © 1991. Reprinted by permission of the University of Pittsburgh Press.

Peter Meinke

Simple Apple Slice

Kansas Senator

2 cooking apples, peeled ,
  cored and sliced into quarters
6 fl oz/175 ml water
1 oz/25 g butter
Some cinnamon

METHOD

Put the apple slices, which must be tart, in a shallow pyrex dish. In a small saucepan boil up water, margarine and cinnamon for about 2 minutes. Pour the mixture over the apples, then bake for about 1 hour in an oven preheated to 180C/350F/Gas Mark 4.

MARIO CUOMO

Former Governor of the State of New York

Big Apple Mousse

2 lb/900 g apples, peeled, cored and chopped

12 oz/350 g light brown sugar

1 cinnamon stick

Juice of $^1\!/_2$ lemon

4 fl oz/110 ml water

3 tbsp powdered gelatine,
  softened in a little water for a few minutes

For the topping

1 pint/575 ml double cream

4 oz/110 g caster sugar

1 tbsp Calvados or brandy (optional)

Serves: 6 to 8

METHOD

Put the apples, brown sugar, cinnamon stick, lemon juice and water in a heavy saucepan and cover tightly. Cook over a medium-high heat until the apples are very tender. Add the softened gelatine to the mixture and stir well to dissolve completely, then remove the cinnamon stick. Place the apple mixture in a bowl and beat with an electric mixer at high speed. Set aside and keep cold. Put the cream in a chilled mixing bowl and whisk it at high speed until it begins to thicken. Add the granulated sugar and the Calvados or brandy, and continue to whisk until soft peaks are formed. Fold the apple mixture into the cream mixture, pour into a serving bowl and refrigerate until set.

Vermont Applesauce

HOWARD DEAN

Governor of the State of Vermont

METHOD

Put the water into a large pan and add the apple quarters. Bring to the boil, reduce the heat and simmer until the apples are beginning to break up, about 20 to 30 minutes. Stir from time to time to prevent them sticking. Put the apples through a food mill or push them through a sieve. Serve hot with nutmeg and cinnamon to taste. Sugar should not be necessary. Custard is an excellent accompaniment.

$^3\!/_4$ pint/425 ml water

8 McIntosh apples or other dessert
  apples, quartered
  (no need to peel and core)

Nutmeg and cinnamon, to taste

Serves: 4 to 6

"Vermont has been growing apples as long as it has been a state - 200 years. This recipe features the Vermont McIntosh apple, which is grown to near perfection in our cool nights and warm days."

Cranberry Cookies

GEORGE ALLEN
Governor of the Commonwealth of Virginia

4 oz/110 g butter, softened
4 oz/110 g caster sugar
6 oz/175 g brown sugar
4 tbs milk
2 tbs orange juice
1 egg
12 oz/350 g self raising flour
$1/_2$ tsp salt
4 oz/110 g nuts, chopped
12 oz/350 g chopped cranberries, fresh if possible

METHOD

In a bowl, cream together the sugar and butter. Beat in the milk, orange juice and egg. After sifting together the flour, baking powder, soda and salt, add to the creamy mixture, a little at a time and blend well. Stir in the the nuts and cranberries. Cover a flat baking tray with baking paper, then spoon on the mixture into small, individual cookies (3 or 4 tsp per drop). Leave a little space between them to allow for expansion. Bake in an oven preheated to 180C/350F/Gas Mark 4 for 10 to 15 minutes.

"These cookies do not brown but will be pretty and good."

JOHN ENGLER
Governor of the State of Michigan

Red Raspberry Pie

METHOD

For the crust, sift the flour into a bowl and rub in the butter or lard until the mixture resembles breadcrumbs. Mix together the egg, vinegar and salt and lightly stir them into the flour mixture with a fork. Gather together the dough and press it into a ball, then divide it in half. Roll out one half and use to line an 8 inch/20 cm plate.

Mix together all the ingredients for the filling and put them into the pie plate. Roll out the remaining pastry and cover the filling with it, making sure that it is pressed down well around the rim of the dish. Cut a couple of slits in the top, then bake in an oven preheated to 200C/400F/Gas Mark 6 for 35 to 40 minutes until the top is golden brown.

For the pie crust
8 oz/225 g flour
4 oz/110 g butter or lard
1 egg
2 tbsp vinegar
A pinch of salt
For the filling
1 lb/450 g fresh or frozen raspberries
3 tbsp ground tapioca
8 oz/225 g granulated sugar
A knob of butter

Serves: 4 to 6

Best Apple Pie

3 oz/75 g light brown sugar

3 oz/75 g granulated sugar

1 tbsp cornflour or 2 tbsp plain flour

$\frac{1}{4}$ tsp cinnamon

$\frac{1}{4}$ tsp nutmeg

A pinch of salt

2 lb/900 g cooking apples, peeled,
  cored and thinly sliced

1 lb/450 g shortcrust pastry

1 oz/25 g butter or margarine

Milk or water, for brushing

Sugar, for sprinkling

Serves: 6

"If the edges are browning too fast, cover with a narrow strip of aluminium foil. Remember to allow it to cool for about an hour before serving with vanilla ice cream."

METHOD

Mix together the sugars, cornflour or flour, cinnamon, nutmeg and salt, then sprinkle this mixture over the apples. Toss gently to mix and leave to stand until the juices begin to run, which will take about 10 minutes.

Meanwhile, roll out half the pastry and use to line a 9 inch/23 cm pie plate, allowing it to overlap the edges of the plate by $\frac{1}{2}$ inch/1 cm. Roll out the remaining pastry to a 12 inch/30 cm round. Fold it into quarters and make 3 slits near the centre of each fold to allow the steam to escape while cooking. Pile the apple mixture into the pastry base and dot with the butter or margarine.

Moisten the rim of the pastry with water, place the folded pastry on top of the pie so that the point is in the centre, then unfold it to cover the apples. Trim the overhang to 1 inch/2.5 cm; turn the edges under and press together to seal, then flute them with a knife. For a crispy, sugary top, brush with a little milk or water and lightly sprinkle with sugar. Bake in an oven preheated to 220C/425F/Gas Mark 7 for 40 minutes, or until the juices bubble through the slits and the apples are tender.

Governor of the State of Georgia

Peach Cobbler

3 oz/75 g plain flour
A pinch of salt
2 tsp baking powder
12 oz/350 g caster sugar
6 fl oz/175 ml milk
4 oz/110 g butter, melted
4 fresh peaches, stoned and sliced

METHOD

Sift the flour, salt and baking powder into a bowl, then mix in 8 oz/250 g of the sugar. Stir in the milk and beat well. Put the melted butter into a baking dish and pour the batter over it but *do not stir.* Mix the peaches with the remaining sugar and arrange them on the batter. Again, do not stir. Bake in an oven preheated to 180C/350F/Gas Mark 4 for 45 to 60 minutes.

Serves: 4 to 6

"Remember, don't stir the batter."

Carolina Apple Cake

Governor of the State of North Carolina

12 fl oz/375 ml vegetable oil or corn oil
1 lb/450 g caster sugar
4 eggs, beaten
12 oz/350 g plain flour
1 tsp salt
2 tsp vanilla extract
1 tsp bicarbonate of soda
3 large apples (about 1 lb/450 g),
  peeled, cored and diced
4 oz/110 g nuts, chopped

For the sauce
1 oz/25 g butter
8 oz/225 g soft brown sugar
4 tbsp milk
2-3 tsp vanilla extract

METHOD

Whisk together the oil, sugar and beaten eggs. Sift the flour and salt and add to the mixture with the vanilla extract. Add the bicarbonate of soda, apples and nuts and mix well. Pour into a greased and floured 10 inch/25 cm ring mould. Bake in an oven preheated to 180C/350F/Gas Mark 4 for 1 hour, or until a skewer inserted in the centre comes out clean. Turn out on to a wire rack.

To make the sauce, put all the ingredients into a saucepan and simmer for 3 minutes, then pour over the warm cake.

Serves: 4 to 6

Kansas Apple Dumplings

1 packet shortcrust pastry

6 cooking apples,
  peeled and cored

3 tbs raisins

3 tbs nuts, chopped

6 oz/175 g brown sugar

8 fl oz/225 ml water

Serves: 6

METHOD

Heat the oven to 220C/425/Gas Mark 7. Prepare the pastry as directed, then roll two-thirds of the dough into a 14 inch/36 cm square and cut into 4 squares. Roll the remaining dough into a 14 x 7 inch/36 x 18 cm rectangle and cut lengthwise into 2 squares. Place an apple on each of the 6 squares.

Mix together the raisins and nuts, then fill the centres of each apple with the mixture. Moisten the corners of one square, then bring the 2 opposite corners of pastry up over the apple and press together. Fold in the sides of the remaining corners as if wrapping a parcel, and bring the other corners up over the apple and press together. Repeat the process with the other 5 squares. Place the dumplings in an ungreased baking dish (size approx.1 $^1/_2$ x 7 $^1/_2$ x 1 $^1/_2$ inches/3.5 x 19 x 3.5 cm.)

In a pan, heat the brown sugar and water to boiling point, making sure the sugar is completely dissolved. Carefully pour the mixture around the dumplings. Bake for about 40 minutes in the hot oven until the crust is golden and the apples tender. During baking, spoon the sugar syrup over the dumplings several times. Serve warm or cool with whipped cream.

Lumpy Milkshake Supreme

"This recipe comes from many hours of delightful and tasty research and a great deal of love. It is a special treat for the entire family. After a long day at the office and time away from home, we gather in the kitchen to create this treat . . . we hope it will become your family favourite as well."

METHOD

Take three generous scoops of vanilla icecream, $^1/_2$ pint/275 ml of milk, and a generous helping of chocolate syrup (the kind used for ice cream). Mush gently and then stir manually, counter-clockwise, with love. Sip through a straw.

EVAN BAYH

Governor of the State of Indiana

Indiana Mint Brownies

4 oz/110 g self-raising flour

4 oz/110 g caster sugar

$^1/_2$ pint/275 ml chocolate-flavoured syrup
  (the type that is served with ice cream)

4 eggs

2 oz/50 g butter, softened

Makes about 40 small brownies

For the mint cream

8 oz/225 g icing sugar

4 oz/110 g butter, softened

1 tbsp water

$^1/_2$ tsp mint extract

3 drops green food colouring (optional)

For the chocolate topping

8 oz/225 g mint-flavoured chocolate or milk chocolate

3 oz/75 g butter

*"Store your mint brownies
in the refrigerator until
needed."*

METHOD

Grease a 13 x 7 x 2 inch/33 x 18 x 5 cm baking tin. In a bowl, beat together the flour, sugar, syrup, eggs and butter with an electric hand mixer on low speed until combined, then beat for 1 minute at medium speed. Pour the mixture into the prepared tin and bake in an oven preheated to 180C/350F/Gas Mark 4 for 20 to 25 minutes, or until the top springs back when pressed lightly with a finger. Put the baking pan on a wire rack and leave to cool.

Meanwhile, prepare the mint cream and the chocolate topping. For the mint cream, put the sugar, butter, water, mint extract and food colouring in a small bowl and beat until smooth.

For the chocolate topping, put the chocolate and butter in a small bowl set over a pan of simmering water and heat until melted. Spread the mint cream over the cooled brownies, then pour the slightly cooled chocolate topping over the mint layer. Cover and chill for at least 1 hour, then cut into squares.

Bien-me-sabe (Coconut Delight)

PEDRO ROSSELLO

Governor of Puerto Rico

2 large ripe coconuts,
  to yield 2 cups of coconut milk
  (or canned coconut milk)
14 oz/400 g granulated sugar
6 egg yolks
16 lady's finger sponge biscuits
3 egg whites
3 tbsp granulated sugar

Serves: 8

METHOD

In a saucepan, combine the coconut milk and sugar and cook over a high heat, without stirring, until boiling. Reduce the heat to moderate and continue to boil until the syrup thickens. Remove from the heat and allow to cool.

Put the egg yolks in a saucepan and gradually blend in the syrup. Cook over a moderate heat, stirring constantly with a wooden spoon, until the mixture boils, then remove immediately from the heat and strain. In 8 deep dessert plates, put 2 lady's fingers and spoon the coconut cream over them. In a bowl, beat the egg whites until they form stiff peaks, then gradually add the sugar and continue to beat to make a meringue mixture. Garnish with this meringue.

JIM GUY TUCKER

Governor of the State of Arkansas

Chocolate Soured Cream Cake

METHOD

Grease and line a deep 8 inch/20cm round cake tin. Cream the butter and sugar together until light and fluffy. Put the cocoa powder in a separate bowl, pour on the boiling water and mix well until smooth. Stir in the soured cream. Gradually add the eggs to the creamed butter mixture, beating well after each addition. Add the soured cream mixture, then fold in the sifted flour. Pour into the prepared cake tin and bake in an oven preheated to 160C/325F/Gas Mark 3 for 1 hour or until a skewer inserted in the centre comes out clean. Cool in the tin for 10 minutes, then turn out on to a wire rack to cool completely.

To make the icing, gently melt the chocolate with the coffee or water in a bowl set over a pan of simmering water. Cool slightly, then add to the soured cream and whisk thoroughly. Chill for 30 minutes and then spread over the top and sides of the cake.

8 oz/225 g butter
8 oz/225 g caster sugar
2 oz/50 g cocoa powder
$\frac{1}{4}$ pint/150 ml boiling water
$\frac{1}{4}$ pint/150 ml soured cream
2 eggs, beaten
8 oz/225 g self-raising flour

For the icing
8 oz/225 g bitter chocolate
2 tbsp black coffee or water
$\frac{1}{2}$ pint/275 ml soured cream

Serves: 4 to 6

Iowa Apple Cake

TERRY E. BRANSTAD

Governor of the State of Iowa

4 oz/110 g butter or margarine

6 oz/175 g granulated sugar

9 oz/250 g soft brown sugar

1 egg

8 oz/225 g plain flour

2 tsp baking powder

1 tsp bicarbonate of soda

1 tsp ground cinnamon

$^1/_2$ tsp ground cloves

12 fl oz/350 ml apple puree

6 oz/175 g raisins

2 oz/50 g walnuts or pecan nuts, chopped

For the cream cheese frosting

6 oz/175 g softened cream cheese

4 oz/110 g softened butter or margarine

2 tsp vanilla extract

8 - 10 oz/225 - 275 g icing sugar, sifted

Cinnamon and nutmeg, to decorate (optional)

Serves: 6

"For a decorative finish, put a paper doily on the frosted cake and then lightly sift over a mixture of cinnamon and nutmeg. Carefully remove the doily."

METHOD

Grease and line a 13 x 9 x 2 inch/33 x 23 x 5 cm baking tin. Beat the butter or margarine in a large mixing bowl for 30 seconds. Add the sugars and egg and beat until combined. Sift together with flour, the baking powder, bicarbonate of soda and spices. Add the flour mixture alternately with the apple puree to the butter mixture, whisking in well. Stir in the raisins and nuts. Pour the mixture into the prepared tin, spreading it evenly. Bake in an oven preheated to 180C/350F/Gas Mark 4 for 30 to 35 minutes, or until a skewer inserted near the centre of the cake comes out clean. Cool the cake in the tin on a wire rack, then turn it out of the tin.

For the frosting, beat together the cream cheese, butter or margarine and vanilla extract until light and fluffy. Gradually beat in enough icing sugar to make a spreadable frosting. Coat the top and sides of the cake with the frosting.

Governor of the State of Mississippi

Mississippi Mud Cake

8 oz/225 g butter

2 oz/50 g cocoa powder

1 lb/450 g granulated sugar

4 eggs, lightly beaten

6 oz/175 g plain flour

A pinch of salt

6 oz/175 g pecan nuts, chopped

1 tsp vanilla extract

Miniature marshmallows,
  to decorate

For the chocolate frosting

1 lb/450 g icing sugar

4 fl oz/110 ml milk

$1^1/_2$ oz/40 g cocoa powder

2 oz/50 g softened butter

METHOD

Melt the butter and cocoa together in a pan, then remove from the heat. Stir in the sugar and beaten eggs. Add the flour, salt, nuts and vanilla extract and mix well. Spoon the mixture into a greased 13 x 9 x 2 inch/33 x 23 x 5 cm baking tin and bake in an oven preheated to 180C/350F/Gas Mark 4 for 35 to 40 minutes or until firm. Remove the cake from the oven and immediately sprinkle marshmallows over the top. To make the frosting, beat together the icing sugar, milk, cocoa powder and butter until smooth. Spread over the hot cake.

"Mississippians can't get enough of this mud!"

Serves: 8

Peanut Butter Oatmeal Cookies

JIM EDGAR

Governor of the State of Illinois

"This is one of Jim and Brenda Edgar's healthy heart recipes."

4 oz/110 g plain flour

$^1/_2$ tsp bicarbonate of soda

7 level tbsp golden syrup

4 tbsp natural peanut butter

2 egg whites

1 oz/25 g granulated sugar

1 oz/25 g soft brown sugar

$^1/_2$ tsp vanilla extract

3 oz/75 g rolled oats

Makes 24 cookies

METHOD

Combine the flour and bicarbonate of soda in a bowl and set aside. Beat together the golden syrup and peanut butter, then beat in the egg whites, sugars and vanilla. Add the flour mixture to the bowl and stir well to combine. Fold in the oats. Drop rounded teaspoonfuls of the mixture onto a greased baking sheet and bake in an oven preheated to 190C/375F/Gas Mark 5 for 8 minutes. Allow the cookies to cool on the baking sheet for 2 minutes before transferring to a wire rack to cool completely.

Chocolate Chip Oatmeal Cookies

ANGUS KING

Governor of the State of Maine

10 oz/275 g plain flour

1 tsp baking powder

1 tsp salt

2 oz/50 g oatmeal

$^{1}/_{4}$ tsp cinnamon

8 oz/225 g butter

6 oz/175 g granulated sugar

5 oz/150 g soft brown sugar

1 tsp vanilla extract

2 eggs, beaten

12 oz/350 g chocolate chips

2 oz/50 g almonds, chopped

Makes 36 cookies

METHOD

In a small bowl, combine the flour, baking powder, salt, oatmeal and cinnamon. In a separate bowl, beat together the butter, sugars and vanilla extract until light and fluffy, then beat in the eggs. Add the flour mixture and then stir in the chocolate chips and almonds. Drop rounded tablespoonfuls of the mixture onto a greased baking sheet on a baking tray and bake in an oven preheated to 190C/375F/Gas Mark 5 for about 10 minutes, until the cookies are light brown. Remove from the oven and transfer to a wire rack to cool.

MARC RACICOT

Governor of the State of Montana

4 oz/110 g granulated sugar

5 oz/150 g soft brown sugar

3 oz/75 g softened margarine or butter

3 oz/75 g white vegetable fat

1 egg

1 tsp vanilla extract

6 oz/175 g white or wholemeal flour

$^{1}/_{2}$ tsp bicarbonate of soda

$^{1}/_{2}$ tsp salt

6 oz/175 g chocolate chips

2 oz/50 g nuts, chopped (optional)

Makes 40 cookies

Chocolate Chip Cookies

METHOD

Beat the sugars, fats, egg and vanilla extract together in a bowl, then stir in all the remaining ingredients. Drop rounded teaspoonfuls of the mixture about 2 inches/5 cm apart on an ungreased baking sheet. Bake in an oven preheated to 190C/375F/Gas Mark 5 for 8 to 10 minutes, until light brown. Cool slightly, then transfer to a wire rack.

LAWTON CHILES

Governor of the State of Florida

Oatmeal Cookies

10 oz/275 g margarine

7 oz/200 g soft brown sugar

4 oz/110 g granulated sugar

1 egg

1 tsp vanilla extract

6 oz/175 g plain flour

1 tsp bicarbonate of soda

1 tsp salt

1 tsp ground cinnamon

$^1/_4$ tsp nutmeg

12 oz/350 g rolled oats

METHOD

Beat the margarine and sugars together until light and fluffy. Beat in the egg and vanilla. Add the flour, bicarbonate of soda, salt and spices and mix well. Stir in the oats. Take large dessertspoonfuls of the mixture and roll them into balls, then place on a greased baking sheet and flatten slightly. Bake in an oven preheated to 190C/375F/Gas Mark 5 for 8 to 9 minutes for chewy cookies or 10 to 11 minutes for crisp ones. Cool on a wire rack.

Makes 30 cookies

The Mansion's Chocolate Pecan Cookies

DAVID M. BEASLEY

Governor of the State of South Carolina

2 oz/50 g vegetable fat

2 oz/50 g butter

3 oz/75 g granulated sugar

2 oz/50 g soft brown sugar

1 large egg, beaten

1 tsp vanilla extract

A squeeze of lemon juice

5 oz/150 g plain flour

$^3/_4$ tsp baking powder

$^1/_3$ tsp salt

$^1/_3$ tsp cinnamon

3 oz/75 g pecans, chopped

7 oz/200 g chocolate chips

METHOD

In a bowl, beat together the vegetable fat, butter and sugars until light and fluffy. Add the egg, vanilla extract and lemon juice, beating well after each addition. Sift the flour, baking powder, salt and cinnamon, then add gradually to the mixture, beating thoroughly until it is creamy. Stir in the nuts, then the chocolate chips. Drop rounded teaspoonfuls of the mixture onto a greased baking sheet and bake in an oven preheated to 180C/350F/Gas Mark 4 for 10 to 12 minutes, until the cookies are light brown. Remove from the oven and transfer to a wire rack to cool.

Makes about 36 cookies

FORREST JAMES

Governor of the State of Alabama

Yeast Cake Biscuits

"This is a recipe of my mother's. My dad was raised on these biscuits and they are still a staple on the dinner table in Opelika."

8 oz/225 g butter or margarine
2 tbsp granulated sugar
1 lb/450 g plain flour, sifted
1 tsp salt
1 tsp baking soda
1 tsp baking powder
1 tsp cream of tartar
12 fl oz/350 ml buttermilk
 (at room temperature)
1 oz/25 g yeast
 dissolved in 2 tbs warm water

Serves: 4 to 6

METHOD

Cream together the butter or margarine and the sugar in a large bowl. In another bowl, sift together the flour, salt, baking soda, baking powder and cream of tartar. Add the mixture alternately with the buttermilk to the creamed butter mixture and mix well, then add the yeast, and mix again. Cover the bowl and leave to rise until it has doubled in bulk, then mash down the mixture. Store in a refrigerator or roll out. Let rise, cut to desired size, then place on a baking tray lined with baking paper. Cook in an oven preheated to 190C/375F/Gas Mark 5 for 10 to 15 minutes. Precooked biscuits may be double-wrapped and frozen, but dough keeps for only 2 days in the refrigerator. The quantities in this recipe can be easily doubled.

Party Rolls

"These rolls freeze well."

JEAN CARNAHAN

Governor of the State of Missouri

METHOD

Mix together the yeast in 2 tbs water, then add the rest of the water and sugar to the bowl, stirring until thoroughly dissolved. Add the margarine, salt and beaten eggs and mix well. Gradually stir in the flour, then knead lightly. Place the mixture in a clean bowl, cover and allow to rise for 2 hours. Punch down and let rise again until it has doubled in size. Roll out and cut to desired size. Place the rolls on a buttered, or greased baking paper lined baking tray and leave to rise for half an hour, then bake in an oven preheated to 190C/375F/ Gas Mark 5 for 10 to 15 minutes.

2 oz yeast
2 tbsp granulated sugar
8 fl oz/225 ml plus 2 tbsp water
2 oz/50 g sugar
4 oz/110 g margarine
1 tsp salt
3 eggs, beaten
1 lb 4 oz/560 g plain flour
A little butter

Makes 50 party-size rolls

Cinnamon Rolls

FRANK KEATING

Governor of the State of Oklahoma

METHOD

Melt the butter or margarine and let it cool slightly. Put the milk in a saucepan, bring to the boil rapidly, then allow to cool till lukewarm. Add the yeast and tbs of sugar to the milk and stir until dissolved. Transfer to a bowl and beat in half the flour and all the salt with a wooden spoon until the mixture is perfectly smooth. Add the melted butter or margarine and eggs, and gradually mix in the rest of the flour. Only use enough flour to make the dough easy to handle. Knead the dough well and place in a clean, greased bowl. Cover and set in a warm place to rise until double in bulk.

In another bowl, mix together the sugars and cinnamon.

Roll out the risen dough to a thickness of about 1/4 inch/60 mm. Coat one side generously with softened butter, then thickly sprinkle the cinnamon and sugar mixture over it. Cut the dough and mixture in half, lengthwise, then carefully roll up the two halves like Swiss rolls. Cut the rolls into 1in/ 2.5 cms slices.

Prepare individual filling cases by placing in them a little softened butter, a little sugar and a tsp of honey. Place the slices in the cases, and leave until the centres rise. Then bake on a shallow baking tin in an oven preheated to 180C/350F/Gas Mark 4 until brown, usually 10 to 12 minutes.

*4 oz/110 g margarine
  or butter*
³/₄ pint/425 ml milk
2 oz/50 g yeast
2 tbs sugar
1lb 8 oz/675 g flour
2 tsp salt
8 oz/225 g brown sugar
8 oz/225 g white sugar
2 tbs cinnamon
A little honey

Makes: 30 rolls

"I'm fond of cinnamon rolls on Sundays before going to church."

ANN W. RICHARDS

Governor of the State of Texas

Jalapeno Cheese Cornbread

METHOD   Serves: 6

Sift together the cornmeal, flour, baking powder and salt in a bowl. Add the dripping. Work into the mix. In a separate bowl, lightly combine the eggs and milk, then add to the main bowl. Beat until smooth and slightly heavier than pancake batter. Add the onion, creamed corn, pepper, cheddar and sugar, and mix in well. Pour into a 10 inch/25 cm buttered baking tin and bake in an oven preheated to 220C/425F/Gas Mark 7 for 25 minutes, until well risen and golden brown.

"A wonderful bread with chicken, pork or vegetables."

5 oz/150 g fine cornmeal
4 oz/110 g plain flour
2 tsp baking powder
¹/₂ tsp salt
2 large eggs
2 tbs dripping, melted
Scant ¹/₂ pint/200 ml milk
1 small green onion, finely chopped
4 oz/110 g creamed corn
2 oz/50 g Jalapeno pepper, chopped
6 oz/175 g Cheddar cheese, grated
1 tbs sugar

Toffee Nut Bars

EDWARD T. SCHAFER

Governor of the State of North Dakota

4 oz/110 g white vegetable fat or butter
4 oz/110 g soft brown sugar
4 oz/110 g plain flour

For the topping
2 eggs
8 oz/225 g soft brown sugar
1 tsp vanilla extract
1 oz/25 g plain flour
1 tsp baking powder
4 oz/110 g pecans or walnuts, chopped
3$^1/_2$ oz/100 g desiccated coconut
Icing sugar, for dusting

METHOD

Cream together the fat or butter and sugar, then stir in the flour, mixing well. Press the mixture into a greased 13 x 9 inch/33 x 23 cm baking tin and bake in an oven preheated to 180C/350F/Gas Mark 4 for 10 minutes. Leave to cool.

To make the topping, beat the eggs thoroughly and then beat in the sugar and vanilla extract. Stir in the flour and baking powder, then the nuts and coconut. Spread this mixture over the base already baked, then bake in an oven preheated to 150C/300F/Gas Mark 2 for 25 minutes, or until the topping is set. Leave to cool, then cut into bars and dust with icing sugar.

Makes about 24 bars

JOHN WAIHEE

Governor of the State of Hawaii

Ono Banana Bread

METHOD

Sift together the flower, baking powder, salt, baking soda and sugar. Add the butter or margarine, eggs and half of the mashed bananas. Stir well to combine the ingredients, then beat for 2 minutes at medium speed with an electric mixer.

Add the remaining bananas and lemon juice. Beat for a further 2 minutes. Fold in $^3/_4$ of the nuts, then pour the mixture into a greased, lined loaf tin (8 $^1/_2$ in/21 cm x $^1/_2$ inch/0.5 cm). Sprinkle the last of the nuts over the top of the batter. Bake in an oven preheated to 180C/350F/Gas Mark 4 for 1 hour.

"This is a great family favourite."

8 oz/225 g plain flour, sifted
2 tsp baking powder
$^3/_4$ tsp salt
$^1/_2$ tsp baking soda
4 oz/110 g cane sugar
4 oz/110 g butter or margarine
2 eggs
3 bananas, mashed
1 tsp lemon juice
4 oz/110 g blanched almonds, chopped

Serves: 6

World's Finest Chocolate Gateau

MICHAEL J. SULLIVAN
Governor of the State of Wyoming

2 oz/50 g dark raisins

2 fl oz/50 ml Scotch whisky, bourbon or coffee

5 oz/150 g self-raising flour

A pinch of salt

6 oz/175 g almonds, ground

7 oz/200 g cooking chocolate

2 oz/50 g butter, unsalted and softened

3 eggs, separated

12 oz/350 g granulated sugar

For the icing

3 oz/75 g dark chocolate

3 oz/75 g caster sugar

3 oz/75 g butter, unsalted

"This is the official dessert which is served at the Governor's residence."

METHOD

Cut a round of waxed paper or baking parchment to fit the base of a 9 inch/23cm cake tin. Butter the sides, or use a springform pan. Put the raisins in the Scotch, bourbon or coffee and soak for 15 minutes. Mix the flour, salt and almonds in a bowl and set aside. Melt the chocolate in 3 tbs of water, in a separate bowl set over a small pan of hot water. When melted, stir in the butter until the mixture is smooth. Very thoroughly beat in the egg yolks, one at a time, with the sugar until the mixture is pale yellow. Transfer the melted chocolate to the bowl and stir in. Add the flour mixture, the soaked raisins and their liquid to the bowl, stirring constantly.

In a separate bowl beat the egg whites until they form soft, shiny peaks. Stir in one-third of the egg white into the chocolate mixture, then fold the now lightened chocolate mixture into the remaining egg whites. Pour the batter into the prepared tin.

Bake the gateau in an oven preheated to 190C/375F/Gas Mark 5 until the top cracks. The cake will appear wet and perhaps not completely cooked. It should have begun to retract from the pan sides and its surface should have cracked or begun to pull away from the sides. Place the cake tin on a cooling rack and let cool for 30 minutes before running a knife round the edge and removing it from the tin. Remove the waxed paper base. To make the icing, melt the chocolate, as before, and blend in the caster sugar and butter until smooth and shiny, then spread evenly and generously over the top.

SIR RICHARD BRANSON

Business Selections

W HO SAYS THAT, IN BUSINESS, there is no such thing as a free lunch? I must have attended one sometime, I just can't remember when. High-level corporate decisions taken over the dinner table are a way of life in the modern world. It may seem a very glamorous life, jetting off to examine a new business trend or sign a major new contract, but with the territory goes enormous responsibility. People's livelihoods depend on making good business decisions. Top executives are never really off duty. There is a constant round of business and social obligations to be met, and contacts to be kept up across the whole political and economic spectrum. Executives can't afford to lose touch.

But away from the high-pressure worlds of business and finance, how do they like to relax? Yes, you've guessed it - over a nice meal they've prepared themselves. You'd be surprised how many tough captains of industry, in private, like to don an apron and potter about in the kitchen. Mind you, someone else usually has to do the cleaning up after them.

In this international section there is a real A to Z flavour - from globe-trotting Sir Richard Branson's Apple and Rhubarb Almond Sponge, to a zucchini vegetable and meat dish from Jean-Pierre Quemard, head of international jewelers Van Cleef and Arpels. There's also Donald Trump's clam chowder (clams are a big favourite in the USA, but something of an acquired taste).

The big surprises? Probably The Body Shop founder Anita Roddick's liking for Dutch Potato Broccoli, a delicious, but highly calorific vegetable dish. Another unexpected favourite is that of HarperCollins US publishing chief George Craig. He may be based in the US but Stovies, a humble, wonderfully tasty traditional dish from the North East of Scotland, are his culinary heart's desire. Be warned. Though they appear to be deceptively simple to make, truly good Stovies are rare outside of Aberdeenshire, where they border on being an art form. Get an Aberdonian to tell you the secret.

LORD WEINSTOCK

Chairman of General Electric Company

"This stock represents the ideal foundation for all manner of soups."

1 small boiling chicken,
 about 2¹/₂ - 3 lb/1.1 - 1.25 kg
4 pints/2.25 litres water
2 onions, chopped
2 - 3 carrots, chopped
2 - 3 celery sticks, chopped
1 - 2 small turnips, chopped
Salt and freshly ground black pepper
Small glass of white wine or sherry
 (optional)
6 oz/175 g white rice or
 thin vermicelli
Chopped fresh parsley, to garnish

Serves: 4 to 6

Chicken Soup

METHOD

Put the chicken in a large pan and add the water and vegetables. Bring slowly to the boil, then reduce the heat, cover with a tight-fitting lid and simmer gently for at least 4 hours. Remove from the heat, strain and set the liquid aside to cool. When it is cold, remove all fat from the top, then return the soup to the boil and cook until it has reduced in volume and the flavour is more concentrated. Season to taste and add the wine or sherry if desired.

Boil the white rice or vermicelli separately, drain and stir it into the soup. Sprinkle with fresh parsley and serve. The flesh from the cooked chicken can be removed from the carcass and added to the soup before serving, if desired.

Stilton Soup

2 oz/50 g butter
2 large onions, chopped
1 lb/450 g potatoes, chopped
1 celery stick, chopped (optional)
2 pints/1.2 litres stock,
 preferably chicken
1 lb/450 g Stilton cheese, chopped
Paprika
Cream, to garnish (optional)

Serves: 6 to 8

ANGUS GROSSART

Merchant Banker

METHOD

Melt the butter in a large pan, add the onions, potatoes and celery, then cover and sweat gently for 30 minutes, stirring occasionally to prevent sticking. Add the stock and simmer until the vegetables are tender, then gradually stir in the Stilton. Puree the soup in a blender, add a little paprika to taste, then serve in very hot soup bowls. A little cream may be added to each portion.

Root Vegetable Soup

PROFESSOR YORAM DINSTEIN

President of Tel Aviv University

"I am afraid I am no cook. However, here is a recipe of a favourite dish prepared by my wife, Ada."

2 white turnips or parsnips, chopped
1 large onion, coarsely chopped
2 stalks of celery, diced
2 carrots, diced
5 potatoes, diced
$1^1/_2$ pints/875 ml water
4 oz/110 g butter
Salt and freshly ground pepper, to taste
1 lb/450 g fresh spinach, de-stalked

Serves: 4

METHOD

Place all the vegetables, except the spinach, in a large saucepan, add the water, butter and salt and pepper. Bring to the boil, then simmer for 40 minutes. The vegetables should be very tender at this point. Add the spinach and simmer for a further 2 minutes until the spinach wilts. Allow to cool slightly, transfer the soup mixture to a blender and puree. Adjust seasoning if necessary. Thin the soup with cream or a little stock (1 chicken cube in a cup of hot water), put back in the pan and heat before serving.

RAE GINGER ELSEN

Canada
President, Women's Entrepreneurial Confederation

"Add a little yogurt to the centre of each soup plate as decoration."

Zucchini Soup

6 medium courgettes, peeled and
  coarsely cut
2 large onions, chopped
$^1/_2$ tsp curry powder
$1^1/_2$ pints/875 ml vegetable or defatted
  chicken stock
Dill and chives, to garnish
1 tbs yogurt, to serve (optional)

Serves: 4 to 6

METHOD

Place the chopped courgettes and onion in a saucepan and sprinkle over them the curry powder. Mix the vegetables gently to ensure all the pieces are coated. Add the stock, cover the pan and bring to a boil. Lower the heat and simmer for 45 minutes. Spoon the mixture into a blender or food processor and puree. The soup can be served hot or cold. Garnish with dill or chives before serving.

3 large potatoes (about 1³/₄ lb/875 g), diced
12 fl oz/350 ml single cream
4 fl oz/110 ml water
4 tbsp smooth peanut butter
8 oz/225 g broccoli,
  chopped into 1-2 inch/2.5-5 cm chunks
1 onion, finely chopped
Freshly grated Parmesan cheese, for topping

Serves: 4 to 6

Dutch Potato Broccoli

METHOD

In a pan, simmer the potatoes gently in the cream and water until tender. Do not drain. Add the peanut butter and simmer gently until thickened. Meanwhile, in a saucepan, cook the broccoli in boiling water until tender when tested with a fork. Drain and add to the potato mixture along with the onion. Stir well to mix and put into a large buttered casserole. Sprinkle generously with grated cheese and bake for 30 minutes in an oven preheated to 180C/350F/Gas Mark 4.

"A firm favourite with many of my friends."

Potato Nests with Caviar

JOKE C.M. VAN DEN BOER

President, World Association of Women Entrepreneurs

"Sprinkle chives over the tops before serving immediately."

Serves: 4

4 large potatoes, unpeeled
1 tbs chives, thinly sliced
3 oz/75 g Sevruga caviar
3 tbs sour cream
1 tsp champagne vinegar
  (or lemon juice)
Chives, to garnish

METHOD

Brush the potatoes well and rinse clean. Put them in a large pan of water, with a pinch of salt, bring to the boil and cook until tender. Meanwhile, mix the sour cream with the rest of the ingredients, except the caviar, and store at room temperature.

Drain the potatoes and peel while still warm. Put the potatoes through a processor, individually, and into four pre-warmed deep plates. Divide the sour cream over the potato nests, then add the caviar.

Stovies

GEORGE CRAIG

Chairman and Chief Executive, HarperCollins Publishers USA

"In this traditional Scots recipe, potatoes are cooked very slowly in the minimum of liquid, with meltingly tender results. Originally developed as a convenient way of finishing up the remains of the Sunday roast, the potatoes were cooked in dripping and gravy and leftover scraps of meat were stirred in at the end."

2 oz/50 g butter or dripping
2 large onions, thinly sliced
2 lb/900 g potatoes,
 sliced about $1/_4$ inch/5 cm thick
About 3 tbsp stock, water or gravy
Salt and freshly ground black pepper
Chopped fresh chives or parsley,
 to garnish

Serves: 4 to 6

METHOD

Melt the butter or dripping in a large heavy-based saucepan, add the onions and cook gently for about 5 minutes, until softened. Add the potatoes and stir well to coat them with the fat. Cover with a tight-fitting lid and cook over a very low heat for about 10 minutes, then stir in the stock, water or gravy. Cover again and cook very gently for about 1 hour or until the potatoes are tender, stirring occasionally to prevent them sticking and adding a little more liquid if they dry out. If you like, turn the heat up at the end to brown and crisp the potatoes slightly. Season to taste with salt and plenty of black pepper, sprinkle with chives or parsley and serve.

TIM WATERSTONE

Founder of Waterstones, booksellers

A little good olive oil
1 medium onion, coarsely chopped,
 per person
1 green pepper, coarsely chopped
2 slices of bacon per person
3 oz/75 g rice per person
1 pint/575 ml vegetable stock

Serves: 2

Bacon Risotto

METHOD

Cook the onions and pepper in a little olive oil in a frying pan until the onion starts to brown, then set aside. Meanwhile, grill the bacon for a minute or so until soft, remove, and dice into medium sized pieces. Wash and drain the rice, then parboil it in a pan for two or three minutes in boiling water. Drain thoroughly. Add the rice to the onion and pepper in the frying pan, then add the diced bacon, and mix gently over a low heat. Add half the stock, and simmer over a very low heat for ten minutes, then add the rest of the stock. Cook over a low to medium heat for 20 minutes, then serve on warm plates.

Manhattan Clam Chowder

2 - 3 rashers of lean bacon, chopped

1 tbsp vegetable oil

1 large onion, cut into $1/_2$ inch/1 cm dice

2 carrots, cut into $1/_2$ inch/1 cm dice

4 celery sticks, cut into $1/_2$ inch/1 cm dice

1 bottle of clam juice

1 large potato, cut into $1/_2$ inch/1 cm dice

1 large tomato, chopped

12 cherrystone clams

Salt and freshly ground black pepper

A pinch of oregano

Serves: 4

METHOD

Fry the bacon in the oil until soft, then remove it from the pan. Add the onion and cook until translucent. Return the bacon to the pan with the carrots, celery and clam juice, topping up with water, if necessary, to cover everything. Bring to the boil and simmer for 10 minutes. Add the potato, tomato, seasoning and oregano and cook until tender. Remove the clams from the shells and chop them finely. Strain the juices and put to one side. Just before serving, add the clams and the strained juice to the chowder and bring to the boil. Adjust the seasoning, to taste.

"As an accompaniment serve your clam chowder with small oyster crackers."

Tuna Noodle Casserole

6 oz/175 g medium noodles

1 x 9 oz/250 g can of tuna, drained

4 fl oz/110 ml salad cream

1 large stick of celery, diced

1 small onion, diced

$1/_2$ green pepper, diced

1 tsp salt

1 can condensed cream of celery soup

4 fl oz/110 ml milk

4 oz/110 g strong cheddar cheese, grated

Serves: 6

"Fast and easy to make."

METHOD

Cook the noodles in boiling, salted water until tender. Drain off the water, then mix in the tuna, salad cream, vegetables and salt with a spoon. In a separate pot, blend the soup and the milk. Heat it through, but don't boil. Add the grated cheese and stir until it melts into the mixture, then pour the sauce over the noodles mixture. Turn everything into a large casserole dish. Bake in a hot oven preheated to 200C/400F/Gas Mark 6 for about 20 minutes.

MME ARMAND DUTRY

Belgium
Honorary President, World Association of Women Entrepreneurs

"I think Morecambe shrimps are the nearest thing to our Belgian crevettes."

Artichoke Hearts with Shrimps

4 globe artichoke hearts, fresh
(Alternatives: tinned or frozen)
4 oz/110 g shallots, chopped
1 knob of butter
8 fl oz/225 ml double cream
$^1/_2$ glass white wine
8 oz/225 g shrimps, peeled
Cheese, grated, to garnish

Serves: 4

METHOD

If using fresh artichokes, prepare them by trimming off the pointed leaves and removing the "choke." Remove most of the stalk. Wash thoroughly, rub with lemon juice and steam gently in a large pot for about 30 minutes, until tender, but firm. Do not overcook. When a single leaf can be pulled out easily, the artichokes are ready. Shred the shallots and, in a pan, cook them in the melted butter until soft. Add the wine, continue to cook and reduce the mixture. When the volume has diminished by about half, add the cream and shrimps. Mix very gently and cook over a low heat for a few minutes. Fill the artichokes with the mixture, sprinkle with cheese and put in a warm oven under the grill until the cheese melts. Serve immediately.

Festive Fishcakes

SIR ERIC AND LADY PARKER

Director and race horse breeder

2 lb/900 g potatoes
4 tbsp double cream
6-8 oz/175-225 g smoked salmon,
  finely chopped
$^1/_2$ tsp horseradish sauce (optional)
A squeeze of lemon juice
Salt and freshly ground black pepper
2 eggs
Flour seasoned with a little
  cayenne pepper and salt for dusting
4 tbsp olive oil

Serves: 4

"We make these at Christmas with leftover smoked salmon."

METHOD

Boil the potatoes in salted water until tender, then drain and mash with the cream. Leave to cool. Mix the smoked salmon, horseradish, lemon juice and plenty of seasoning into the potatoes, then bind the mixture together with one of the eggs to make a firm dough. Divide it into 8 cakes. Beat the remaining egg and dip the fishcakes in it, then roll them in the seasoned flour. Fry in olive oil for about 2 minutes per side, until golden. Serve straight away, with a mixed salad.

SIR IAN AND LADY VALLANCE

Chairman of British Telecom

Prawns with Mushrooms

METHOD

Melt the butter in a pan and fry the onion and red pepper until soft. Stir in the flour, then add the tomatoes, herbs and wine. Season to taste and cook gently for 15 minutes. Add the mushrooms and prawns and simmer for a further 5 minutes. Serve on a bed of rice.

Serves: 3 to 4

1 oz/25 g butter
1 small onion, chopped
$^1/_2$ red pepper, sliced
1 oz/25 g plain flour
13 oz/375 g can of chopped tomatoes
1 tsp fresh oregano, chopped
1 tsp fresh basil, chopped
$^1/_4$ pint/150 ml dry white wine
Salt and freshly ground black pepper
4 oz/110 g mushrooms, sliced
8 oz/225 g peeled prawns

Plaice with Cockles

NICKY JOYCE

4 plaice fillets
$^1/_2$ pint/275 ml cockles
1 oz/25 g butter
  (or 1 tbsp sunflower oil)
Salt and freshly ground pepper, to taste

Serves: 4

"Simple, yet tangy with a real sea flavour, this dish serves equally well as a starter on its own or as a main course."

METHOD

Wash the fillets, put half the cockles in the centre, and roll them up. Place the rolled fish seam-side down in a fireproof dish and sprinkle the remaining cockles over the fish. Brush the fish with the butter or oil, (don't use olive oil; it is too heavy), and add seasoning. Cover the dish with a lid or foil. Cook in a moderate oven preheated to 170C/325F/Gas Mark 3 for 30 minutes.

NB: *As a main dish, double the quantities and serve with whole new potatoes, cooked in milk, then sprinkled with dried thyme and grated nutmeg. The potatoes should be put in the oven, in an oven-proof open dish, with 3 tbs of the milk, to cook beside the fish, for the last 15 minutes.*

RICHARD COLE-HAMILTON

Chairman of the Forte Group

Chairman's Chicken with Broccoli

"A filling meal with plenty of flavour."

METHOD

Cook the broccoli for a few minutes until just tender, then drain. Put the soup, mayonnaise and lemon juice in a pan and heat gently, stirring well, to make the sauce. Layer the ingredients in a large casserole dish in the following order: broccoli, chicken, sauce, cheese, breadcrumbs. Cook in an oven preheated to 180C/350F/Gas Mark 4 for 40 to 50 minutes, until browned on top.

12 oz/350 g broccoli, chopped
2 x 10 oz/275 g cans of condensed chicken soup
$^1/_4$ pint/150 ml Hellmann's mayonnaise
Juice of $^1/_2$ lemon
$1^1/_4$ lb/575 g cooked chicken, chopped
3 oz/75 g Cheddar cheese, grated
2 oz/50 g fresh breadcrumbs

Serves: 4

ADELE SCHEELE

New York
Management consultant, lecturer and author

"Always serve piping hot."

METHOD

Make up the marinade, mixing together all the ingredients, then pour into a large shallow pan which has been lightly greased with butter. Place the chicken breasts on the mixture, then place on top the thinly sliced onions and a sprinkling of saffron, if using. Place the pan under a preheated grill and cook for 10 minutes, basting regularly. Turn over the breasts and grill for another 10 minutes until tender and cooked right through. Serve with either boiled rice, pita or naan bread and a tomato and cucumber side salad.

Easy Chicken Tandoori

6 chicken breasts, boned
   and skinned
1 large onion, thinly sliced
1 tsp saffron, optional

Serves: 6

For the marinade

1 pint/575 ml yogurt, low or non-fat
1 tsp cumin, ground
1 tsp ginger, ground
1 tsp chilli pepper, ground
1 tsp paprika
1 tsp salt
1 tsp pepper, freshly ground
1 garlic clove, pressed or chopped

Chicken in Cider

4 cooked chicken breasts, skinned
4 oz/110 g butter or margarine
6 oz/175 g mushrooms, thinly sliced
1 large onion, finely chopped
1^1/$_2$ oz/40 g plain flour
7 fl oz/200 ml medium sweet cider
5 tbsp tomato ketchup
1 tsp paprika (optional)

Serves: 4

"Ideally, this recipe should be made the day before."

MAY & DONALD STORRIE

Estate agent

METHOD

Place the chicken breasts in a casserole. In a frying pan, melt half the butter or margarine and lightly cook the mushrooms and onion before adding them to the casserole. Melt the remaining butter or margarine in a saucepan and stir in the flour a little at a time to make a roux. Then gradually add the cider, stirring continuously to avoid lumps. If the sauce does become lumpy, put it through a blender and return to the saucepan. Add the tomato ketchup and the paprika, and cook gently for 2 to 3 minutes, then pour the sauce over the chicken. Leave to marinate for 24 hours if possible. Approximately 30 minutes before serving, place the casserole in an oven preheated to 190C/375F/Gas Mark 5 and heat through. Do not overheat as the ingredients are already cooked. Serve with rice or new potatoes, broccoli and carrots.

Mole Poblano de Guajalote (Chicken in Chocolate Sauce)

Serves: 4

METHOD

Heat the oil in a pan and fry the onion, garlic and chillies over a low heat until softened. Add the chicken and toss until the cubes are sealed on all sides. Stir in the tomatoes, chicken stock, cloves, cinnamon and seasoning. Bring to the boil, then turn down to a simmer and cook, covered, for 20 minutes or until the chicken is tender. Add the almonds and half the sesame seeds and continue to cook, uncovered, for 10 minutes. Add the chocolate and stir until it has melted into the sauce. Toast the remaining sesame seeds in a dry pan and sprinkle them over the chicken. Serve with plain boiled rice and salad.

4 tbsp oil
1 onion, finely chopped
3 garlic cloves, crushed
3 red chillies, deseeded and chopped
$1^1/_2$ lb/675 g boneless chicken breasts, diced
13 oz/375 g can of chopped tomatoes
$^1/_2$ pint/275 ml chicken stock
5 cloves
1 tsp cinnamon
Salt and freshly ground black pepper
2 tbsp ground almonds
2 tbsp sesame seeds
2 squares of dark bitter cooking chocolate

JEAN-PIERRE QUEMARD

Managing Director, Van Cleef & Arpels, international jewellers

Provencale Stuffed Vegetables

3 zucchini (courgettes)
2 onions
6 oz/175 g beef, minced
4 large beef tomatoes
1 garlic clove, minced
1 egg
3 slices of bread
Milk
Salt and pepper
1 oz/25 g butter

Serves: 2 to 3

METHOD

Boil the zucchini and onions. When cooked, scrape out the insides and save the pulp. Carefully cut off the tops of the tomatoes. Scrape out the insides, discarding the seeds, and saving the tomato pulp. In a pan, cook the minced meat with the onions and garlic, then add the pulp from the other vegetables.

Put some milk in a shallow dish, beat in the egg, then soak the bread in the mixture. Add the soaked bread to the pan, season to taste and mix well. Season the empty tomato skins with salt before filling them with the stuffing mixture. Sprinkle breadcrumbs over the top and put a small knob of butter on each stuffed tomato. Pour a little water in an oven dish, then place the stuffed tomatoes in it. Bake at 200C/400F/Gas Mark 6 for 30 to 40 minutes.

SIR JOHN HARVEY-JONES

Marinated Kebabs

Business consultant, TV trouble-shooter

1¹/₂ - 2 lb/675 - 900 g lean lamb,
  cut into 2 inch/5 cm cubes
6 rashers of bacon
4 - 6 oz/110 - 175 g button mushrooms
6 small tomatoes
Juice of ¹/₂ lemon
Fresh or dried marjoram
Vegetable oil, for frying

For the marinade
¹/₂ pint/275 ml plain yogurt
2 garlic cloves, crushed
1 tsp chopped fresh ginger root
  or 1 tsp ground ginger
1 tsp chilli powder or cayenne pepper
1 very large onion, coarsely chopped
Salt and freshly ground black pepper

METHOD

Mix together all the marinade ingredients in a shallow dish, add the cubes of lamb and leave to marinate for 3 to 8 hours (the longer the better).

Preheat the grill to high. Remove the meat and onion from the marinade, draining the onion well. Cut each bacon rasher into 3 pieces and roll up. Thread the meat, mushrooms and bacon rolls onto skewers, adding a tomato at each end. Place under the hot grill and cook for about 10 to 15 minutes or until tender. Turn the kebabs frequently, sprinkling them at each turn with the lemon juice and a pinch of marjoram.

While the kebabs are cooking, fry the onion in a little vegetable oil until browned and softened. Serve the kebabs with plain boiled rice and the fried onion, and drizzle over them the juices that will have collected in the grill pan during cooking.

Serves: 3

"Don't forget to use the rich juices, they make this meal."

Venison Sausage Casserole

MARCUS GREGSON

Chief Executive of merchant bankers Samuel Montagu, London

"This is a winner for those of us who have to watch the dreaded cholesterol as venison has very little fat and is one of the few red meats allowed."

METHOD

In a large frying pan, saute the sausages in the oil until browned, then transfer them to a heatproof casserole dish. Add the sugar to the remains of the oil and saute the shallots until they are honey-coloured, then transfer them to the casserole. Add the stock and port to the pan and boil furiously until the liquid is reduced to half its original volume. Season and stir in the redcurrant jelly until melted. Pour the mixture into the casserole and simmer gently, uncovered, for 45 minutes. Add the mushrooms, if using, 10 minutes before the end of the cooking. Serve with a puree of potatoes and celeriac.

8 venison sausages
2 tbsp olive or sunflower oil
1 tsp sugar
1 lb/450 g shallots, chopped
2 pints/1.2 litres game or chicken stock
3 fl oz/75 ml port
Salt and freshly ground black pepper
1 tbsp redcurrant jelly
6 oz/175 g mushrooms, sliced (optional)

Serves: 4

PATTY DE DOMINIC

Chair of the U.S. Business Women's Delegation to the United Nations Conference on Women, China

METHOD

Rinse the spinach thoroughly in warm water to clean and wilt. Shake off any excess water. Slice the tomatoes. Split four pitta breads in half, and arrange the spinach on the open faces, covering as if for a pizza.

Top with tomatoes and, if using, the grated cheese. Put the halves under the grill for about a minute, until the spinach is crisp and the pitta bread slightly browned.

1 large bunch of spinach, fresh
4 large fresh tomatoes, chopped or sliced
4 pitta breads or English muffins
Cheese, grated, to taste (optional)

Popeye Pizzarelli

PETER WOOD

Chief Executive of Direct Line Insurance

Fettucini al Filetto

1 tbsp olive oil

1 lb/450 g fillet steak, cut into strips

8 oz/225 g mushrooms, chopped

1 small red pepper, finely sliced

$\frac{1}{2}$ oz/15 g butter

4 tbsp tomato sauce or passata

Salt and freshly ground black pepper

1 lb/450 g fresh fettucini or tagliatelle

7 fl oz/200 ml single cream

Freshly grated Parmesan cheese, to serve

Chopped fresh parsley, to garnish

Serves: 4

METHOD

Heat the oil in a large frying pan and saute the steak over a high heat for 5 minutes. Add the mushrooms, red pepper and butter and cook for 8 minutes at a lower heat. Add the tomato sauce and seasoning. Meanwhile, cook the pasta in boiling salted water for 2 to 3 minutes, until al dente, then drain and add it to the steak and sauce. Mix well and stir in the cream. Serve sprinkled with cheese and garnished with parsley.

"Only use the best fillet steak for this dish."

LORD HANSON

Chairman of Hanson plc

Yorkshire Pudding

"It is important to serve at once. Yorkshire Pudding should not wait for anyone!"

$^1/_2$ pint/275 ml milk

or $^1/_4$ pint/150 ml each milk and water

1 tbsp melted butter

6 oz/175 g plain flour

Salt and freshly ground black pepper

2 eggs

Serves: 6 to 8

METHOD

Put the milk, melted butter, flour and salt and pepper in a bowl and beat until smooth. Beat in the eggs, one at a time. The batter should be no thicker than whipping cream. Leave in the refrigerator for 2 hours. Grease 1 large baking tin or 6 to 8 individual patty tins and place in an oven preheated to 230C/450F/Gas Mark 8 until very hot. Pour in the batter and bake for 15 minutes, then reduce the heat to 180C/350F/Gas Mark 4 and cook for a further 20 minutes, until well risen and golden brown.

Apple and Rhubarb Almond Sponge

1 lb/450 g cooking apples, peeled,
  cored and sliced

1 lb/450 g rhubarb,
  cut into 1 inch/2.5 cm pieces

Grated zest and juice of 1 orange

3 oz/75 g demerara sugar

2 oz/50 g sultanas

For the sponge topping

3 oz/75 g butter

3 oz/75 g caster sugar

2 eggs, beaten

A few drops of almond essence

3 oz/75 g self-raising flour

1 oz/25 g ground almonds

A pinch of salt

A little milk

1-2 tbsp flaked almonds

SIR RICHARD BRANSON

Founder of Virgin

METHOD

Put the apples and rhubarb into a saucepan with the orange zest and juice, sugar and sultanas. Simmer for about 15 minutes, then transfer to a greased ovenproof dish.

To make the topping, cream together the butter and sugar until light and fluffy. Beat in the eggs and the almond essence, then gently fold in the flour, ground almonds and salt. Add enough milk to make a dropping consistency, then spoon the mixture over the fruit. Sprinkle the flaked almonds over the top and bake in an oven preheated to 180C/350F/Gas Mark 4 for 30 to 35 minutes, until the sponge is well risen and golden brown. Serve hot with custard or cream.

Serves: 6

LORD YOUNGER OF PRESTWICK

Banker and former Secretary of State for Scotland

Apricot and Orange Mousse

METHOD

Soak the apricots in the brandy for 30 minutes, then simmer gently for 30 minutes, until soft and plump. Remove from the heat, add the orange juice and puree in a blender. Put the egg yolks and orange zest in a bowl and whisk, gradually adding the sugar, until the mixture becomes thick and pale. Fold in the apricot puree. Put 4 tablespoons of water into a small saucepan and sprinkle the gelatine over it. Heat gently until the gelatine has completely dissolved, then stir it into the apricot mixture. Whip the cream until thick but not stiff and then fold it into the apricot mixture.

In a separate bowl, whisk the egg whites until they form stiff peaks, then use a metal spoon to fold them lightly but thoroughly into the apricot mixture. Pour into a serving dish and sprinkle flaked almonds over the top. Leave in the fridge to set before serving.

8 oz/225 g dried apricots
3 fl oz/75 ml brandy
Grated zest and juice
of 2 oranges
3 eggs, separated
3 oz/75 g caster sugar
$1/_2$ oz/15 g gelatine
$1/_2$ pint/275 ml double cream
Toasted flaked almonds,
to decorate (optional)

Serves: 6 to 8

"Wherever possible, buy the best-quality dried apricots. They should be plump and ready to eat."

Skibo Castle Meringue Slice

PETER DE SAVARY

Business entrepreneur

"This is a Scottish recipe which I inherited when purchasing Skibo Castle in Sutherland. The recipe was given to a local lady in 1946 by her grandmother, who acquired it from the then housekeeper of Skibo Castle."

3 oz/75 g butter
2 oz/50 g caster sugar
2 egg yolks, beaten
7 oz/200 g plain flour
a pinch of salt

For the topping
2 egg whites
4 oz/110 g caster sugar
3 - 4 oz/75 - 110 g dates, chopped

Serves: 4

METHOD

Cream the butter and sugar together until pale and fluffy, then beat in the egg yolks. Add the flour and salt and work until the mixture resembles pastry. Press it into a small Swiss roll tin and bake in an oven preheated to 180C/350F/Gas Mark 4 for 30 minutes. Remove from the oven but leave the oven on.

To make the topping, whisk the egg whites until stiff. Whisk in half the sugar until the whites stiffen again, then fold in the remaining sugar. Carefully fold in the dates then spread the mixture over the base. Return to the oven and bake for another 30 minutes. Cool and cut into slices to serve.

HAIM BEN SHAHAR

Professor, Tel Aviv University

Chocolate Mousse Cake

"This mousse cake can be decorated with whipped cream or the cream can be folded into the mousse mixture before it is spread over the meringue base."

5 oz/150 g cooking chocolate
4 eggs, separated
4 tbsp cognac or orange liqueur
1 tsp vanilla extract
4 oz/110 g caster sugar
8 inch/20 cm pre-prepared meringue base
½ pint/275 ml double cream, whipped

Serves: 6

METHOD

Melt the chocolate in a bowl set over a pan of hot, but not boiling, water. Add the egg yolks very slowly to the melted chocolate, then stir in the spirit and the vanilla extract. In a separate bowl, whisk the egg whites until stiff, then whisk in half the sugar until the whites stiffen again. Fold in the remaining sugar. Gently fold the egg whites into the chocolate mixture. You have the option at this stage to fold in the whipped cream to the mousse before pouring it onto the meringue base. Chill in the refrigerator for 8 hours or overnight, until set.

BRIAN GILDA

Chairman of Peoples Motor Group, Scotland

Bread and Butter Pudding

6 large slices of white bread,
crusts removed
1 oz/25 g softened butter
Grated zest of $^1/_2$ orange
4 eggs
$^1/_2$ pint/275 ml milk
$^1/_2$ pint/275 ml single cream
4 tbsp caster sugar
$^1/_2$ tsp vanilla extract
4 tbsp currants
1-2 tbsp melted butter
Icing sugar, for dusting

Serves: 4 to 6

METHOD

Spread the bread generously with the butter and cut each slice into 3 fingers. Lay these in a well-buttered 3 pint/1.75 litre ovenproof dish (it should be about half full). Sprinkle with the orange zest. In a mixing bowl, beat the eggs with a fork then beat in the milk, cream, sugar and vanilla extract. Strain this mixture over the bread. Leave the pudding to stand for 15 to 20 minutes until the bread is well soaked. Sprinkle over the currants and brush with the melted butter.

Place the dish in a baking tin and pour boiling water into the tin to come two-thirds up the sides of the dish. Bake in an oven preheated to 160C/325F/Gas Mark 3 for 40 minutes or until the pudding is firm to the touch. Sift icing sugar over the top and serve hot.

BRENDA ROSSMANN

England
National President of the Women Chiefs of Enterprises - International

2 oranges

6 eggs, medium

8 oz/225 g sugar, caster

8 oz/225 g almonds, ground

1 tsp baking powder

Flourless Orange Cake

Serves: 4

METHOD

After slicing off the tops, wrap the two oranges separately in Glad Wrap or a suitable alternative, and micro-wave for 6 to 8 minutes at low heat until mushy. Scoop out the fruit of the baked oranges, removing any heavy pith. Place it and all the other ingredients in a blender or mixer, and blend until smooth. Pour the mixture into a baking tin lined with baking parchment. Bake in an ordinary oven preheated to 180C/350F/Gas Mark 4 for an hour, or for a little longer if it is still too moist. Allow the tin to cool a little, then turn out onto a cooling rack. Before serving, sprinkle the cake with icing sugar and serve with thick cream.

Scripture Cake

INGREDIENTS

1) 10 oz/275 g butter

2) 10 oz/275 g soft brown sugar

3) 5 eggs

4) 2 tbsp honey

5) 1 lb/450 g raisins

6) 1 lb/450 g figs

7) 6 oz/175 g almonds, chopped

8) 10 oz/275 g plain flour

9) 2 tsp baking powder

10) A pinch of salt

11) 2 tsp mixed spice

12) 3 tbsp milk

Well, did Sir Douglas Hardie's recipe for Scripture Cake in the Church and State Section have you stumped? Here are the ingredients and method:

METHOD

Serves: 6 to 8

Grease and line a deep 10 inch/25 cm cake tin. Cream the butter and sugar together until light and fluffy. Gradually beat in the eggs, one at a time, then beat in the honey. Stir in the fruit and nuts. Sift in the flour, baking powder, salt and spices and mix well. Add the milk to give a dropping consistency. Place in the prepared tin, level the top and bake in an oven preheated to 140C/275F/Gas Mark 1 for $4^1/_2$ hours, until a skewer inserted in the centre comes out clean. Cover the top with aluminium foil or brown paper for the last 2 hours to prevent burning.

The Solution

Lemon Syllabub

"In Elizabethan times, one of the favourite wines in Britain was a still dry white wine produced at Sillery, in the Champagne district of France. Bub was a slang term for a bubbly drink . . . By association, syllabub came to describe a drink or sweet made by mixing a frothy cream with still wine."

1 lemon, peeled
Lemon rind
2 fl oz/50 g brandy
3 oz/75 g sugar, caster
$^1/_2$ pint/275 ml double cream
$^1/_4$ pint/150 ml sweet,
  white wine
Rind of a lemon,
  to garnish

Serves: 2 to 4

METHOD

Peel the lemon thinly with a potato peeler. Squeeze out the juice and add enough brandy to make the liquid up to $2^1/_2$ fl oz/60 ml. Pour the liquid into a small bowl, add the lemon peel and leave to stand for at least six hours.

When ready, strain the liquid through a fine sieve, then stir in the sugar, making sure it dissolves completely. In a separate bowl, whip the cream until it thickens, creating soft peaks. Mix the wine into the lemon and brandy mixture, then add the liquid to the cream, while continuing to whisk. The cream should absorb all the liquid and still have a firmness to it, standing in soft peaks. Spoon the cream mixture into individual glasses or dessert dishes and chill in the refrigerator for at least three hours.

For the garnish, thinly peel a lemon and cut the skin into narrow strips. Blanch them for 2 to 3 minutes in a shallow pan of boiling water, drain, and serve the syllabub with a cluster of lemon strips on top as decoration.

Johnny Beattie

Scotland, the Land I Love

WHEN GOD MADE THE GARDEN OF EDEN, He must have left a little bit over to create Scotland. It is the most beautiful country in the world. For all my travels, I will always come back to it, because it is my home. Living anywhere else, on a permanent basis, would be unthinkable. All my closest friends and family are here, and just as importantly, so is my heart. Scotland is a special place.

Words can't really do justice to its scenic beauty, from the islands to its glens and bens, rivers and lochs. I have seen them in all their seasons, and they still take the breath away every time. When you add to that the great sense of history which exists, where-ever you turn, you have something pretty wonderful.

But of course it is the people who make Scotland special. There is a natural warmth and friendliness about Scots, and a spontaneous hospitality which makes a visit to our shores an unforgettable experience. Forget the hoary old jokes about Scots being mean; when their hearts are touched, they are the most generous people on earth. They will dig deep in their pockets to help. They'll give of their time, too, which is a much more precious gift. There is a great, and natural sense of social justice among Scots. They believe in helping those who need it. It's a national characteristic which never fails to surface when it is needed. All this I know from personal experience.

Being Celts, my fellow Scots are also quite, quite maddeningly suspicious of their own home-grown success stories; still far too machismo for my liking, and I wouldn't want to be anywhere else in the world. For the record, in case any over-seas industrialists and businessmen are reading this (while messing up the kitchen - see Business Section introduction), Scotland is also a modern, hi-tech, forward-looking nation with a skilled labour pool internationally renowned for its stability, reliability and hard work. Among other things, about one in ten of the world's personal computers are made here. For non-European companies, it's also a fine base from which to service the European Community.

And - if you're still in the kitchen, Sir or Madam Chief Executive - Scotland also produces some of the finest quality foodstuffs in the world. Lobster, crab and fresh salmon enjoy legendary, and richly deserved, international reputations. So too do our succulent Scots beef and dairy produce. Our home-produced vegetables, in season, are unrivalled in quality. Then of course there is our matchless Scotch whisky. What more could anyone want?

Well, quite a lot, judging from this Section. It's a pretty mixed bag, from just about as varied a clientele as you'll find in the book. It has everything from Heavenly Chicken to Naughty Pasta. There's a recipe for Breakfast in Excess which begins: "Large doses of everything which is bad for you . . ." a strange recipe from former London Police Commissioner Sir David McNee for mince with poached eggs; and from actor Rikki Fulton the British Navy version of the Australian Outback's Bushman's Stew, where everything - and I mean everything - goes into the pot. To introduce a note of sanity into the proceedings, I've added on another section at the end from family and friends, including my late mother's hand-written recipe for her famed German Biscuits.

Smoked Salmon Mousse

DOUGIE DONNELLY

TV sports presenter

8 oz/225 g smoked salmon offcuts
Juice of $^1/_2$ lemon
$^1/_4$ pint/125 ml Hellmann's mayonnaise
$^1/_2$ pint/275 ml whipping cream
Freshly ground black pepper
1/4 tbs. gelatine
2 tbs water

Serves: 6 to 8

METHOD

Chop the smoked salmon offcuts very finely in a food processor, reserving a few pieces for decoration. Add the lemon juice and mayonnaise and process briefly. Put 2 tablespoons of water in a small bowl, sprinkle over the gelatine and leave for a few minutes until spongy. Meanwhile, whip the cream and gently fold it into the salmon mixture. Season with black pepper, then stir in the melted gelatine, transfer to a serving dish and leave to set. Serve garnished with the reserved salmon.

"To really impress, line small ramekin dishes with larger pieces of smoked salmon, add the mousse mixture and fold over the ends of the smoked salmon to enclose the mousse completely. Leave to set in the fridge, then turn out on to serving plates. Serve garnished with lemon wedges and skinned, finely chopped tomatoes, and accompanied by brown bread."

ROBERT AND SHONA LIGHTBODY

Bakery chain proprietors

Smoked Salmon Sausages with Cucumber Salad

6 long slices of smoked Tay salmon,
 plus 8 oz/225 g smoked salmon trimmings
Juice of 1 lemon
$1^1/_2$ tbsp horseradish
A good pinch of cayenne pepper
Salt and freshly ground black pepper
3 leaves of gelatine
1 pint/575 ml double cream

Serves: 6

For the dressing
$^1/_4$ pint/150 ml olive oil
1 garlic clove, roughly chopped
$^1/_2$ medium fennel bulb, diced
1 large sprig of dill
1 tbsp salt
1 star anise, crushed
1 tbsp caster sugar
4 tbsp white wine vinegar
Freshly ground black pepper
Pernod, to taste

For the salad
2 large cucumbers
3 tomatoes, skinned,
 deseeded and chopped

METHOD

Puree the smoked salmon trimmings in a food processor with the lemon juice, horseradish, cayenne and salt and pepper. Soak the gelatine in $^1/_4$ pint/150 ml of the cream until softened, then heat gently to dissolve. With the processor running, slowly add the gelatine mixture to the pureed salmon until well blended, then gradually add the remaining cream. Transfer the mixture to a bowl, check the seasoning and chill for about 1 hour. Place each slice of smoked salmon on a sheet of cling film and pipe or spoon the filling down the centre of each one. Then roll up the slices in the cling film and squeeze gently to form sausage shapes. Chill in the fridge until set.To make the dressing, heat the oil, garlic, fennel, dill, salt and star anise in a pan until it is hot to the touch. Set aside to cool and infuse. Place the sugar, vinegar and a little pepper in a basin, then strain in the oil infusion and whisk well to make a dressing. Add Pernod to taste.

To make the salad, shred the cucumbers into long thin strips, like spaghetti. Put the tomatoes in boiling water to help in skinning, then deseed and chop finely. Toss the shredded cucumbers with the tomatoes and some of the dressing. Put some of the salad in the centre of each serving plate and place a sausage on top. Serve with brown bread.

Fish Fillets in Cheese Sauce

JOHNNY BEATTIE

Comedian

1 oz/25 g butter

1 oz/25 g plain flour

$^1/_2$ pint/275 ml milk

$^1/_2$ tsp Dijon mustard

$^1/_2$ tsp cayenne pepper

Salt and freshly ground black pepper

5 oz/150 g Cheddar cheese, grated

1 1b/450 g cod or haddock fillets, poached

4 cream crackers, buttered

Serves: 2 to 3

METHOD

Melt the butter in a saucepan, add the flour and cook for 1 minute, stirring. Gradually whisk in the milk, stirring constantly, until the sauce simmers and thickens. Add the mustard, cayenne pepper and other seasoning, and 3 oz/75 g of the cheese. Place the fish in an ovenproof dish and pour over the cheese sauce. Crumble over the cream crackers and sprinkle over the remaining cheese. Bake in an oven preheated to 190C/375F/Gas Mark 5 for 20 to 25 minutes until golden.

DR LEWIS KELMAN

"As a doctor interested in weight control and a talented boiler of eggs, wholly dependent on my lovely lady to avoid starvation, might I suggest my recipe for a healthy adult diet and lifestyle."

Ingredients

Saturated fats (solid at room temperature): Trim it off!

Polyunsaturated fats (mainly oil): No more than one-eighth of daily intake

Fibre and starches (including sugars): About one quarter of food intake

Protein (lean meat, fish, or other sources if vegetarian): Once or twice daily in moderate amounts

Eggs: Occasionally

Milk (skimmed) Up to half pint/275 ml daily

Fruit: A daily helping

Vegetables: Bung them on! Go light on potatoes

Bread: The staff of life for vitamin content; a few slices

Frying pan: Throw it away

Tobacco: Never

Alcohol: Small doses, if at all

Exercises: Within your capabilities and only if it's fun

Surround it all with love, given and received, and maintain an ever-open mind.

Dietician

SIR D. BRUCE PATULLO

Governor of the Bank of Scotland

Cheesy Shrimps

1¹/₂ oz/40 g butter
1¹/₂ oz/40 g plain flour
¹/₂ pint/275 ml milk
Salt and freshly ground black pepper
A pinch of mustard powder
3 oz/75 g Cheddar cheese, grated
6 oz/175 g shrimps, or peeled prawns

Serves: 4

METHOD

Melt the butter in a pan, stir in the flour and gradually add the milk, stirring until it boils and thickens. Season to taste with salt, pepper and mustard, then stir in most of the cheese. Add the shrimps or prawns and pour into 4 greased ramekin dishes. Sprinkle the remaining cheese on top, then bake in an oven preheated to 150C/300F/Gas Mark 2 for about 5 minutes, or until hot and bubbling.

"This dish makes an excellent starter and should be served with brown bread and butter."

Tuna Fish Casserole

PEGGY O'KEEFE

Singer

6 oz/175 g tagliatelle
2 x 7 oz/200 g cans of tuna, drained
¹/₂ pint/275 ml soured cream
4 oz/110 g peas, cooked
Salt
Freshly ground black pepper
2 oz/50 g fresh breadcrumbs
3 oz/75 g cheese, grated

Serves: 4

METHOD

Cook the pasta in a large pan of boiling salted water until al dente, then drain. Mix together the pasta, tuna, soured cream and peas and season to taste. Transfer the mixture to a casserole dish, sprinkle the breadcrumbs and grated cheese on top and bake in an oven preheated to 200C/400F/Gas Mark 6 for 25 minutes, until the topping is golden brown.

Sunday Brunch

DR ROBERT LOW
Gynaecologist

"It really is a most enjoyable dish and as yet I haven't poisoned anyone!"

3 - 4 eggs

Salt and freshly ground pepper, to taste

3 - 4 rashers of smoked bacon

2 slices of black pudding

A little butter

3 oz/75 g mushrooms

A generous pinch of ground garlic

2 - 3 oz/50 - 75 g smoked salmon,
  cut into fine strips

Serves: 2

METHOD

Gently scramble the eggs in a bowl with a little seasoning, and set aside. Lightly grill the bacon and black pudding. In a pan, melt a little butter, add the garlic and stir in. Add the mushrooms, and sautee over a low heat. Pour in the egg mixture and cook gently. Just before it is ready to serve, and while it is still runny, add the salmon strips. Serve on hot plates.

DAVID SHAW
Theatrical producer

2 eggs

2 slices of black pudding

2 slices of square sausage

2 tomatoes

6 large mushrooms

2 tattie scones

1 slice of bread
  (preferably Scottish square,
  outside heel!)

lard (as much as you need)

Salt and pepper

Serves: 1

Breakfast in Excess

"Large doses of everything that is bad for you."

METHOD

First of all, try and remember in which order they go into the big frying pan. As some things cook faster than others, I am told by people who really know about cooking that the secret is to have everything ready at the one time. My method is more simple than that. As the pan can't take everything at the one time anyway, cook the first lot, eat it, then have a second course, or you end up with shrivelled bacon, mushy eggs and you wonder where the mushrooms have gone.

Then put in too much salt, too much pepper, drink mugs of tea with too much sugar in it, eat toast with too much butter on it and stand by whilst your daughters lecture you on the dangers of cholesterol, salt, meat and every other excess. Finally, as it is by now afternoon and the sun is over the yardarm, take a large wine of the country with water and 'get tore into' the Sunday papers.

Flaky Mushroom and Feta Pie

PETER MORRISON
Singer

2 large onions, chopped

2 tbsp oil

2 garlic cloves, chopped

4 very large open-cap mushrooms, sliced

3 oz/75 g feta cheese, crumbled

2 tbsp white breadcrumbs

1 tsp dried or 2 tsp fresh thyme

Salt and freshly ground black pepper

1 large egg, beaten

12 oz/350 g puff pastry

Serves: 4

METHOD

Fry the onions in the oil until they begin to colour, then add the garlic and mushrooms and fry for a further 5 minutes. Tip the mixture into a bowl and allow to cool, then add the cheese, breadcrumbs, thyme, seasoning and egg, reserving a little egg to glaze the pie.

Roll out the pastry to an oblong about 14 x 12 inches/ 35 x 30 cm and spread the filling down one half of it. Brush the edges with water and fold the pastry over, making a pie 14 x 6 inches/35 x 15 cm in size. Seal the edges and brush with the reserved egg, cut a few slashes in the top and bake in an oven preheated to 220C/425F/Gas Mark 7 for 35 to 40 minutes, or until well risen and golden brown.

ARCHIE MCPHERSON

TV and radio sports presenter

Fresh Tagliatelle
with Bacon and Pesto

1 tbsp olive oil
2 garlic cloves, chopped
12 oz/350 g bacon, cut into strips
1 1b/450 g fresh egg tagliatelle
$^{1}/_{4}$ pint/150 ml double cream
1 jar of pesto
1 oz/25 g Parmesan cheese, freshly grated
Salt and freshly ground black pepper
Fresh basil leaves and black olives, to garnish

Serves: 4

METHOD

Heat the oil in a large saucepan, then add the garlic and bacon. Cook over a medium heat for 5 to 6 minutes, stirring occasionally. Meanwhile, cook the pasta in a large pan of boiling salted water, until al dente. Drain the pasta, add it to the bacon and stir in the cream, pesto, cheese and seasoning to taste. Cook gently for 1 to 2 minutes just to heat through, then transfer it to a warmed serving dish. Garnish with basil and olives and serve immediately.

BRENDA COCHRANE

Scottish singer

METHOD

Saute the bacon, onion and mushrooms in the olive oil until tender, adding the herbs, salt and pepper. Meanwhile, cook the pasta in boiling salted water with a little olive oil, until al dente. Drain the pasta and return it to the warm pan. Add the bacon mixture, then add the cheese and cream and stir until the cheese has melted. Serve on heated plates or in bowls.

Serves: 4

Naughty Pasta

6 rashers of back bacon, fat removed, cut into small strips
1 medium onion, chopped
4-8 oz/110-225 g mushrooms, chopped
1 tbsp olive oil
1 tsp fresh or freeze-dried oregano
1 tsp fresh or dried mixed herbs
Salt and freshly ground black pepper
14 oz/400 g penne or other pasta
3-4 oz/75-110 g strong Cheddar cheese, grated
$^1/_4$ pint/150 ml half-fat double cream, such as Delight or Elmlea

---

"I usually serve this with a green salad dressed with olive oil, lemon juice and salt. It's simple but absolutely delicious, along with warm French rolls. No butter is needed as the pasta sauce is very rich. The cream and cheese in this recipe make it a bit of a nightmare for those of us who can easily put on pounds. I only make this now and again."

Singapore Fried Vermicelli

TV actor/writer

1 packet Chinese-flavoured vermicelli

1 packet Chinese-flavoured noodles

8 oz/225 g quorn or other meat substitute,
  cut into 1 inch/2.5 cm cubes

3 tbsp cornflour

3 tbsp groundnut oil

1 tbsp finely chopped fresh ginger root

1 garlic clove, crushed

3 spring onions, sliced

7 oz/200 g can of water chestnuts, drained

4 oz/110 g button mushrooms, thinly sliced

1 tbsp hot-sweet Chinese sauce

$^1/_2$ red pepper, sliced into strips

$^1/_2$ green pepper, sliced into strips

1 tbsp soy sauce

METHOD

Cook the vermicelli and noodles according to the instructions on the packet, then drain thoroughly and set aside. Roll the quorn in the cornflour to coat. Heat the oil in a wok, then add the ginger and cook for 1 minute. Add the quorn, garlic, spring onions and water chestnuts and cook for another minute, stirring constantly to prevent sticking. Add the mushrooms and hot sauce, then add the vermicelli and noodles and stir-fry for 1 minute. Stir in the peppers and cook for another minute, then add the soy sauce, stir and serve.

Serves: 2

*"Don't forget
the
groundnut
oil . . .
it adds
a lot
of
character
to the
meal."*

RIKKI FULTON

Film, TV actor and comedian

Pot Mess

METHOD

"This is an unattractive name for a delicious time and money saving soup concocted on the mess decks of Her Majesty's larger ships. Every month, just before the victualling allowance is credited to each mess, it is the practice to clear out every particle of food left over from the previous month. To do this, every scrap and can of edible left-over food is piled willy-nilly into a large pot and heated through. Sounds awful . . . tastes wonderful!

It's best to start with canned soup as a base into which you can put any kind of meat or poultry, beef, pork spam, corned beef, etc, all diced up and chucked in beside canned peas, baked beans, tomatoes, etc. Amazingly, the flavour is nearly always the same . . . absolutely delicious. It's great for small informal parties, or those supper breaks at the end of the third rubber of Bridge."

Heavenly Chicken

MR LESLIE AND ALMA WOLFSON

Scottish Chairman, Tel Aviv University Trust

2 roasting chickens, cut into 8 portions

8 fl oz/225 ml Italian salad dressing

9 oz/250 g jar of apricot jam

1 packet of dried onion soup mix,
preferably French onion soup

Serves: 4

METHOD

Place the chicken pieces in two roasting pans. Combine the remaining ingredients for a few seconds in a food processor or blender, then pour over the chicken and allow to marinate in the refrigerator for a few hours, or overnight. Bake uncovered in an oven for about an hour at 180C/350F/Gas Mark 4 until nicely browned. Baste occasionally; the chicken will have a barbecued appearance and flavour. Serve with rice.

As variations, you can use Thousand Island dressing and apricot jam; French dressing and apricot or peach jam; or any bottled low-calorie dressing and diet jam.

"Eat one chicken and put the other away in the freezer."

Rikki Fulton

JACK MILROY AND MARY LEE

Husband and wife variety stars

Chicken Baked with Herbs

1 chicken leg
1 tomato, finely chopped
2 shallots, finely chopped
1 tsp chopped fresh tarragon
1 tsp chopped fresh chives
2 tbsp chicken stock or dry white wine
$^1/_2$ tsp olive oil
Squeeze of lemon juice
Salt and freshly ground black pepper

Serves: 1

METHOD

Put the chicken leg in a small shallow ovenproof dish or 2 sheets of aluminium foil folded up all round to make a container. Cover the chicken with the tomato, shallots and herbs, then pour in the stock or wine. Add the olive oil and lemon juice and season well. Place in an oven preheated to 180C/350F/Gas Mark 4 and cook for 35 to 40 minutes, until the chicken is tender. Serve with rice.

Chicken Stuffed with Haggis

JIMMY LOGAN

Actor and comedian

"Turkey or pheasant can be used instead of chicken. A little whisky can be added to the gravy to complement the haggis; it sharpens the palate. My Aunt Jean always called it 'seasoning.' She lived to be 90!"

METHOD

1 haggis

2 oz/50 g butter

1 onion, chopped

1 oz/25 g raisins

1 dessert apple, Granny Smith, peeled, cored and chopped

1 banana, sliced (optional)

3-4 1b/1.25-1.8 kg chicken

Serves: 4

Take the haggis out of its skin and break it up into small pieces. Melt the butter in a large frying pan, add the onion and raisins and fry gently until the onion is softened. Add the haggis, apple and banana, and fry gently for 3 to 4 minutes. If using the stuffing, make it up according to the instructions on the packet, leave to cool, then combine thoroughly with the haggis mixture. Stuff the chicken, place in a roasting tin and cook in an oven preheated to 190C/375F/Gas Mark 5 for about 1 hour 20 minutes, increasing the oven temperature to 220C/425F/Gas Mark 7 for the last 25 minutes to brown and crisp the skin. The chicken is cooked when a skewer inserted at the base of the leg produces clear juices.

Meatballs
with Hungarian Sauce

12 oz/350 g beef steak, minced
1 onion, finely chopped
Salt and freshly ground black pepper
3 tbsp oil

For the sauce
2 oz/75 g butter
2 onions, sliced
4 oz/110 g button mushrooms, sliced
1 tbsp plain flour
2 level tbsp paprika
7 oz/200 g can of tomatoes, chopped
2 tbsp tomato puree
1 tbsp lemon juice
$1/_2$ pint/275 ml beef or chicken stock
4 tbsp soured cream (optional)

Serves: 4

FRANK PIGNATELLI

Director of Education, Strathclyde Regional Council

METHOD

Mix together the minced beef and onion and season to taste. With floured hands, shape the mixture into 1 inch/2.5 cm meatballs. Heat the oil in a shallow pan and fry the meatballs for about 10 minutes. Set aside but keep warm.

For the sauce, melt the butter in a pan and fry the onions until softened. Add the mushrooms and cook for a few minutes, until tender. Add the flour and paprika and cook, stirring, for 1 to 2 minutes. Stir in all the remaining ingredients except the soured cream and simmer for 4 to 5 minutes. Add the meatballs to the sauce, heat gently and drizzle over the soured cream, if using.

"Serve the meatballs with plain boiled noodles."

Steak Balmoral

ANDY CAMERON

Stand-up comedian and TV actor

$1/_2$ onion, chopped
4 oz/110 g mushrooms, chopped
1 oz/25 g butter
2 fillet steaks
$1/_4$ pint/150 ml double cream
3 tbsp whisky
13 oz/375 g can of asparagus spears, drained
1 oz/25 g Parmesan cheese, freshly grated

Serves: 2

METHOD

Saute the onion and mushrooms in the butter until tender, then set aside and keep warm. Grill the steaks until done to your liking, then set aside and keep warm also. Pour the cream and whisky into the saute pan, bring to the boil, stirring, then cook until reduced and thickened. Place the onion and mushroom mixture on top of the steaks and cover with the asparagus spears. Coat everything with the sauce, sprinkle with the cheese and brown under the grill. Serve immediately.

ANDY CAMERON

SIR DAVID MCNEE
Former Commissioner, London Metropolitan Police

Mince with Poached Eggs

8 oz/225 g steak, minced
Salt and freshly ground pepper
1 beef stock cube
2 eggs

Serves: 2

METHOD
In a saucepan, season to taste and cook the mince with enough water to cover for 45 minutes. When ready, crumble in the stock cube for browning, and stir in. Drop in 1 egg per person into the mince and cook to taste, soft, medium or hard. Serve with bread or toast and butter.

"This was our family's Saturday lunch for as long as I can remember. I don't know why, except that Saturday morning was always a very busy time for my mother and this dish was easily prepared."

Baked Ham in Cider

JIM CASSIDY
Editor, Sunday Mail

2-3 1b/900 g - 1.25 kg gammon
Cloves
1 tbsp mustard, more if necessary
2 tbsp brown sugar, more if necessary
$^3/_4$ pint/ 425 ml cider

For the sauce
$1^1/_2$ tbsp cornflour
$^1/_4$ pint/150 ml milk
2 tsp fresh parsley, chopped

Serves: 4 to 6

METHOD
Wash the ham, then soak it in cold water for 2 to 3 hours. Dry the ham, score the fat into diamonds and stud it with cloves. Place it in a roasting tin, spread the mustard and brown sugar over the ham, then pour the cider around it. Cover with foil and bake in an oven preheated to 190C/375F/Gas Mark 5 for $1^1/_2$ to 2 hours. For the last 25 minutes, remove the foil and add more mustard and brown sugar if necessary.

To make the sauce, pour the cider from the ham into a pan and then add the cornflour, mixing well. Stir in the milk and parsley, bring to the boil and cook for 2 minutes, stirring all the time. Serve the sauce separately.

Spicy Lamb Burgers

DR SANDY MCINTOSH

Medical practitioner

1 level tsp cumin seeds

1 level tsp coriander seeds

1 small onion, quartered

1 garlic clove, peeled

3 tbsp chopped fresh coriander leaves

Juice of $\frac{1}{2}$ lime

4 oz/110 g cashew nuts, roasted and salted

1 green chilli, deseeded

Salt and freshly ground black pepper

12 oz/350 g shoulder of lamb, minced

4 tbsp oil

Serves: 4

METHOD

Heat the cumin and coriander seeds in a dry frying pan for a few minutes, until lightly browned, then grind them to a powder. Put all the ingredients except the lamb and the oil in a food processor and chop them fairly coarsely. Put them in a bowl with the lamb and mix thoroughly with your hands. Shape the mixture into burgers and fry in the oil for 3 to 5 minutes on each side, until cooked through. Alternatively, if you want to barbecue them, chill the burgers in a refrigerator for about 2 hours to firm them up first.

EVELYN COWAN

Author and journalist

Stuffed Cabbage Leaves

12 green cabbage leaves, preferably Savoy

4 oz/110 g rice, previously cooked

12 oz/350 g minced beef

1 tbsp grated onion

2 tbsp tomato puree

juice of 1 lemon

1 tbsp chopped fresh parsley
  or thyme (optional)

Salt and freshly ground black pepper

About $\frac{1}{2}$ pint/275 ml boiling beef stock

1 oz/25 g soft brown sugar

Serves: 4

METHOD

Put the cabbage leaves in a bowl, cover with boiling water and leave for 2 to 3 minutes. Drain them, dry with a cloth, then cut away the hard central core. In a bowl, mix the rice with the beef, then add the onion, half the tomato puree, a squeeze of lemon juice and the parsley or thyme. Stir well and season to taste. Put a spoonful of the mixture in the centre of each cabbage leaf and fold over like a parcel. Pack the stuffed leaves closely in a casserole dish and just cover them with the well-seasoned boiling stock, to which has been added the remaining tomato puree, the sugar and the remaining lemon juice. Cover and cook in an oven preheated to 180C/350F/Gas Mark 4 for about 35 minutes.

SIR FITZROY MACLEAN

Author and world traveller

Boeuf Stroganoff

2 oz/50 g butter

1¹/₂ 1b/675 g fillet steak,
  cut into 1 x ¹/₄ inch/2.5 cm x 60 mm strips

1 onion, finely chopped

8 oz/225 g mushrooms, chopped

1 small tomato, skinned and diced

8 fl oz/225 ml soured cream

Salt and freshly ground black pepper

Serves: 4

METHOD

Heat half the butter in a pan, add the beef and fry for 5 to 7 minutes. In another frying pan, saute the onion in the remaining butter for a few minutes, then add the mushrooms and tomato and cook gently until tender. Add the vegetables to the meat and pour over the cream. Heat through, season to taste, and serve immediately.

"This dish should always be served with sauteed potatoes."

Peaches Baked with Cinnamon

ALISTAIR McDONALD

Singer

14 oz/400 g can of peach halves in syrup

2 tsp ground cinnamon

4 oz/110 g soft brown sugar

2 tbsp kirsch or brandy (optional)

6 fl oz/175 ml double cream

Serves: 2 to 3

METHOD

Drain the peach halves, reserving the syrup, and place them cut-side up on a baking tray. Mix together the cinnamon and sugar and sprinkle over each peach. Drizzle over the kirsch or brandy, and bake in an oven preheated to 200C/400F/Gas Mark 6 for about 20 to 25 minutes, until the sugar has melted and is slightly caramelized.

Add 2 tablespoons of the reserved syrup to the cream and whip until it forms soft peaks. Serve the hot peaches with the cream.

Cheese Scones

MARY SANDEMAN
Pop singer

"These delicious little scones are very light and spongy, rather like American muffins."

4 oz/110 g plain flour
4 oz/110 g Cheddar cheese, grated
$^1/_2$ tsp salt
A pinch of cayenne pepper
3 tsp baking powder
1 egg
$^1/_4$ pint/150 ml milk

Makes 12 scones

METHOD

Put all the dry ingredients in a bowl and mix well. Lightly beat together the egg and milk, pour onto the flour mixture and stir together to make a soft dough. Spoon into well-greased patty tins and bake in an oven preheated to 200C/400F/Gas Mark 6 for about 10 to 12 minutes, until well risen and golden brown.

HUGH AND JEAN ADAM
Director of Rangers Pools

Clootie Dumpling

6 oz/175 g self-raising flour
6 oz/175 g mixed dried fruit
4 oz/110 g suet
4 oz/110 g dark brown sugar
1 tsp baking powder
1 tsp ground ginger
1 tsp mixed spice
1 tbsp treacle
1 egg
About 4 tbsp milk

Serves: 8

METHOD

Half fill a large pan with water, put an inverted plate in the bottom and bring to the boil. Mix all the ingredients together, adding enough milk to make a soft dough. Dip a pudding cloth (or a large linen or cotton tea towel) in hot water, then lay it flat and sprinkle it with flour. Place the pudding mixture in the centre, pull the sides of the cloth together and tie them securely with string. Put the dumpling on top of the plate in the pan of water and simmer for 3 to 4 hours, topping up with water if necessary. The water should come about three-quarters of the way up the dumpling. Serve with cream or custard.

Sozzle Cake

4 oz/110 g butter

6 oz/175 g caster sugar

2 large eggs

8 oz/225 g self-raising flour

1 tsp salt

2tbs milk

4 oz/175 g dried fruit

4 oz/175 g assorted nuts

2 tsp lemon juice

9 oz/250 g brown sugar

Scotch whisky

"Before you start, sample the whisky. To be sure the whisky is of the highest quality, pour one level cup into a glass and drink it as fast as you can, then repeat. Good, isn't it? Now go ahead. But before you start, sample the whisky . . ."

Serves: 4 to 6

METHOD

With an electric mixer, beat one cup of butter in a large fluffy bowl. Add one teaspoon of the thugar and beat again. Meanwhile, make sure the whisky is of the highest quality. Try another top-up. Open another bottle if necessary.

Add two large eggs, fried druit and beat til high. If druit gets stuck in beaters, just pry it loose with the drewscriver. Sample the whisky again, checking for tonscisticity. Next, sift three cups of salt or anything. Sample the whisky. Sift half a pint of lemon juice. Fold in chopped butter and strained nuts. Add one babblespoon of brown sugar, or whatever colour you can find, and wix mell. Grease the oven and turn cake tin to 360 gredees.Now pour the whole mess into the oven and bake. On second thoughts, don't bother. Check the whisky again and go to bed.

TRANSLATION: *Don't sample the whisky. Beat together the butter and caster sugar until smooth. Add the eggs and brown sugar and beat well until light and fluffy. Sift the flour with the salt, then fold into the mixture with 2 tbs milk. Stir in the dried fruit and nuts, and the lemon juice, then add 8 tbs whisky and mix again. Pour the mixture into a greased cake tin and bake in an oven preheated to 180C/350F/Gas Mark 4 for approx. 35 minutes, or until a knife inserted near the centre comes out clean. Turn out onto a cooling rack.*

Family Favourites

Creamed Broccoli and Cauliflower Soup

Mrs Joan Doherty

Sister of Vera Weisfeld

"This is a simple soup which is quick to make and tastes really delicious."

6 oz/175 g broccoli, divided into florets
6 oz/175 g cauliflower, divided into florets
1 pint/575 ml milk
$1^1/_2$ pints/875 ml water
1 chicken stock cube
$^1/_4$ pint/150 ml double cream
$^1/_2$ tsp nutmeg
Salt and freshly ground black pepper
Squeeze of lemon juice

METHOD

Put the broccoli and cauliflower into a saucepan with the milk and water, then crumble in the stock cube. Bring to the boil and simmer until the florets are very tender. Remove from the heat and puree in a blender or food processor. Return to the pan, add the cream and reheat gently, then season with the nutmeg, salt and pepper and lemon juice.

Serves: 4 to 6

Mrs Irene Watt

Family friend

METHOD

Put the stock and vegetables in a large pan, bring to the boil and simmer for 45 minutes, then liquidize in a blender or food processor. Return to the pan, add the milk and Worcestershire sauce and reheat gently. Just before serving, stir in the cream and garnish with the parsley and mushrooms.

"Don't forget the Worcester sauce. It makes all the difference."

Cream of Christmas Soup

1 pint/575 ml turkey stock
2 carrots, chopped
2 onions, chopped
4 celery sticks, chopped
1 potato, chopped
$^1/_2$ pint/275 ml milk
1 tbsp Worcestershire sauce
$^1/_4$ pint/150 ml double cream
Fresh parsley, chopped
A few mushrooms, finely sliced
 to garnish

Serves: 4 to 6

MALCOLM AND ANGELA McNEIL

Caesar Salad

Family friends

Serves: 4 to 6

2 thick slices of bread, cut into $^1/_2$ inch/1 cm cubes

3 garlic cloves, crushed

8 tbsp good-quality olive oil

2 Cos or Little Gem lettuces, torn into bite-sized pieces

2 oz/50 g can of anchovies, drained, rinsed and chopped

1 tbsp lemon juice

2 oz/50 g fresh Parmesan cheese, finely grated

1 egg, boiled for 1 minute

Salt and freshly ground black pepper

METHOD

Put the bread cubes in a pan with the crushed garlic and half the olive oil and fry over a moderate heat until crisp and golden. Set aside. Toss the lettuce leaves in the remaining olive oil in a salad bowl, then toss in the anchovies, lemon juice and Parmesan cheese. Break the soft-cooked egg into the salad and toss gently with salt and pepper to taste. Serve garnished with the fried bread cubes.

MRS MARIE PHILLIPS

Recipe for the Home

Family friend

TAKE half a cup of friendship, one cup of thoughtfulness and cream together with a pinch of powdered tenderness.

BEAT very lightly in a bowl of loyalty, with one cup of faith, one of hope and one of love. Be sure to add a teaspoonful each of gaiety and the ability to laugh at little things.

MOISTEN with the sudden tears of heartfelt sympathy, then bake in a good-natured pie.

Serves the World

Potted Herrings

JACK AND BETTY HARVIE

Family friends

METHOD

Sprinkle each herring fillet with salt, pepper and cornflour. Roll up the fillets and place them in an ovenproof dish. Pour over the wine or vinegar and water and lay the onion slices and bay leaves on top. Cover and bake in an oven preheated to 150C/300F/Gas Mark 2 for 1 hour. Serve hot with new potatoes or cold with salad.

6 herring fillets

Salt and freshly ground black pepper

$1^1/_2$ tsp cornflour

4 fl oz/110 ml good quality white wine vinegar or cider vinegar

4 fl oz/110 ml water

1 medium onion, thinly sliced

2 bay leaves

Serves: 2 to 3

152

ANDREW SIM

Family friend

Haddy Monte Carlo

6 oz/175 g smoked haddock fillet
$\frac{1}{4}$ pint/150 ml milk
1 oz/25 g butter
1 egg, lightly poached

Serves: 1

METHOD

Simmer the smoked haddock fillet in water just to cover until cooked (approximately 8 minutes). Drain, then add the milk and butter. Heat slowly for a few minutes but do not boil. Serve the fish with plenty of milk from the pan and a soft poached egg on top.

Scampi Auld Reekie

BOBBY AND MARIE LOUDEN

Family friends

2 oz/50 g butter
1 large Spanish onion, finely sliced
1 lb/450 g jumbo scampi
1 large or small measure of whisky, to taste
$\frac{1}{4}$ pint/150 ml double cream
Salt and freshly ground black pepper

Serves: 3 to 4

METHOD

Heat the butter in a frying pan, add the onion and saute until tender. Add the scampi and stir gently for about 2 minutes. Turn down the heat and add the whisky, stirring gently. Simmer for 30 seconds, then add the cream, cover the pan and cook for 2 minutes. Season to taste and serve hot, with boiled rice or pitta bread.

"A marvellous starter which takes less than five minutes to rustle up."

VERA WEISFELD

Co-founder of The Weisfeld Foundation

African Stew

"The dish that started it all . . . out of this recipe grew this book. For an even more succulent stew, I recommend preparing it the night before. This brings out the full flavour of the ingredients. Reheat gently before serving."

METHOD

Heat the butter, margarine or oil in a large pan, add the onions, carrots, peppers and garlic and fry very gently until soft. Add the cubed beef and fry briskly until the meat is sealed and brown. Stir in the tomato puree, spices, salt and vinegar, then pour in the stock and bring to the boil. Simmer gently for 2 hours or until the meat is tender, stirring occasionally. Mix the peanut butter and flour together and add to the simmering stew a little at a time, stirring until the stew thickens. Stir in the wine. Serve with creamed potatoes or rice.

Serves: 4

"If you like you can add or substitute some ingredients."

$1^1/_2$ oz/40 g butter or margarine, or 2 tbsp oil

2 medium onions, chopped

2 medium carrots, sliced

1 green pepper, sliced

1 red pepper, sliced

1-2 garlic cloves, chopped

$1^1/_2$ lb/675 g best stewing steak, cut into cubes

2 level tbsp tomato puree

$^1/_4$ level tsp ground cloves

$^1/_4$ level tsp ground ginger

A pinch of cayenne pepper or a shake of Tabasco sauce

1- 2 level tsp salt

1 tsp vinegar

$^1/_2$ pint/275 ml beef stock

2 level tbsp smooth peanut butter

1 level dsp plain flour

A dash of red or white wine (optional)

154

A striking pictorial study of Vera and Gerald Weisfeld on their mercy mission to Bosnia with badly needed supplies.

MRS CELINA O'LOUGHLIN

Sister of Vera Weisfeld

Brandy Cream Sauce

"This luxurious sauce can be served with ice cream, steamed or baked puddings or fruit tarts, or even used as a topping for trifle."

METHOD

Beat the egg until it is light and fluffy, then beat in the melted butter and the icing sugar, salt and brandy. Gently fold in the whipped cream, then cover and chill. Stir before using. The sauce keeps well in the refrigerator.

Serves: 4

1 egg
2 oz/50 g melted butter
6 oz/175 icing sugar
A pinch of salt
4 tbsp brandy
7 fl oz/200 ml double cream,
  lightly whipped

Meringue Casings

KAY CASSELLS

Family friend

METHOD

Whisk up four egg whites in a bowl until stiff. Gently fold in 6 oz/175 g caster sugar, ensuring it is well mixed. Spoon onto a greaseproof paper in small amounts. Cook in an oven preheated to 170C/325F/Gas Mark 3 for 15 minutes, then lower the heat to 110C/225F/Gas Mark 1/4 and bake for a further 75 minutes, until hard. Cool and store.

BRIAN AND DOROTHY LEVINE

Family friends

Hazelnut Meringue

METHOD

Whip the egg whites until they are very stiff. Add the caster sugar gradually, beating it in until the mixture forms stiff peaks. Add the vanilla essence and vinegar, and fold in the hazelnuts. Divide the mixture into two and place in two 8in/20 cms sandwich tins lined with baking parchment. Bake in an oven preheated to 190C/375F/Gas Mark 5 for 30 to 40 minutes. Allow to cool. To make the topping and filling, whisk up the double cream. Place a layer of cream, followed by a layer of raspberries, on one of the two meringue halves, and gently place the second meringue on top. Save some of the cream and raspberries to use as topping, then dust with icing sugar.

4 egg whites
9 oz/250 g caster sugar
$^3/_4$ drops vanilla essence
$^1/_2$ tsp white vinegar
4 $^1/_2$ oz/125 g ground hazelnuts

For the topping
$^1/_2$ pint/275 ml double cream
$^1/_2$ lb/275 g fresh raspberries
1 tbs icing sugar

Serves: 4 to 6

156

Honey Cake

DR ADRIAN AND MYRNA WHITESON

Family friends

"Although this is a traditional honey cake recipe, we always use golden syrup. You could, of course, substitute honey for all or some of the syrup."

1 lb/450 g tin golden syrup

$^1/_4$ pint/150 ml vegetable oil

4 fl oz/110 ml cold tea

4 oz/110 g caster sugar

1 tsp ground ginger

1 tsp mixed spice

$^1/_2$ tsp bicarbonate of soda

3 eggs, separated

12 oz/350 g self-raising flour, sifted

Flaked almonds, to decorate

Serves: 4 to 6

METHOD

Grease a 2 lb/900 g loaf tin or 2 deep round tins. Mix together the syrup, oil, tea, sugar, ginger, mixed spice and bicarbonate of soda. A blender or food processor is ideal for this. Add the egg yolks and blend in.

In a separate bowl, whisk the egg whites until stiff. Fold the flour and the egg whites into the mixture and pour the batter into the prepared tins. Scatter almonds over the top. Bake in an oven preheated to 180C/350F/Gas Mark 4 for 1 hour (or 40 minutes for 2 round cakes) until the top is firm and the sides are shrinking away from the tin slightly. Leave to cool in the tin for about 10 minutes, then turn out onto a wire rack to cool completely.

GEOFFREY AND CAROLE NATHAN

Family friends

Reina's Banana Chartreuse

METHOD

Make up the jellies with the boiling water. Pour about $^1/_2$ inch/1 cm of jelly into the bottom of a chilled 3 pint/1.75 litre mould and, when it is slightly set, slice 1 banana evenly over it. Place the remainder of the jelly in the refrigerator until it begins to set. Mash the remaining bananas with the lemon juice to prevent discolouration. Whisk the cream until it forms soft peaks, then beat in the slightly gelled jelly. Add the mashed bananas and pour into the mould. Leave in the refrigerator overnight. When ready to serve, run a thin knife round the top edge of the mould to loosen the contents, then immerse the mould in boiling water for 10 seconds only. Run cold water over a serving dish and place it on top of the mould, invert and turn out. Keep refrigerated until ready to serve.

2 packets of lemon jelly

1 pint/575 ml boiling water

6 bananas

Juice of 1 lemon

1 pint/575 ml double cream

Serves: 6 to 8

TERRY AND SADIE CARLIN

German Biscuits

8 oz/225 g plain flour
5 oz/150 g butter, softened
2 oz/50 g caster sugar
Red currant jelly
4 oz/110 g white icing sugar
2 - 3 tbs. water
Glace cherries (optional)

Makes 12 German biscuits

METHOD

In a bowl, knead together by hand the flour, butter and sugar until it forms a smooth dough. Roll out to approx. 1/4 inch/0.5 cm thickness and cut into 2 inch/5 cm rounds with a round pastry cutter. Bake in a slow oven preheated to 170C/325F/Gas Mark 3 until lightly coloured. For the topping, put the icing sugar in a bowl and add just enough water to mix it into a smooth paste. Spread the icing over the biscuits, with a half glace cherry or a dab of jelly in the centre. For more colour, scatter Hundreds and Thousands on the icing.

Water Bread

MAURICE AND JACQUELINE HART

Family friends

2 oz/50 g fresh yeast

4 oz/110 g granulated sugar

1¹/₄ pints/725 ml warm water

2¹/₄ lb/1kg strong plain flour

4 fl oz/110 ml oil

2 tsp salt

1 egg beaten with 1 tbsp water,
  to glaze

Poppy seeds, to decorate

Makes 3 loaves

METHOD

Dissolve the yeast and 2 teaspoons of the sugar in 4 fl oz/110 ml of the warm water. Sift the flour into a very large bowl. Make a well in the centre and pour in the remaining water, the oil, the remaining sugar, the salt and the yeast mixture. Mix until a soft dough is formed. Knead by hand for 10 to 15 minutes, or in an electric mixer with a dough hook for 5 minutes, until smooth but not sticky. Place the dough in a greased bowl, cover it with a tea-towel and leave to rise until doubled in bulk.

Punch down the risen dough and knead lightly. Divide it into 9 balls for braided loaves or into 3 balls for tin loaves and leave to rest for 10 minutes. To make braided loaves, roll each of the 9 balls into a rope 10 inches/25 cm long. Take 3 ropes and pinch them together at one end. Pleat them together, then tuck the ends under to seal. Repeat with the remaining dough to make 2 more loaves. Place them on a baking sheet. If you are making tin loaves, simply press the 3 balls of dough into three 1 lb/450 g loaf tins. Brush with the beaten egg and sprinkle with poppy seeds. Leave to rise for 20 to 30 minutes, then bake in an oven preheated to 180C/350F/Gas Mark 4 for 45 minutes to 1 hour, or until the loaves are browned and sound hollow when tapped underneath. Cool on a wire rack.

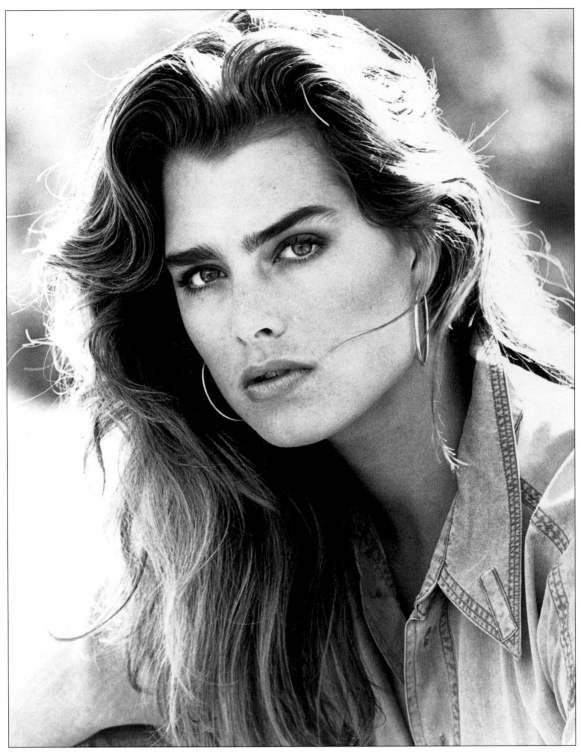

BROOKE SHIELDS

World Showbusiness

I T WAS WALLIS SIMPSON, FOR WHOM A KING GAVE UP A CROWN, who once observed, "You can never be too rich or too thin." She could very well have been talking about international showbiz. Keeping in shape for the unforgiving eye of the camera lens is an exceptionally important part of a star's life. As very public figures, away from the film set, they are constantly "on parade" - from official photo calls and public appearances to vigilant paparazzi dogging their footsteps in search of candid (and frequently unflattering) shots .

Some stars have a love-hate relationship with their weight, others seem to sail through life untroubled by calories. What the public often doesn't see are the personal trainers who put many of them through rigorous daily exercises, or the fairly rigid control they exercise over what they eat. Not unnaturally, this section reflects a fairly high degree of awareness of calorific content, as in Liz Taylor's Spicy Chicken dish. There are also more than a few pasta dishes. What is clear from this Section is that is possible to eat well, and enjoy tasty, imaginative meals which won't pile on the pounds, if taken in moderation.

Honor Blackman's Hot Avocado Parcels and Jenny Agutter's Cucumber and Walnut Chilled Soup are two particularly unusual dishes. For anyone on a controlled diet, walnuts are an excellent ingredient. A sprinkling of roughly crushed walnuts can inject fresh flavour into even the most "tired" of dishes. I've even heard of people who surreptitiously carry a few around with them when asked out to dinner parties.

It's not all calorie counting, however. Tom Hanks shows he's no Forrest Gump, weighing in with a simple to make Creamy Cheesecake. On this side of the Atlantic, where British stars seem more relaxed about what they eat. Liam Neeson recommends an Irish Stew with a pint of Guinness as part of the stock; Michael Caine plumps for Carrot Cake and its equally delicious counterpart, Banana Cake. These are pretty heavyweight offerings. When well made, carrot cake is superb. Too often, though, we are subjected to stodgy versions which could provide the building trade with an alternative source of material.

After a helping or two of the better version, however, we'll probably have to opt for the irrepressible Rolf Harris's Bachelor's Scrambled Egg and Tomato, to redress the balance - although I have to say the other dishes sound a lot more attractive.

Vegetable Health Soup

BROOKE SHIELDS

Film star

"This soup may be served hot or cold with a dab of low-fat cottage cheese in the centre."

1 tbsp vegetable oil

1 large onion, chopped

2 medium Granny Smith apples, peeled, cored and chopped

2 large dashes of Worcestershire sauce or chilli sauce

12 oz/350 g broccoli (including stalks)
  or cauliflower or carrots, chopped

2 pints/1.2 litres chicken stock

Fresh parsley or mint, chopped, to garnish

Serves: 4

METHOD

Heat the oil in a large frying pan and saute the onion and apples, sprinkled with Worcestershire or chilli sauce, until softened. Set aside. Steam or parboil the vegetables until tender. Heat the chicken stock in a pan, add all the ingredients except the parsley and simmer for 10 minutes, then puree in a blender or food processor. Serve garnished with parsley in winter, mint in summer.

LEWIS GILBERT

Film Director of Shirley Valentine

Soupe de Poisson Tafflet

4 white fish steaks, such as cod or hake

A knob of butter

1 large onion, thinly sliced

1 tbsp fresh parsley, chopped

1 level tsp sugar

Salt and freshly ground black pepper

1 pint/575 ml milk

5 oz/150 g frozen peas, preferably petits pois

8 oz/225 g vermicelli

Serves: 4

METHOD

The secret is to cook the fish, butter, onion, parsley, sugar, salt and pepper very slowly in the milk in a covered pan, so that it merely simmers gently and does not curdle. The milk should be scarcely bubbling and the fish should take about 20 minutes to cook.

Cook the peas and vermicelli separately in boiling salted water until tender, then drain well. Serve the vermicelli, peas and milk in soup bowls. Serve the fish on separate plates or add it to the soup, if you prefer.

"This is a good meal if you are feeling rather delicate."

Cucumber and Walnut Soup

"This soup should be served well chilled and is delicious even in winter. Chopped fresh chervil or mint would be a lovely addition in summer."

4 oz/110 walnuts

1 or 2 garlic cloves, peeled

$1^{1}/_{2}$ tbsp olive oil

$^{1}/_{2}$ cucumber, finely diced

Salt and freshly ground black pepper

$^{1}/_{4}$ pint/150 ml soured cream

About $^{3}/_{4}$ pint/425 ml buttermilk
  or yogurt

Serves: 4

METHOD

With a pestle and mortar, crush the walnuts with the garlic and olive oil (do not use a blender as the soup should retain some texture). Mix thoroughly with the diced cucumber and add salt and pepper to taste. Stir in the soured cream and then dilute with enough buttermilk or yogurt to make a thick soupy consistency. Chill for several hours before serving.

Lentil Soup

GLENDA JACKSON, MP

Stage and film star politician

1 oz/25 g butter

1 onion, chopped

2 garlic cloves, crushed

1 tsp cumin

8 oz/225 g red lentils

1 tomato, chopped, or 7 oz/200 g can of tomatoes

1³/₄ pints/1 litre chicken stock

Salt and freshly ground black pepper

A squeeze of lemon juice

Fresh parsley, chopped, to garnish (optional)

Serves: 4

METHOD

Melt the butter in a pan, add the onion and garlic and cook them gently for 2 to 3 minutes. Stir in the cumin and lentils, then add the tomato and stock. Simmer for 30 to 45 minutes until the lentils are very soft. Liquidize the soup in a blender or food processor. Return the soup to the pan, reheat gently and season with salt and pepper and a little lemon juice. Garnish with parsley.

NIGEL HAVERS

Screen and stage star

METHOD

Melt the butter in a frying pan and add the chopped onion and garlic. Saute until soft but not brown. Remove the onion and garlic from the pan and set aside. Add to the pan the chicken livers, salt and pepper and the bouquet garni, opened and sprinkled over the chicken livers. Cook for approximately 5 to 8 minutes, leaving the chicken livers slightly pink in the centre. Do not overcook. Pour the entire contents of the pan, together with the onion and garlic, into a blender or food processor and blend well, adding the brandy while the machine is switched on. Pour into a pate dish and, when firm and cool, cover with clarified butter and garnish with parsley.

Serves: 6

Chicken Liver Pate

4 oz/110 g butter

1 medium onion, chopped

1 large garlic clove, chopped

1 lb/450 g fresh or frozen chicken livers

Salt and freshly ground black pepper

1 dried bouquet garni sachet
  or 1 tsp dried mixed herbs

2 tbsp brandy

Clarified butter and sprigs of parsley, to serve

Susan's Salad

A few lettuce or chicory leaves

1 banana, chopped

2 carrots, grated

2 tomatoes, sliced

A handful of raisins

4 oz/110 g cottage cheese or mild goat's cheese

4 oz/110 g fresh pineapple, chopped, or strawberries

6 blanched almonds

A little grated fresh ginger root (optional)

SUSAN HAMPSHIRE

Fim star, cookery writer

For the dressing

1 tsp fresh chives and parsley, chopped

1 tbsp walnut oil

1 tsp lemon juice or cider vinegar

Onion salt, to taste

Freshly ground black pepper

Serves: 2

METHOD

Arrange the lettuce or chicory on 2 serving plates and divide the remaining ingredients between them. If you are using the ginger, sprinkle it over the cheese. Mix together all the ingredients for the dressing, pour it over the salad and serve.

SUSAN HAMPSHIRE

HONOR BLACKMAN

Hot Avocado Parcels

HONOR BLACKMAN
Film and television star

2 tsp lemon juice
2 tsp lime juice
1¹/₂ tsp sweet chilli sauce
1 firm avocado, peeled, stoned
  and cut into ¹/₄ inch/5 mm cubes
1 cooked chicken breast,
  cut into small cubes
1 plum tomato, deseeded and diced
3 oz/75 g Gruyere cheese,
  cut into ¹/₄ inch/5 mm cubes
8 sheets of filo pastry
2 oz/50 g butter, melted
Salt and freshly ground black pepper
Lemon or lime wedges, to serve

Serves: 4

METHOD

Sprinkle the lemon juice, lime juice and chilli sauce over the diced avocado, making sure it is well coated. Mix the avocado with the chicken, tomato, cheese and salt and pepper. Lay 1 sheet of filo pastry on a work surface, brush with melted butter, then cover with another sheet of pastry. Brush the edges with butter and place a quarter of the avocado mixture in the centre. Fold the filo over the filling to enclose it completely (just like wrapping a Christmas parcel). Repeat with the remaining filo and filling to make 4 parcels. Place the parcels on an oiled baking tray, seam sides down, brush with more melted butter and bake in an oven preheated to 180C/350F/Gas Mark 4 for 20 minutes. Serve with lemon or lime wedges and a crisp salad.

EDWARD FOX
Film star

My Favourite Lunch

"I am afraid that I am not a good cook nor even a moderate one, however my favourite lunch at this time of year is:-
steak and kidney pudding with mashed potatoes (plenty of pepper) and cabbage (practically raw) followed by treacle tart with cream and lemon."

169

MICHAEL WINNER

170

Scrambled Eggs

MICHAEL WINNER
Film producer

"This is not my favourite recipe - it is my only one! Ava Gardner told me Frank Sinatra did his scrambled eggs like this when we discussed cooking."

METHOD

Take the eggs and add a lot of milk - you have to do this by intuition. Whisk long and thoroughly with an electric whisk. In the meantime heat a large frying pan with butter melted to just under sizzling. When the eggs are at their frothiest pour speedily into the pan. Keep moving them around with a wooden spoon; the whole thing takes only a few minutes. Add caviare, chopped smoked salmon or just have 'em alone or on toast.

ROLF HARRIS
TV entertainer

Bachelor Scrambled Eggs and Tomato

Butter or margarine
1 spring onion, finely chopped
  (optional)
Milk
2 eggs
Salt
Freshly ground black pepper
1 tomato, cut in half

Serves: 1

METHOD

First, melt a small splodge of butter or margarine in a frying pan and drop in the spring onion, if using. Cook over a low heat for a short while then add a slosh of milk ...too much and the eggs will be watery. Take the pan off the heat while you break the eggs into it. Add a dusting of salt to each egg and as much pepper as you like, then put the pan back on a low heat (it must be a low heat as nothing is worse than little black horrible tasting burnt bits in scrambled egg) while you graunch up the eggs with a wooden spoon and generally scramble them around. Meanwhile, place the tomato halves under a hot grill, flat side down and cook until the skin shrivels up and starts to go black, then turn them over, add a dusting of salt and grill the flat side. The scrambled eggs should be just starting to solidify, so take the pan off the heat for a tick while you pop in your beautifully grilled tomato. The skin on the smooth side just comes away but you will need to cut out the core on the other half of the tomato. Put the pan back on the heat while you squelch up the tomato with the wooden spoon. Don't dry it up too much. Mix the eggs and tomato thoroughly and serve.

SAM NEILL

Film star

Late Scrambled Eggs

METHOD

Melt 2 large knobs of butter in a heavy saucepan, then remove from the heat. Break in 6 free-range eggs and add a couple of splashes of milk. If you have been righteous, also add a dab of cream! Put in some chopped fresh parsley and black pepper and beat a little with a fork, not too much as you want to get some white bits on completion. Cook over a moderate heat, stirring with a wooden spoon and adding some chopped smoked salmon about halfway through. When still a little runny, serve on brown toast, accompanied by champagne and coffee.

Serves: 2

Champ

JEREMY IRONS

Film star

10 spring onions
 (green part as well as white)
 or 2 leeks, chopped
4 fl oz/110 ml milk
1¹/₂ lb/675 g potatoes
Salt and freshly ground black pepper
4 tbsp butter, melted

METHOD

Serves: 4

In a pan, cook the spring onion or leeks in the milk until softened, then drain and set aside, reserving the milk. Boil the potatoes until tender in salted water, then drain and mash. Season to taste and add the spring onions or leeks. Beat well together and add enough of the hot milk to make the potatoes creamy and smooth. Place the mixture in a warmed deep dish, make a well in the centre and pour in the hot melted butter. Serve immediately.

Champ can also be make with chopped parsley, chives, young nettle tops or young green peas. For a supper dish, scrambled eggs are often served in the centre, sprinkled with chopped parsley.

JEREMY IRONS

Potato Cakes

"I got this recipe from my mother, who often used to make these potato cakes for tea. They are delicious with bacon."

2 1b/900 g potatoes, peeled,
  boiled and mashed
2 oz/50 g butter
About 6 oz/175 g plain flour
Salt and freshly ground black pepper
Vegetable oil, for frying (optional)

Makes 12 potato cakes

METHOD

Put the mashed potatoes into a bowl and mix in the butter. Sieve the flour onto the potatoes, mixing as you go, until you have a stiff dough. Add salt and pepper to taste. Roll out the mixture on a well-floured board to a thickness of $^1/_2$ inch/1 cm, then cut into squares or other shapes with a knife or a pastry cutter. Cook on an ungreased hot griddle or in a little vegetable oil in a heavy frying pan until the potato cakes are brown on both sides, turning them halfway through. Serve them split and buttered.

Irish Colcannon

HELEN MIRREN

Film and TV star

1 1b/450 g kale or cabbage, finely chopped

7 - 8 fl oz/200-225 ml milk or cream

2 small leeks or green spring onion tops,
  chopped

2 1b/900g potatoes, preferably Irish, diced

Salt and freshly ground black pepper

A pinch of ground mace

4 tbsp butter, melted

Serves: 4

METHOD

Cook the kale or cabbage in a large pan of boiling water until very tender, then drain and keep warm. Put the milk or cream in a small pan with the leeks or spring onions and simmer until soft. In another saucepan, cook the potatoes until tender, then drain and mash them. Mix in the leeks or onion tops and enough milk or cream to give a creamy consistency. Add the kale or cabbage and season with salt, pepper and mace. Drizzle with the melted butter and serve immediately.

TOPOL

The unforgettable 'Fiddler on the Roof'

Gefilteh Fish

1 large onion, sliced

4 - 5 carrots, sliced

1 tsp salt

$^1/_2$ tsp black pepper

3 tbsp sugar (if of Russian descent)

or 6 tbsp sugar (if of Polish descent)

$^1/_2$ pint/275 ml water

For the fishcakes

1 carp, to give about 2 1b/900 g flesh,
  filleted and minced

3 onions, finely chopped

3 hard-boiled eggs, finely chopped

1 egg

A few tbsp breadcrumbs or plain flour

Serves: 4

METHOD

For the fishcakes, mix together the minced carp and the other ingredients adding breadcrumbs or flour to bind, if necessary. Divide into 12 oval fishcakes, 1 inch/2.5 cm thick.

Spread the sliced onion over the base of a wide casserole dish. Cover the base with half the carrots and sprinkle them with the salt, pepper and sugar. Pour over the water, then cover the carrots with a layer of 6 to 8 fishcakes. Arrange the remaining carrots on top, add another layer of fishcakes and pour over enough water to cover everything. Bring to the boil and then simmer for 2 hours on a low heat. Leave to cool, then remove the fishcakes from the liquid. Place on a serving platter and decorate with the carrot slices. Strain the liquid off the onions (which should be discarded) and put it in a separate container. Put the fishcakes and liquid in the refrigerator. The liquid will turn to jelly. Serve the fishcakes cold, topped with a little jelly.

JANE ASHER

Actress, cookery writer

Four-Cheese Pasta

"This is one of my favourites. The melted cheese perfectly complements the pasta and makes it wonderfully creamy. Use any cheeses as long as they roughly correspond to the types given here. As it is very rich, serve small portions and follow with a sharply dressed green salad."

2 tbsp olive oil

1 garlic clove, crushed

1¼ lb/560 g pasta

¼ pint/150 ml single cream

2 oz/50 g each Gruyere,
   Bel Paese and Dolcelatte cheeses, diced

2 oz/50 g Parmesan cheese, freshly grated

Salt and freshly ground black pepper

Serves: 6

METHOD

Heat the oil in an ovenproof casserole, add the garlic and remove the dish from the heat. Cook the pasta in boiling salted water for about 8 minutes or until it is al dente, then drain and toss in the garlic oil. Add the cream, the cheeses and the seasoning and mix well. Place in an oven preheated to 220C/425F/Gas Mark 7 just long enough for the cheese to melt. Serve immediately.

Pasta al Burro

FELICITY KENDAL

Stage and television actress

8 oz/225 g spaghetti

2 - 3 tbsp olive oil

2 oz/50 g butter

2 large garlic cloves, finely chopped

A large bunch of parsley, finely chopped

Freshly ground black pepper

Freshly grated Parmesan cheese, to serve

Serves: 2

METHOD

Cook the spaghetti in a large pan of boiling salted water until it is al dente. Meanwhile, heat the oil in a pan and melt in dollops of the butter. When the oil and butter are hot but not sizzling, add the garlic and parsley. Drain the spaghetti and toss it thoroughly with the garlic and parsley sauce. Serve immediately with lots of black pepper and Parmesan cheese, accompanied by a green salad.

JANE ASHER

JENNY SEAGROVE

Penne Arrabiata

METHOD

Put a fair amount of olive oil in a large pan and add the onion and garlic. Cook gently over a low heat, constantly moving the pan around. Add the chilli and then the tomatoes to the pan. Season to taste and cook until the tomatoes are softened. In a separate pan, in boiling salted water, to which a dash of olive oil has been added, cook the penne until the pasta is al dente. Leave the pot uncovered during the boil. Drain the penne and pour over it the hot sauce. Toss well to ensure that the penne is married with the sauce and serve with a lovely Italian red wine.

JENNY SEAGROVE

Film star

Some Extra Virgin olive oil
1 large onion, chopped
Garlic cloves to taste, finely chopped
Hot red chilli peppers to taste,
  finely chopped
4 large tomatoes, roughly chopped
Salt and freshly ground black pepper
6 oz/175 g penne

Serves: 2

"Robert and Del Webber first cooked this for me at their beach house in Malibu, California. Now it is a favourite dish of mine in Italian restaurants."

SUSANNAH YORK

Film star

Pasta Cosa Nostra

METHOD

Heat the olive oil in a pan, add the garlic, onion and peppers and cook gently for 5 minutes, until softened. Add the mushrooms and cook for a few minutes longer, then stir in the tomatoes, herbs, tomato puree, seasoning and olives, and red wine if you have it. Let the sauce simmer while you cook the pasta. Drop the pasta into a large pan of boiling salted water to which you have added about a teaspoon of olive oil, and cook until al dente. Drain well and serve with the sauce and plenty of Parmesan cheese.

Serves: 6

1 - 2 tbsp olive oil
2 - 3 garlic cloves, chopped
1 onion, chopped (optional)
1 green pepper, finely sliced
$1/2$ red pepper, finely sliced
8 oz/225 g mushrooms, sliced (optional)
1 lb/450 g fresh tomatoes, chopped
  or 2 x 13 oz/375 g cans of tomatoes, chopped
2 bay leaves
A pinch of dried oregano, to taste
2 tsp tomato puree
Salt and freshly ground pepper
2 oz/50 g black olives, stoned and halved
4 fl oz/110 ml red wine (optional)
$1^1/_2$ lb/675 g fresh pasta
  (my favourite is green tagliatelle)
Freshly grated Parmesan cheese, to serve

MICHAEL CRAWFORD

Stage and TV entertainer

METHOD

Cook the pasta in boiling salted water, until al dente, then drain. Toss in 1 tsp of olive oil and set aside. Into a large, deep frying pan, over a moderate heat, put in the olive oil and briefly saute the onions until tender. Add the tomatoes, ham, garlic and wine. Stirring occasionally, cook gently for about 5 minutes until some of the liquid is absorbed. Add the herbs, the sugar and red peppers. Don't season with salt, there is enough in the ham. Cook gently for 5 more minutes, to reduce the sauce. Taste and correct the seasoning, if necessary. Pour the sauce over the pasta, sprinkle with cheese, and serve.

"This is a quick and delicious version of Salsa Amatriciana. But remember to take out the red peppers before serving."

Salsa Michele

1 lb/450 g tagliatelle, fettucine or linguine pasta (fresh, if possible)

2 tbs good olive oil

1 large onion, chopped

2 x 14 oz/400 g cans of plum tomatoes, peeled and coarsely chopped

8 oz/225 g Parma ham, coarsely chopped

6 cloves of fresh garlic, minced

Glass of white wine (like Pinot Grigio)

2 tbs fresh oregano, chopped (packed tight to measure)

3 tbs fresh basil, chopped (packed tight to measure)

A pinch of sugar

1 - 2 dried red peppers, to taste

2 oz/50g Parmagioni cheese, grated (optional)

Serves: 3 to 4

Spiced Basmati Rice

Oil for frying

1 large onion, finely chopped

2 small dried red chillies, chopped, or to taste

1 heaped tsp garam masala

3 garlic cloves, crushed

1 tsp salt (more if stock is unsalted)

1 pint/575 ml vegetable stock (made with organic vegetable stock cubes if possible)

Serves: 4

JULIE CHRISTIE

Film star

METHOD

Pick over the rice and then wash it in several changes of water until the water runs nearly clear. Pour 2 pints/1.2 litres of fresh water over the rice and let it soak for 30 minutes, then leave to drain in a sieve or colander for 20 minutes.

Heat some oil in a heavy bottomed saucepan, add the onion and fry over a moderate heat until slightly browned. Add the rice, chillies, garam masala, garlic and salt. Stir gently for 3 to 4 minutes until all the grains of rice are well coated. If the rice begins to stick in the pan, turn the heat down slightly. Pour in the stock and bring to the boil. Cover with a very tight-fitting lid and cook on the lowest possible heat for 25 minutes.

Chicken with Sage

Film star

4 boneless chicken breasts

2 tbsp plain flour, seasoned with salt and pepper

1 tbsp olive oil

$^1/_2$ oz/15 g butter

2 tbsp fresh sage, chopped

4 thin slices of prosciutto or bacon, chopped

$^1/_4$ pint/150 ml dry white wine

1 pint/575 ml chicken stock

Serves: 4

METHOD

Dust the chicken breasts with the seasoned flour. In a large heavy pan, lightly fry them on both sides in the olive oil and butter until golden brown. Add the sage, prosciutto or bacon, wine and stock. Cover and simmer for about 40 minutes until the chicken is tender. Remove the chicken, but keep warm. Increase the heat and boil until the liquid is reduced by half. Pour it over the chicken and serve immediately, with a green salad and French bread.

JACK LEMMON

Film superstar

8 corn tortillas

$^1/_2$ pint/275 ml soured cream

1 tsp ground cumin

1 tsp chilli powder

$^1/_2$ tsp salt

5 spring onions, sliced

$1^1/_2$ 1b/675 g cooked chicken, diced

12 oz/350 g mild taco sauce (Old El Paso)

6 oz/175 g Cheddar cheese, grated

$^1/_2$ small avocado, peeled, stoned and sliced

2 oz/50 g black olives, sliced

Serves: 4

Chicken Tortilla Casserole

METHOD

In a small frying pan, heat the tortillas, one at a time, over a low heat until softened, about 30 seconds per side. Set aside. In a large bowl, combine the soured cream, cumin, chilli powder and salt and stir until well blended. Stir in the spring onions and chicken pieces.

Spread about a third of the taco sauce in an 11 x 7 inch/ 28 x 18 cm oven proof dish. Cut one tortilla into quarters, then place it in the dish with the point of each quarter in a corner of the dish. Layer 3 whole tortillas in the dish. Spread half the chicken mixture over the tortillas. Spoon a third of the taco sauce over the chicken. Sprinkle with three-quarters of the cheese, then layer the remaining 4 tortillas as before. Top with the remaining chicken mixture and taco sauce. Cover and bake in an oven preheated to 190C/375F/ Gas Mark 5 for 20 minutes. Remove the lid, sprinkle with the remaining cheese and bake for 20 minutes longer. Let the casserole stand for 10 minutes before serving. Garnish with the avocado slices and olives.

DAVID LODGE

Actor

METHOD

Put the rice in a pan with the salt and chicken stock. Bring to the boil, stir once, then cover the pan tightly and cook gently for 15 minutes. In a separate pan, heat the oil and 1 oz/25 g of butter, add the onion and fry for 5 minutes. Add the chicken pieces and fry until golden, then season to taste. Stir in the raisins, almonds, apricots and cinnamon, then add just enough water to cover everything. Simmer gently until the apricots are tender and the liquid has reduced.

Heat the remaining butter in a large saucepan and add half the rice, then the chicken and apricot mixture and finally the rest of the rice. Cover the pan and cook over a very gentle heat for a further 10 minutes. Serve with petit pois or any vegetable of your choice.

Chicken Polo

12 oz/350 g long grain rice

1¹/₂ tsp salt

1¹/₂ pints/850 ml chicken stock
  (made with 2 stock cubes)

2 tbsp oil

3 oz/75 g butter

1 large onion, finely chopped

4 boneless chicken breasts, chopped

Salt and freshly ground black pepper

3 oz/75 g raisins

2 oz/50 g split almonds

4 oz/110 g dried apricots, chopped

¹/₂ tsp cinnamon

Serves: 4

Spicy Chicken

2 tsp curry powder

1 tsp cumin

¹/₂ tsp ground ginger

¹/₂ tsp turmeric

¹/₂ garlic clove, crushed

1 onion, finely chopped

1 tsp grated fresh ginger root

*1 medium chicken, skinned
  and cut into serving pieces*

Serves: 4

ELIZABETH TAYLOR

Screen superstar

METHOD

Combine all the ingredients except the chicken in a bowl. Coat the chicken pieces with this mixture, pressing it well into the flesh, and refrigerate for at least 3 hours, preferably longer. Cook on a moderately hot barbecue or under a preheated grill for approximately 30 minutes or until tender, turning once.

"As you know, weight gain and weight loss is a subject I know something about . . . I firmly believe that starvation diets and excessive calorie counting are counter-productive to long-term weight loss and a healthy lifestyle. My recipes are satisfying, well seasoned and delicious, as well as low in calories."

ELIZABETH TAYLOR

183

SIR ANTHONY HOPKINS

SIR ANTHONY HOPKINS

Film star

1 tsp garlic, finely chopped

1 tsp fresh ginger root, finely chopped

7 fl oz/200 ml vegetable oil

1 1b/450 g onions, chopped

2 large green chillies, finely chopped

2 x 13 oz/375 g cans of tomatoes, chopped

8 oz/225 g small potatoes, cut into 2 x 1 inch/5 x 2.5 cm pieces

8 fl oz/225 ml yogurt

2 1b/900 g chicken fillets, cut into 2 x 1 inch/5 x 2.5 cm pieces

Fresh coriander leaves and garam masala, to garnish

Serves: 6

Chicken Vindaloo

For the whole masala

$^1/_4$ oz/7 g cumin seeds

5 cloves

2 x 1 inch/2.5 cm pieces of cinnamon

5 black cardamom pods, lightly crushed

5 bay leaves

For the powdered masala

1 tsp salt

1 tsp turmeric

1 tsp paprika

1 tsp ground cumin

1 tsp chilli powder

METHOD

Pound together the garlic and ginger to a paste. Heat the oil in a large pan until very hot, then add all the ingredients for the whole masala. Blast for a few minutes over a very high heat, then reduce the heat, add the onions and fry until golden brown, stirring occasionally. Stir in the garlic/ginger paste and chillies and cook for 5 minutes, then add the tomatoes and potatoes and cook for 7 minutes. Stir in all the ingredients for the powdered masala and cook for 5 minutes. Add the yogurt and cook for another 5 minutes, then finally add the chicken and cook over a gentle heat for 10 minutes. Raise the heat slightly and continue to cook until the chicken and potatoes are done. Serve sprinkled with coriander leaves and garam masala.

Lamb Casserole

2 chicken or beef stock cubes

$1^1/_2$ tsp plain flour

$^1/_4$ pint/150 ml water

4 lamb chops, trimmed

2 onions, sliced

Salt and freshly ground black pepper

Fresh or dried rosemary and thyme, to taste

4 rashers of lean bacon

1 glass of red wine, such as Rioja

Serves: 2

BOB HOSKINS

Film and television star

METHOD

Crumble the stock cubes in a saucepan and mix with the flour, then blend in the water. Bring to the boil and simmer until the gravy has thickened. Put the lamb chops in a heavy casserole and place the onions on top. Add seasoning and herbs to taste. Add the bacon and cover with the gravy. Cook in an oven preheated to 170C/325F/Gas Mark 3 for $1^1/_2$ hours. For the last 20 minutes, add the wine, leave the lid off the casserole and raise the temperature to 180C/350F/Gas Mark 4.

LIAM NEESON

Glens of Antrim Irish Stew

LIAM NEESON

Film star

"Serve with good bread, a bottle of red wine, such as Margaux '85, and Van Morrison's 'Celtic Twilight' playing in the background."

1 oz/25 g butter

2 1b/900 g lamb or beef, cubed

1 large onion, coarsely chopped

2 carrots, chopped

1 tbsp plain flour (optional)

$1/_2$ pint/275 ml beef stock

2 tbsp tomato puree

$1/_2$ tbsp sugar

2 potatoes, cubed (optional)

1 bottle of Guinness or
  a large glass of red wine

1 bouquet garni
  (sprig of parsley, sprig of thyme,
  1 bay leaf tied up in muslin)

Salt and freshly ground black pepper

Tabasco sauce

METHOD

Melt the butter in a large pan and fry the meat in it until browned on all sides. Do not crowd the pan; brown the meat in two or three batches if necessary. Remove the meat from the pan, add the onion and carrots and cook until slightly softened. Return the meat to the pan, add the flour, if using, then stir in the stock, tomato puree and sugar. Bring to the boil and then reduce the heat to a simmer. Add the potatoes, if using, the Guinness or wine, the bouquet garni and salt and pepper to taste. Cook over a low heat for about 1 to $1^1/_2$ hours or until the meat is tender. While the stew is simmering, add 4 or 5 drops of Tabasco, to taste.

Serves: 4

ANDREW MACDONALD

Film Producer of Shallow Grave

Lamb Goulash in Sheepskin

METHOD

In a large pot, brown the lamb and the onions together for a few minute until the onions are translucent. Add the paprika and stir in well. Stir in the caraway seeds and salt to taste. Add the peppers, cover tightly and cook for 30 minutes over a low heat. Do not add any liquid. Remove the pot from the heat and wrap it in one or more sheepskin rugs or coats. Leave overnight and unwrap in the morning and allow to cool. When ready to eat, heat up very gently. The meat will be incredibly tender. Serve with baked potatoes, or penne-type pasta, or, more authentically, home-made gnocchi or noodles, with a cucumber salad on the side.

4 1b/1.75 lean lamb,
  cut into 1 - 2 inch/2.5 - 5 cm chunks

2 1b/900 g onions, chopped medium-fine

4 tbsp mild powdered paprika

1 tsp caraway seeds

Salt, for seasoning

2 red sweet peppers, coarsely chopped

10 fl oz/275 ml soured cream (optional)

2 tbsp plain flour (optional)

Serves: 8

187

Creamy Cheesecake

METHOD

For the base, mix together the crumbled biscuits, sugar and melted butter. In a 10in/25 cm springform pan, press the mixture firmly onto its base. Chill until required.

For the filling, beat the cream cheese with an electric mixer until soft. Add the eggs, sugar and vanilla and continue to mix for 5 minutes. Take the prepared base out of the fridge and pour the mixture into the pan. Bake in an oven preheated to 190C/375F/Gas Mark 5 for 50 to 55 minutes.

For the topping, whip together the cream, vanilla and sugar. Spread generously on top of the hot cake and bake for 5 minutes. Allow to cool completely before chilling for several hours. Serve with your favourite fruit topping.

Serves: 6 to 8

For the base
1 small packet digestive
*   biscuits, crumbled*
1 tbs caster sugar
3 tbs butter, melted

For the filling
3 x 8 oz/225 g cream cheese,
*   softened*
4 eggs
8 oz/225 g caster sugar
2 tsp vanilla essence

For the topping
$1/_2$ pint/275 ml sour cream
2 tsp vanilla essence
1 tbs caster sugar

Favourite Lemon Pie

3 oz/75 g caster sugar
$3^1/_2$ tbsp cornflour
About 4 fl oz/110 ml boiling water
4 egg yolks, lightly beaten
1 oz/25 g butter
Grated zest and juice of 2 lemons
A pinch of salt
Prebaked pastry case, 8 inch/20 cm

For the meringue
2 egg whites
2 oz/50 g caster sugar

Serves: 4 to 6

METHOD

To make the filling, put the sugar, cornflour and water in a saucepan and stir constantly over a low heat until the mixture is thick and smooth. Add the egg yolks, butter, lemon zest and juice and salt. Cook gently, stirring all the time, for 2 to 3 minutes until the mixture thickens. Do not let it boil. Pour into the pastry case.

To make the meringue, whisk the egg whites in a bowl until they form stiff peaks. Add the sugar 1 tablespoon at a time, beating well between each addition. Cover the pie with meringue mixture and bake in an oven preheated to 180C/350F/Gas Mark 4 for 10 to 15 minutes, or until the top is light brown. Cool slightly before serving.

Carrot Cake

MICHAEL CAINE

Film star

"A banana cake can be made in the same way."

METHOD

Grease and line an 8 inch/20 cm round cake tin. Sift the flour, cinnamon and baking powder together in a bowl, then stir in the walnuts, raisins and sugar. In a separate bowl, mix together the eggs, carrots, melted butter and oil, then stir this mixture into the seasoned flour. Stir in the milk to give a soft dropping consistency. Transfer the mixture to the prepared tin and bake in an oven preheated to 160C/325F/ Gas Mark 3 for 60 to 70 minutes, until well risen and firm. Leave to cool in the tin for 10 minutes, then turn out on to a wire rack to cool completely.

8 oz/225 g self-raising flour

1 tsp cinnamon

2 tsp baking powder

2 oz/50 g walnuts, chopped

6 oz/175 g raisins

5 oz/150 g soft brown sugar

2 eggs, beaten

6 oz/175 g carrots, grated

2 oz/50 g butter, melted

4 tbsp corn or vegetable oil

2 tbsp milk

Serves: 6

Bloody Mary

MICHAEL GRADE

Show business mogul

Tomato juice	Celery salt	Vodka
Tomato ketchup	Tabasco sauce	Chilli vodka
Lemon juice	Worcestershire	Grapefruit juice
French mustard	sauce	Celery stick
Salt and black pepper	Dry sherry	Beef bouillon
Garlic salt	Ice	Ground nutmeg

"Hic!"

Darling Vera & Gerald.

Love Always. Edna xxx

DAME EDNA EVERAGE

TV and Stage

DEAR OH DEAR. AMID THIS BUNCh of culinary vandals, Rab C Nesbit (Gregor Fisher), the string vested Govan philosopher, emerges as a positive gourmet, with his recipe for Aromatic Chicken. Baked Beans on Toast - from Mr Bean (Rowan Atkinson), naturally - cornflakes from John Cleese; Lenny Henry's Killer Chilli; French Toast from Robbie Coltrane (who puts up a most spirited defence for it); even TV astronomer Patrick Moore weighs in with a Martian pancake, which turns out to be the humble Rarebit. Desserts made from crumbled biscuit bases are common; and what are we to make of Dawn French's Mars Bar Fondue?

Ah well, that's show business - British style. It's difficult to believe that such highly talented people have such lowly aspirations in the kitchen. Let's be charitable, put aside Lenny Henry's first cookery ingredient - a lucky rabbit's foot - and assume there's quite a lot of practical joking going on.

Fortunately, the Section also contains a fair sprinkling of more adventurous dishes. We're indebted to Michael Aspel for raising the tone of the Section with his fish dish, Halibut with Leeks and Black Olives and Terry Wogan's Chicken and Asparagus Casserole. Other commendable dishes which won't have folk breaking out into a nervous rash over having to do something more complex than use the tin-opener include Joanna Lumley's Cheese and Lentil Gratin and Gloria Hunniford's slightly simpler Cheese Strata. Both are, dare we say it, absolutely fabulous.

The main emphasis here tends to be on traditional fare. That extends through to the sweet end of the menu as well, with Ronnie Corbett's rich chocolate cake and Stewart Hall's Christmas cake. If you are looking for something a bit lighter, try making Stephen Fry's honey buns. Yes we know, given the general standard of this section, it looks like a confection dreamed up by Einstein, but in reality the recipe is simple to follow and quick to make.

ROBBIE COLTRANE

TV and film actor

New York Diner French Toast

"I got this recipe from a short-order cook in a New York diner many years ago. It's very simple and delicious and although everyone thinks they can make French toast it ain't necessarily so! The secret is the thickness of the bread, the ratio of milk to egg (which should be 50-50) and the vanilla. There are lots of ways to serve this. My favourite is with a sprinkling of lemon or lime juice, then just dusted with icing sugar. You could put maple syrup on the toast and serve with crisp bacon, or top it with two fried or poached eggs and a sprinkling of grated cheese."

2 large eggs

4 fl oz/110 ml milk

1 tsp vanilla extract

A pinch of salt

1 small white loaf (must be good quality), cut into slices $^1/_2$ inch/1 cm thick

1 oz/25 g butter

1 tbsp oil

METHOD

Serves: 2 to 3

Beat the eggs, milk, vanilla and salt together until smooth, then pour the mixture into a wide shallow dish. Dip each slice of bread briefly into the mixture, until wet but not soaked through. Melt the butter and oil in a frying pan and fry the dipped bread over a fairly high heat until golden brown, turning to cook the other side.

Cullen Skink

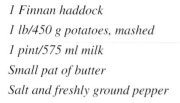
TV's best known grumbler, Richard Meldrew

1 Finnan haddock
1 lb/450 g potatoes, mashed
1 pint/575 ml milk
Small pat of butter
Salt and freshly ground pepper

Serves: 1 to 2

METHOD

Skin the haddock, put it in a pan and cover with boiling water. Simmer for about 5 minutes, or until the fish is cooked. Remove, and take out the bones. Return the bones to the stock and boil for about 30 minutes.

Meanwhile, flake the cooked fish. Also boil the potatoes in a pan of salted water until tender, strain and mash.

Strain the fish stock through a sieve into another pan, and add to it the fish flakes and the milk. Bring to the boil. Add enough mashed potatoes to make a creamy consistency, season, add the butter and serve hot.

BBC television producer

Grandma's Soup

Serves: 4 to 6

1 marrow bone, cut into 3 pieces
  (ask your butcher to do this)
1 lb/450 g shin beef, cubed
3¹/₂ oz/100 g lentils
1 leek, chopped
A little butter and oil
3 carrots, grated
¹/₂ turnip, grated
1 small can of tomato puree
1 tsp sugar
Salt and freshly ground black pepper

METHOD

Put the marrow bone and beef in a large stockpot, add water to cover and simmer for 1 hour. Skim off the fat, then add the lentils and continue simmering for 30 minutes. Meanwhile, in a separate pan, sweat the leek in a little butter and oil. Add the leek, carrots and turnip to the stockpot and simmer for another 30 minutes. Remove the marrow bone, stir in the tomato puree, sugar, and salt and pepper to taste, then serve.

JOHN CLEESE

1) Buy a packet of Cornflakes. 2) Open the cardboard box. 3) Open the sort of plastic packet inside the box. 4) Pour the contents (sort of yellowy-brownish bits of things) on to a plate. 5) Buy a bottle of milk. 6) Take the top off the thin end of the bottle. 7) Invert the bottle gently over the Cornflakes making sure that the milk does not go over the edge of the plate.

Comedy film and TV star

Carrot and Apple Salad

4 large carrots, grated
2 large eating apples, peeled,
  cored and finely chopped
2 oz/50 g sultanas
2 oz/50 g walnuts, chopped
Juice of ¹/₂ lemon
Freshly ground black pepper
1 tbsp fresh parsley, chopped

Serves: 4

METHOD

Put the carrots and apples in a bowl and mix with the sultanas, walnuts and lemon juice. Season with pepper, then sprinkle the chopped parsley over the top. Chill for 1 hour before serving.

RICHARD BRIERS

Stage and TV entertainer

"This makes a tasty, crunchy salad to have with a snack for a summer lunch."

Cheese Strata

"Prepare this dish the night before serving. As a variation, you can add ham or prawns to the layers."

8 slices firm-textured white bread,
  with crusts, cubed
10 oz/275 g strong Cheddar cheese,
  grated
8 eggs
2 oz/50 g butter, melted
1 pint/575 ml milk
$^{1}/_{2}$ tsp dry mustard

Serves: 6

METHOD

Butter a large souffle dish or a ceramic or stoneware casserole. Put a layer of bread in the dish, then a layer of cheese and repeat these layers until the ingredients are used up, ending with cheese. Put the eggs, melted butter, milk and mustard in a blender and process for 30 seconds until thoroughly combined. Pour onto the bread and cheese and refrigerate overnight. The next day, bake in an oven preheated to 180C/350F/Gas Mark 4 for 45 to 60 minutes until firm in the centre and light brown. Serve immediately.

GLORIA (CENTRE) WITH FANS.

Cheese and Lentil Gratin

JOANNA LUMLEY

TV comedy star

"Serve with home-made tomato sauce. This dish is also excellent served cold with a crisp green salad."

1 tbsp oil

1 onion, chopped

1 carrot, chopped

1 celery stick, chopped

6 oz/175 g red lentils

1 garlic clove, crushed

$^3/_4$ pint/425 ml water

4 oz/110 g cheese, grated

2 tbsp fresh parsley, chopped

1 egg, beaten

Salt and freshly ground black pepper

2 tbsp wholemeal breadcrumbs

2 tbsp sesame seeds

METHOD

Heat the oil in a pan, add the onion and fry until soft, then add the carrot, celery, lentils, garlic and water. Bring to the boil, cover and simmer for 20 minutes, until all the water has been absorbed. Add three-quarters of the cheese, the parsley and the egg to the lentil mixture and stir thoroughly. Season well, spoon into a $1^1/_2$ pint/875 ml shallow ovenproof dish and smooth the top. Mix the breadcrumbs with the sesame seeds and the remaining cheese and spread over the lentil mixture. Bake in an oven preheated to 180C/350F/Gas Mark 4 for 45 minutes until the topping is golden brown and crisp.

Serves: 4

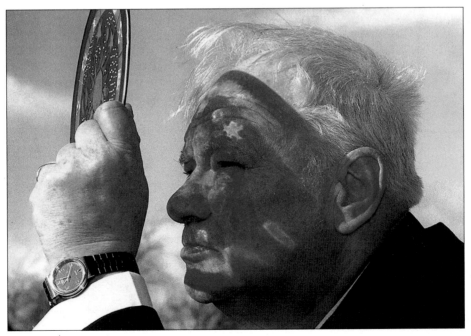

PATRICK MOORE

Astronomer, author and TV presenter

Selsey Rarebit

"Not very original, I suppose, but I like it. Clap two of these together, face to face, and it is transformed into a Martian pancake!"

METHOD   Serves: 1

Take a slice of bread (I prefer white) and toast it on one side. Butter the other side and then arrange on it some grated or sliced cheese, some finely chopped peppers and onion, if you like, salt and pepper to taste and a sliced tomato. Put it back under the grill and cook until the cheese bubbles.

Halibut with Leeks and Black Olives

> *"A light meal to which the olives give a very distinctive flavour."*

2 oz/50 g butter

4 leeks, thinly sliced

8 large black olives, stoned and chopped

2 tbsp dry white wine

$^1/_2$ pint/275 ml fish stock or water

Salt and freshly ground black pepper

4 x 6 oz/175 g halibut steaks

2 tbsp fresh parsley,chopped

Serves: 4

METHOD

Heat the butter in a large shallow pan. Add the leeks and olives and cook briskly until the leeks are soft. Add the wine and fish stock or water, season with salt and pepper and stir well. Add the fish and bring to simmering point. Simmer very gently for 10 minutes, then turn the steaks and simmer for a further 10 minutes. Remove the fish from the pan and keep warm. Simmer the cooking liquid for 3 to 4 minutes to concentrate the flavour. Pour it over the fish, sprinkle with parsley and serve.

Baked Beans on Toast

ROWAN ATKINSON

Mr Bean Recipe

1 can of baked beans

2 slices of bread, toasted

METHOD

Heat the beans in a pan until they go all bubbly. Pour them over the toast and serve.

Serves: 1

Pasta Stewartoto

ALLAN STEWART

Stage and TV entertainer

1 oz/25 g butter

Generous pinch of garlic salt

2 chicken breasts, chopped into cubes

1 can plum tomatoes, chopped

2 oz/50 g Cheddar cheese, grated

6 oz/175 g spaghetti (or other pasta)

1 tbs olive oil

Serves: 2

METHOD

Melt the butter in a deep, heavy bottomed frying pan, and add the garlic salt. Stir and cook for one minute, then add the chicken pieces and cook for 5 to 10 minutes, until they are cooked through and slightly brown on the outside. Add the chopped tomatoes to the pan, bring to the boil, then simmer for 4 to 5 minutes. Add the cheese, and stir in until melted.

Meanwhile, boil the spaghetti in a saucepan of salted water with 1 tbs of olive oil. When cooked, drain and let it cool. Then add it to the frying pan and reheat. Serve with a final sprinkling of grated cheese on top.

"Any self-respecting Italian chef would turn in his trattoria at this, but I like it . . . It's perfect after a show."

JONATHAN DIMBLEBY

TV journalist and author

Bel's Walnut Pasta

METHOD

6 - 8 oz/175 - 225 g spaghetti

3 spring onions, chopped

About 4 tsp walnut oil

2 oz/50 g walnuts, chopped

4 tbsp fresh parsley, chopped

2 oz/50 g cheese, preferably Emmenthal,
   coarsely grated

Freshly ground black pepper

Cook the spaghetti in a large pan of boiling salted water until al dente. Meanwhile, gently cook the spring onions in the walnut oil until tender, then stir in the walnuts. Drain the pasta, tip it into a heated bowl and immediately pour the walnut mixture over it. Add the parsley and cheese and toss together thoroughly with the pasta.

Serves: 2

"Serve immediately in warm bowls with plenty of freshly ground black pepper."

Chicken and Asparagus Casserole

TERRY WOGAN

TV and radio star

6 chicken breasts

About 1$^{1}/_{4}$ pints/725 ml chicken stock

1 large can of green asparagus spears,
   drained

1 can of condensed mushroom soup

$^{1}/_{2}$ pint/275 ml double cream

2 tbsp medium sherry

4 heaped tbsp Cheddar cheese, grated

$^{1}/_{2}$ tsp paprika

Salt and freshly ground black pepper

METHOD

Gently poach the chicken breasts in chicken stock to cover for 15 minutes. Grease a large shallow casserole dish which will take the chicken breasts in one layer. Arrange the drained asparagus in the dish and then place the chicken breasts on top. Put the soup, cream and sherry in a saucepan and heat gently, stirring constantly, until it simmers. Season to taste, after checking, then pour the sauce over the chicken and asparagus. Sprinkle the cheese and paprika on top. Bake in an oven preheated to 200C/400F/Gas Mark 6 for 20 minutes.

Serves: 6

"Wait until the top is golden and bubbling before serving."

Aromatic Chicken

GREGOR FISHER
(Rab C Nesbitt)
Comedian and TV actor

3 - 4 lb/1.25 - 1.75 kg chicken

2 tsp salt

3 slices of fresh ginger root, finely
   shredded

2 tbsp fresh coriander leaves, chopped

3 tbsp soy sauce

A pinch of five-spice powder

3 tbsp sherry

Oil for deep-frying

Serves: 4

METHOD

Rub the chicken thoroughly with the salt both inside and out and leave to dry overnight. Mix the ginger with the coriander, soy sauce, five-spice powder and sherry and rub the chicken with this mixture twice over a period of several hours. Leave to dry in an airy place. Roast the chicken for $1\frac{1}{2}$ hours in an oven preheated to 150C/300F/Gas Mark 2. Drain it, allow it to cool, then cut it into quarters. Place them in a wire basket and deep fry in hot oil for 6 to 7 minutes, by which time the skin should have become quite crispy.

"Serve with a crisp green salad or lightly cooked cabbage."

ELAINE C. SMITH

TV comedy star

Tropical Chicken Kebabs

6 skinless, boneless breasts,
   cut into 1¹/₂ inch/4 cm cubes
2 tbsp medium sherry
Freshly ground black pepper
2 mangoes or peaches, skinned,
   stoned and cut into 1 inch/2.5 cm cubes
12 bay leaves
2 tbsp olive oil
2 tbsp coconut, coarsely shredded
Juice of ¹/₂ lime

Serves: 6

METHOD

Toss the chicken cubes in the sherry with a little black pepper. Push the cubes onto 6 skewers, alternating them with the mango or peach and the bay leaves, then brush with the oil. Cook under a preheated grill or on a barbecue for 8 to 10 minutes, turning occasionally, until golden. Sprinkle with coconut and lime juice and cook for a few seconds longer. Serve immediately with a green salad or rice, after discarding the bay leaves.

Lambingtons

1 tbsp olive oil
1 onion, finely chopped
2 chillies, finely chopped
1 garlic clove, crushed
1 inch/2.5 cm piece of fresh
   ginger root, finely chopped
1 lb/450 g cooked lamb, minced
¹/₂ bunch of fresh coriander,
   finely chopped
¹/₂ bunch of fresh mint,
   finely chopped
2 oz/50 g fresh breadcrumbs
1 egg
Salt and freshly ground black pepper
2 oz/50 g butter
3 oz/75 g desiccated coconut
Sprigs of parsley, to garnish

Serves: 4

DAME EDNA EVERAGE

(Barry Humphries)
Mega-star of the universe

METHOD

Heat the oil in a pan, add the onion, chillies, garlic and ginger and fry gently until the onion is translucent. Remove the pan from the heat and transfer the contents to a bowl. Add the lamb, coriander, mint, breadcrumbs, egg and seasoning to the bowl and mix with your hands (first ensuring they are clean; always check for grubby nails) until they bind together. Shape the mixture into 3 inch/8 cm patties and fry gently in butter in the pan for 2 to 3 minutes until golden brown on all sides. Remove and quickly roll in coconut (not you, possum - THE PATTIES!). Garnish with parsley and serve with rice.

"When mixing by hand, remove all jewellery, except earrings and tiara."

The Lenny Henry Killer Chilli

LENNY HENRY

Comedian and TV star

Serves: 4

Lucky rabbit's foot (optional)
2 large onions, chopped
2 green peppers, chopped
3 oz/75 g butter
1 lb/450 g minced beef
13 oz/375 g can of tomatoes
1 tbsp tomato puree
Chilli powder, to taste
A pinch of mixed spice

A pinch of ground cloves
A pinch of dried oregano
4 oz/110 g mushrooms, chopped
15 oz/425 g can of kidney beans,
   drained
A dash of Tabasco sauce
2 beef stock cubes
1 glass of red wine

"You're going to need all the luck you can get, because I certainly don't know what I'm doing!"

METHOD

In a large pan, fry the onions and peppers in the butter until the onions are fairly translucent. Add the meat and fry until brown, then add the tomatoes and stir for a couple of minutes until bubbling noisily. Add the tomato puree and stir until the mixture thickens slightly, then add the spices, oregano and mushrooms and cook, stirring, for 2 minutes. Add the kidney beans and give the mixture a good stir. Add the Tabasco and crumble in the stock cubes, then add the wine and stir again. Simmer for about an hour, stirring occasionally. After this time, the mixture should be a lovely dark brown colour and quite thick. If there is a layer of fat on top, remove it with a spoon. Serve with boiled rice or pitta bread.

BILL OWEN

TV star of Last of the Summer Wine

Compo's Casserole

METHOD

Place the vegetables in a large ovenproof casserole. Toss the steak in a little seasoned flour. Heat the oil in a pan and fry the meat cubes until sealed on all sides, cook them in batches if necessary. Remove from the pan with a slotted spoon and put in the casserole with the vegetables. Add the soup, wine and tomatoes, plus the garlic or herbs and cook in an oven preheated to 180C/350F/Gas Mark 4 for about 2 hours, until the steak is tender.

Serves: 4

2 carrots, diced
1 parsnip, diced
1 medium onion, diced
1 small turnip and equivalent
   portion of swede, diced
2 celery sticks, diced
1 lb/450 g lean chuck steak,
   cut into cubes
A little seasoned flour
4 tbsp oil
1 can of beef soup
1 glass of red wine
13 oz/375 g can of tomatoes
2 garlic cloves, chopped.

BARBARA WALTERS — Mother's Stuffed Cabbage Rolls

American TV anchorwoman

1 lb/450 g lean chuck steak, minced

Salt and freshly ground black pepper

1 tsp celery salt

2 tbsp tomato ketchup

1 egg

2 crackers, crushed

8 large cabbage leaves from a Savoy
   or other green cabbage

1 onion, chopped

6 fl oz/175 ml bottled chilli sauce

2 tbsp redcurrant jelly

8 fl oz/225 ml water

Serves: 4

METHOD

In a large bowl combine the meat, salt, pepper, celery salt, ketchup, eggs and crackers. Mix with your hands until everything is well combined. Blanch the cabbage leaves in a large pan of boiling water for 5 minutes, then drain and refresh under cold water. Cut out and discard the central cores of the leaves. Divide the meat mixture into 8, shape into rolls and place each portion on a cabbage leaf. Fold the top of each leaf over the mixture, then fold in the sides and roll up into a parcel. Spread the chopped onion over a lightly greased 8 x 10 inch/20 x 25 cm ovenproof dish and arrange the cabbage rolls on top. Combine the chilli sauce, redcurrant jelly and water in a saucepan and stir over a medium heat until the jelly melts. Pour it over the cabbage rolls. Cover the dish tightly with foil and bake in an oven preheated to 190C/375F/Gas Mark 5 for 2 hours. Remove the foil and brush the rolls with the sauce. Continue to bake, uncovered, for 40 minutes or until the sauce is thick and syrupy and the cabbage rolls are glazed. Serve the rolls with the sauce spooned over them

Mars Bar Fondue — DAWN FRENCH

Comedienne, TV actress, scriptwriter

3 Mars bars

Fresh fruit, cut into cubes
   or marshmallows

Serves: 2

METHOD

Cut the Mars bars into cubes and melt them in a bowl set over a pan of very hot water, stirring occasionally. Put the cubes of fruit or marshmallows on fondue forks and dip them into the mixture. Eat immediately!

Nutty Apple Crumble

BOB HOLNESS

TV quizmaster of Raise the Roof

$1^1/_2$ lb/675 g cooking apples, peeled,
  cored and thinly sliced
1 oz/25 g caster sugar

For the topping
8 oz/225 g plain flour
4 oz/110 g butter or margarine
3 oz/75 g caster sugar or soft brown sugar
1 oz/25 g mixed nuts, chopped
2 oz/50 g pecan nuts, chopped
1 oz/25 g sunflower seeds
A few pecan nuts, halved, to decorate

METHOD

Place the apples in a buttered 3 pint/1.75 litre pie dish, sprinkling the sugar between the layers. To make the topping, sift the flour into a bowl, cut up the butter or margarine and rub it into the flour until the mixture resembles breadcrumbs. Stir in the sugar, mixed nuts, pecans and sunflower seeds. Spoon this crumble mixture over the apples, place the dish on a baking tray and bake for 40 minutes in the centre of an oven preheated to 190C/375F/Gas Mark 5. Scatter the pecan halves over the top and bake for a further 5 minutes. Serve hot with custard, cream or vanilla ice cream.

Serves: 4 to 6

JIMMY YOUNG

Radio chat show presenter

Alicia's Crunchy Peach Crumble

6 oz/175 g plain flour
$^1/_2$ tsp salt
3 oz/75 g chilled butter, diced
3 oz/75 g Demerara sugar
4 fresh peaches, skinned,
  stoned and sliced
or $1^1/_2$ lb/675 g canned sliced peaches,
  drained

Serves: 6

METHOD

Sift the flour and salt into a bowl, then add the butter and rub in lightly with your fingertips until the mixture resembles fine breadcrumbs. Add the sugar and mix well. Arrange the peaches in a medium-sized, shallow overproof dish and cover them with the crumble mixture. Bake in an oven preheated to 200C/400F/ Gas Mark 6 for 25 minutes or until the top is golden brown. Serve warm with whipped cream, ice cream or custard.

"You can use other fruits for this recipe, such as nectarines, apples, blackberries or apricots. If you want the crumble to be less crunchy, put the sugar in a blender for a few seconds or use caster sugar instead."

ROSS KING

TV presenter of Pebble Mill

Pineapple Delight

1 medium packet of digestive biscuits
  (8 - 10 oz/225 - 275 g)
2 oz/50 g butter

For the filling
6 oz/175 g icing sugar
4 oz/110 g butter
14 oz/400 g can of crushed pineapple,
  well drained
$^1/_2$ pint/275 ml double cream
1 chocolate flake bar

Serves: 6

METHOD

Crush the digestive biscuits to make crumbs. Melt the butter and then stir in the biscuit crumbs. Spread the mixture into a greased 9 inch/23 cm springform cake tin and bake for 20 minutes in an over preheated to 190C/375F/Gas Mark 5. Leave to cool completely.

For the filling, cream together the icing sugar and butter. Stir in the drained crushed pineapple and spread the mixture over the cold base. Whip the double cream in a bowl and spread it on top.

"Lightly crush the chocolate flake and sprinkle it over the cream."

Ginger Surprise

GARY WILMOT

Stage and TV personality

METHOD

Whip the cream in a chilled bowl until it is stiff. Put a little sherry into a saucer and briefly dunk 2 ginger biscuits into it. Sandwich them together with a little whipped cream. Repeat with the remaining biscuits, pressing them all together to make a long train. (If you do not have a long enough plate for this, you can be artistic and curve the train to fit another shape of plate). Use the remaining cream to cover the biscuits completely. Refrigerate for at least 4 hours. The biscuits and cream merge together and it is almost impossible to tell how the dessert was made.

Serves: 4

"If you have been over-generous with the sherry, the cream may discolour round the edges. If so, decorate with fresh fruit or grated chocolate."

$^1/_2$ pint/275 ml whipping cream, chilled
$^1/_4$ pint/150 ml sherry
1 packet of ginger biscuits
  (about 8 oz/225 g)
Fresh fruit or grated chocolate,
  to decorate (optional)

STEPHEN FRY

Stage and TV star

Honey Buns

2 eggs
3 oz/75 g caster sugar
1 tsp soft dark brown sugar
$3^1/_2$ oz/100 g self-raising flour
A pinch of salt
$^1/_2$ tsp baking powder
$3^1/_2$ oz/100 g butter, melted and cooled
1 tbsp clear honey, plus extra for glazing

Makes about 20 buns

METHOD

Whisk together the eggs and sugars until the mixture is pale and thick. Sift together the flour, salt and baking powder and fold them into the mixture. Set aside to rest for 30 minutes, then stir in the melted butter and honey. Spoon into bun cases and bake in an oven preheated to 180C/350F/Gas Mark 4 for about 10 to 15 minutes, until well risen and golden. Drizzle over a little more honey while the buns are still warm.

CAROLE SMILLIE

TV presenter

Mum's Bread and Butter Pudding

METHOD   **Serves 2 to 3**

Fill a casserole with layers of thick white bread and butter, cut into strips. In between each layer add sultanas, brown sugar, some double cream and cinnamon. Pour a little milk over the whole contents and cook in a hot oven, 180C/350C/Gas Mark 4 until it smells wonderful.

Christmas Cake

STUART HALL

TV presenter

8 oz/225 g butter

8 oz/225 g caster sugar
 or soft brown sugar

8 oz/225 g plain flour

$^1/_4$ tsp salt

1 level tsp mixed spice

$^1/_2$ level tsp baking powder

4 eggs, lightly beaten

1 lb/450 g currants

8 oz/225 g raisins

4 oz/110 g glace cherries,
 chopped

2 oz/50 g chopped mixed peel

4 oz/110 g blanched almonds,
 chopped

A little milk (optional)

4 - 5 tbsp brandy (optional)

Serves: 8 to 10

"Store in an airtight tin for a few days before icing."

METHOD

Line a deep 8 inch/20 cm cake tin with greaseproof paper. Cream the butter and sugar together until pale. Sift together the flour, salt, mixed spice and baking powder. Add a little beaten egg and flour alternately to the creamed fat, beating well between each addition, until it is used up. Stir in the fruit, mixed peel and almonds, and, if necessary, a little milk to make a heavy, dropping consistency. Place the mixture in the cake tin and tie a piece of greaseproof paper round the outside of the tin to come about 3 inches/8 cm above the rim. Smooth the top and make a slight depression in the centre. Bake in an oven preheated to 170C/325F/Gas Mark 3 for 30 minutes, then reduce the heat to 140C/275F/ Gas Mark 1 and bake for a further 3 to $3^1/_2$ hours. If necessary, cover loosely with aluminium foil or brown paper after 2 hours to prevent the cake burning. Leave the cake to cool in the tin, then turn it out on to a wire rack and remove the paper. If you like, you can prick the bottom of the cake with a skewer and sprinkle brandy over it.

Rich Chocolate Cake

4 oz/110 g good quality plain chocolate,
  roughly chopped
$^1/_4$ pint/150 ml milk
2 oz/50 g cocoa powder
A few drops of vanilla extract
8 oz/225 g butter
6 oz/175 g caster sugar
4 eggs, separated
4 oz/110 g plain flour
2 oz/50 g ground rice
2 level tsp baking powder
2 oz/50 g chocolate, roughly grated,
  to decorate

For the chocolate buttercream
8 oz/225 g good quality plain
  chocolate
6 tbsp milk
6 oz/175 g unsalted butter
4 oz/110 g icing sugar, sifted

Serves: 4 to 6

*"No honestly, the calories aren't at all horrific if you close
your eyes while you're eating it."*

METHOD

Generously butter and line a deep 9 inch/23 cm springform cake tin. Put the chocolate in a pan with the milk, cocoa powder and vanilla extract. Stir over a very gentle heat until the chocolate has melted, then set aside.

In a bowl, beat the butter until soft, then add the sugar and beat again until pale and fluffy. Add the egg yolks to the mixture one at a time, and fold in. In a separate bowl, sift together the flour, baking powder and ground rice, then stir them into the egg and butter mixture. Stir in the melted chocolate.

In a separate bowl, beat the egg whites until fairly stiff and roughly stir 2 tablespoons into the cake mixture to soften it. Then lightly fold in the remaining egg white with a metal spoon. Turn the mixture into the prepared tin and bake in an oven preheated to 160C/325F/Gas Mark 3 for about 1 hour or until firm and well risen. The cake is ready when a warmed skewer or knife inserted into the centre comes out clean. Cool in the tin for 10 minutes, then turn out on to a wire rack and leave to cool completely.

To make the chocolate buttercream, melt the chocolate in a pan with the milk over a very gentle heat. In a bowl, beat the butter and icing sugar together until light and fluffy, then beat in the melted chocolate. Leave to cool for 30 minutes.

Split the cake in half horizontally and spread with a third of the buttercream. Sandwich together, cover the top and sides with the remaining buttercream and dust with the grated chocolate.

RONNIE CORBETT

SIR CLIFF RICHARD

A Taste of Music

FROM FISHERMAN'S PIE TO SANTIAGO ALMOND SPONGE CAKE, this short Section is a tremendously diverse reflection of the stars' tastes. Some, like country music star Johnny Cash, Sir Harry Secombe and Rod Stewart, stick very much to their own national backgrounds. The Johnny Cash recipe is for an authentic hot Mexican or Texas Chilli (written down by him for the first time). Rod Stewart sent us copious instructions on the art of making roast chicken with stuffing and gravy - lovingly detailing every careful step of preparation.

Sir Harry's contribution is a much adored traditional Welsh recipe called Teisen Lap. A mixed dried fruit and dough mix (using, if possible, buttermilk), it is still often cut into rounds and cooked on an open griddle. Although the ingredients are slightly different, it resembles very much the Apple Fadge which many country folk will remember mothers and grandmothers making. Served piping hot, straight from the griddle, it was always a delicious and filling treat. And there were never any left-overs.

While on the subject of baking, an increasingly lost art in these days of instant cake mixes, Shirley Bassey's Santiago Almond Sponge Cake is worthy of attention. Almonds impart great flavour to cakes, and you can adjust their quantities to suit personal tastes.

Among the main courses, Jim Kerr, of Simple Minds, shows himself to be a dedicated kitchen craftsman with a brown rice vegetable curry. Lulu reveals herself to be extremely figure conscious with another vegetable dish for one, her imaginative and tasty Baked Potato with Avocado and Broccoli, while percussionist Evelyn Glennie weighs in with another vegetarian dish, Butter Beans in Sesame, which makes an ideal curry accompaniment.

Cliff Richard's secret passion, however, is a real eye-opener. The Peter Pan of pop, whose lithe, slim figure and youthful appearance are a showbiz by-word, loves an ultra-sweet concoction called Transkei Mud, whose ingredients are caramelized condensed milk, double cream, crumbled digestive biscuits and a couple of bars of mint chocolate. With tastes like that, we thought of banishing him to the Stage and TV Section to join obvious soul-mates like Mars Bar Fondue addict Dawn French!

Potted Shrimps with Mushrooms

SIR ANDREW LLOYD WEBBER
Composer

"This is probably the simplest recipe ever for a delicious starter or savoury, but do make sure you have defrosted the potted shrimps before you make it, otherwise they go leathery. Don't tell your guests you made this in two minutes flat!"

4 tbsp medium dry sherry

6 oz/175 g button mushrooms, sliced

A pinch of nutmeg or mace

8 oz/225 g potted shrimps, defrosted if frozen

Squeeze of lemon juice

4 slices of toast, crusts removed

Serves: 4

METHOD

Put the sherry in a frying pan, add the mushrooms and spice and bring to the boil. Simmer for about 1 minute, then add the potted shrimps - without the butter if you are worried about cholesterol - and lemon juice. Bring back to the boil, then serve immediately on the toast.

LULU
Singer and film star

Baked Potato with Avocado and Broccoli

"It's very tasty and non-fattening, a great combination."

1 large baking potato

1 avocado

A few broccoli florets

Salt and freshly ground

black pepper

Serves: 1

METHOD

Bake the potato in an oven preheated to 200C/400F/Gas Mark 6 for about an hour, until soft, then cut it in half. Scoop out the flesh and mash it with the avocado flesh, then fill the potato skins with this mixture. Steam the broccoli florets until they are tender but not soggy and place them on top of the filled potato. Sprinkle with a little salt and pepper, then serve.

Kerr's Curry

Pop star
Simple Minds

METHOD

Put the rice into a large pan, add the water and bring to the boil. Reduce the heat and simmer for 35 minutes or until the rice is tender. Meanwhile, cook the potatoes and cauliflower in separate pans until just tender and then drain. Heat the oil in a large pan and lightly fry the mushrooms, onion, garlic, ginger and chillies for a few minutes until softened. Add the tomatoes and curry powder and cook for 1 minute, then add the coconut milk or yogurt and coriander and simmer for 10 minutes. Add the potatoes and cauliflower and simmer for 15 minutes. Garnish with parsley sprigs and serve with the boiled rice.

10 oz/275 g long grain brown rice

$1^1/_2$ pints/850 ml water

2 lb/900 g potatoes, diced

1 small cauliflower, divided into florets

1 tbsp oil

8 oz/225 g mushrooms, sliced

1 large onion, chopped

3 garlic cloves, finely chopped

$^1/_2$ inch/1cm piece of fresh ginger root, finely chopped

3 hot chillies, finely chopped

13 oz/375 g can of tomatoes, chopped

2 tsp hot Madras curry powder

$^1/_2$ can of coconut milk
 or $^1/_4$ pint/150 ml yogurt

$^1/_4$ tsp ground coriander

Fresh parsley sprigs, to garnish

Serves: 4 to 6

Jenny's Cumin Cabbage

Pop singer

METHOD

Blanch the cabbage in boiling salted water for 1 to 2 minutes until almost tender, then drain through a sieve and put aside. Melt the butter in a pan and cook the onion until it is soft. Add the cumin seeds and cook for a few minutes, then toss in the cabbage and keep turning it over until it is thoroughly heated. Season with salt and pepper and serve.

1 small white cabbage, chopped
  (1 x $^1/_2$ inch/2.5 x 1 cm pieces)
2 oz/50 g butter
1 large onion, sliced
$^1/_2$ tbsp cumin seeds
Salt and freshly ground black pepper

Serves: 4 to 6

KIM APPLEBY

Pop singer

Fisherman's Pie

METHOD

Melt 1 oz/25 g of the margarine in a large frying pan and cook the onion and celery until tender but not brown. Stir in the peas and sweetcorn, mix together and season. Add the fish and the prawns, if using, and transfer the mixture to a 3 pint/1.75 litre ovenproof dish.

In a small saucepan, melt 1 oz/25 g of the remaining margarine and stir in the flour. Cook gently for 1 minute, then remove from the heat and gradually stir in the milk. Return the pan to the heat and stir constantly until the sauce thickens. Remove from the heat again, stir in the egg yolk and pour the sauce over the fish and vegetables.

Mix the remaining margarine into the mashed potatoes together with just enough milk to make them creamy. Pipe or spoon the potato over the fish and vegetable filling. Bake in an oven preheated to 190C/375F/Gas Mark 5 for 40 minutes.

3 oz/75 g margarine
1 large onion, chopped
4 celery sticks, chopped
8 oz/225 g frozen peas
7 oz/200 g canned sweetcorn kernels,
  drained
Salt and freshly ground black pepper
2 lb/900 g white fish fillets,
  skinned and diced
  (halibut, coley, haddock or cod)
6 oz/175 g peeled prawns (optional)
$1^1/_2$ oz/40 g plain flour
$^3/_4$ pint/425 ml semi-skimmed milk
1 egg yolk
2 lb/ 900 g potatoes, boiled and mashed
A little milk

Serves: 4 to 6

JOSE CARRERAS

World opera star

My Favourite Sandwich

Serves: 1

"Take a large slice of Italian ciabatta bread, rub it with the cut side of half a ripe, flavoursome tomato and sprinkle on a little salt. Drizzle over a very little olive oil and two drops only of balsamic vinegar. Then cover the bread with carpaccio (very thinly sliced Italian raw beef) and top with slivers of Parmesan cheese."

Butter Beans in Sesame

EVELYN GLENNIE

Solo percussionist

4 fl oz/110 ml oil

1 tsp cumin seeds

1 large onion, chopped

4 oz/110 g sesame seeds, finely ground

1 tbsp ground coriander

13 oz/375 g can of chopped tomatoes

2 tsp salt

2 tsp sugar

1 tsp chilli powder

1 tsp turmeric

2 x 15 oz/425 g cans of butterbeans, drained

2 sprigs of fresh coriander, chopped, to garnish

Serves: 4

METHOD

Heat the oil in a pan, add the cumin seeds and fry until they begin to crackle. Add the onion and fry until it is soft and translucent. Add the ground sesame seeds and fry for 3 to 5 minutes, then add the ground coriander and fry for a further minute. Stir in the tomatoes, salt, sugar, chilli powder and turmeric. Mix well and simmer for 10 to 15 minutes. Add the drained beans and stir to coat them with the sauce. Simmer until the beans are thoroughly hot. Sprinkle with the chopped coriander and serve with chapatis.

"This is a good accompaniment to meat curries, or it can be served as a vegetarian main course."

ROD STEWART   Roast Chicken with Stuffing and Gravy

Rock superstar

"Leftover stuffing can be used to make stuffing balls. Roll spoonfuls of the mixture into balls, place them in an ovenproof dish and bake for the last 45 minutes of cooking time."

---

4 lb/1.75 kg chicken

1 tbsp oil

For the stuffing

$^1/_2$ loaf white bread,
  processed into breadcrumbs

1 medium onion, finely chopped

1 egg, lightly beaten

$^1/_2$ tsp dried mixed herbs

Salt and freshly ground black pepper

A little milk (optional)

For the gravy

2 onions, roughly chopped

2 carrots, roughly chopped

2 celery sticks, roughly chopped

2 garlic cloves, roughly chopped

3 tomatoes, roughly chopped,
  or $^1/_2$ can of chopped tomatoes

4 fl oz/110 ml dry white wine

3 tbsp plain flour

1 pint/575 ml stock

Serves: 4

METHOD

Remove the fatty pieces from the cavity of the chicken, wash the chicken thoroughly, then dry and set aside. To make the stuffing, mix together all the ingredients in a bowl. The mixture should be moist. If it is too dry, add a little milk. For the gravy, mix together all the ingredients except the flour and stock in a bowl.

Fill the cavity of the chicken with the stuffing, leaving the stuffing fairly loose. Tie the chicken legs together with twine, place the bird in a large roasting tin, brush with the oil and season with salt and pepper. Cook in an oven preheated to 220C/425F/Gas Mark 7 for 15 to 20 minutes, then reduce the heat to 200C/400F/Gas Mark 6 for another 30 minutes. Add all the gravy ingredients to the tin and cook for $1^1/_2$ hours at 190C/375F/Gas Mark 5. The chicken is done when a skewer inserted at the base of the leg produces clear juice. When cooked, remove the chicken from the tin and set aside, but keep warm.

To finish the gravy, put the roasting tin on top of the stove over a moderate heat and sprinkle on the flour. Blend with the vegetables, stirring constantly for 4 to 5 minutes, then add the stock, increasing the quantity if the mixture is too thick. Bring the gravy to a gentle boil, then strain through a sieve into a saucepan. Keep warm.

To serve, carve off the chicken's thigh and leg sections, slice the breast and wings. Cut away the breastbone and remove the stuffing whole. Slice the stuffing and arrange with the chicken pieces on a hot serving platter. Serve the gravy separately.

Rod Stewart

JOHNNY CASH

Country music superstar

METHOD

Heat the oil in a large pan, add the meat chunks and some salt and fry over a high heat until the meat is browned on all sides. Stir in the chilli powder and, if you want a thicker stew, the flour or cornmeal. Cook for a few minutes, then pour in the water. Bring to the boil, then reduce the heat to a simmer and add the tomatoes, onion, green pepper, garlic, kidney beans, sage, dried chilli flakes and the sugar, if using. Simmer for $1^1/_2$ to 2 hours, until the meat is very tender, adding more water if necessary. Adjust the amount of chilli and salt to taste and then serve accompanied by cream crackers or water biscuits.

"You can vary the amount of chilli powder in this to suit your own taste. A hot Mexican or Texas chilli seasoning mix gives the best result, and adding some sugar will help to bring out the flavour of the chilli."

Chilli

4 tbsp vegetable oil

$1^1/_2$ lb/675 g sirloin steak,
  cut into bite-sized cubes

Salt

1 - 2 tbsp chilli powder, to taste

2 oz/50 g plain flour or cornmeal
  (optional)

$^1/_2$ pint/275 ml water

6 large tomatoes, chopped

1 large onion, chopped

1 large green pepper, chopped

2 - 4 garlic cloves, crushed

15 oz/425 g can of red kidney
  beans, drained

2 tbsp chopped fresh sage
  or 1 tbsp dried sage

Dried red chilli flakes, to taste

4 tbsp sugar (optional)

Serves: 4

Santiago Almond Sponge Cake

3 size 2 eggs

8 oz/225 g caster sugar

4 oz/110 g butter, softened

6 oz/175 g self-raising flour

4 fl oz/110 ml water

1 lb/450 g ground almonds

Grated zest of $^1/_2$ lemon

Icing sugar and a few chopped
  or flaked almonds, to decorate

Serves: 4 to 6

SHIRLEY BASSEY

Singing star

METHOD

Put the eggs, sugar, butter, flour and water in a bowl and beat together until light and fluffy. This can be done in a blender or food processor. Tip in the ground almonds and grated lemon zest and mix well. Put the mixture into a lined, well-greased 8 inch/ 20 cm cake tin. Level the surface and bake in an oven preheated to 180C/350F/Gas Mark 4 for about 1 hour, or until a skewer inserted in the centre comes out clean. Leave to cool in the tin for 10 minutes, then turn on to a wire rack to cool completely. Sift over icing sugar and decorate with almonds.

Transkei Mud

METHOD

First, caramelize the condensed milk by boiling the can, unopened and well covered with water, in a pressure cooker for 20 minutes or in a saucepan for $1^1/_2$ hours. Do not allow the saucepan to boil dry. Leave to cool for about 1 hour. Whisk the double cream until it forms soft peaks. Add the caramelized condensed milk a spoonful at a time and mix together thoroughly. Grate 4 to 6 pieces of mint chocolate into the mixture, then layer it in a serving dish with the digestive biscuits, there should be 3 layers of each. Refrigerate for 8 hours or overnight. Garnish with grated mint chocolate before serving.

1 can of condensed milk
$^1/_2$ pint/275 ml double cream
6 - 7 oz/175 - 200 g digestive biscuits
1 - 2 bars of mint chocolate,
  such as Aero or Blitz

Serves: 6

SIR HARRY SECOMBE
Singer and TV presenter

Teisen Lap

" 'Teisen' means cake and 'lap' means plate, so this is a 'plate cake.' It is made all over Wales, but sometimes the mixture is cut into rounds and cooked on a griddle."

8 oz/225 g plain flour
1 heaped tsp baking powder
$^1/_2$ tsp grated nutmeg
4 oz/110 g butter
4 oz/110 g granulated sugar
4 oz/110 g mixed currants and
  raisins or sultanas
2 eggs, beaten
3 - 5 fl oz/75 - 150 ml cream,
  milk or buttermilk

Serves: 4 to 6

METHOD

Sift the flour, baking powder and nutmeg into a bowl and rub in the butter. Stir in the sugar and dried fruit, then mix in the eggs and gradually add enough cream, milk or buttermilk to make a fairly soft mixture. Beat well. Put the mixture in a shallow 8 inch/20 cm round tin or on a large ovenproof plate. Bake in an oven preheated to 180C/350F/Gas Mark 4 for 40 minutes. The cake is done when a skewer inserted in the centre comes out clean. Remove from the oven and turn out to cool on a wire rack.

GIANNI VERSACE

Authors, Artists & Designers

I N THE WORLD OF LITERATURE, food has always featured prominently. But fact is often stranger than fiction. The celebrated diarist Dr Johnson, who would write most critically about the standard of fare offered at his friends' dinner tables, would think nothing of pouring lobster sauce over his plum pudding. Equally odd-ball tastes were displayed by the poet Shelley, a vegetarian, who munched his way through life from pockets filled with dry bread, leaving a trail of crumbs behind him. In more modern times, George Orwell, author of Animal Farm and 1984, would never eat tripe because he once lived over a tripe shop in Wigan, and world-famous thriller writer Alistair MacLean used to bring back the bacon - literally - every time he returned to Switzerland because of an abiding passion for good Scottish rashers at breakfast time, which he cooked himself, having given strict instructions to his housekeeper never to touch the pan's carefully amassed bacon fat.

We can't promise quite such unusual insights in this Section, although it is intriguing that Jackie Collins, whose sizzling blockbuster novels set in the glitzy world of the international jet set, loves Shepherd's Pie. The over-all impression, though, is one of creativity which is entirely logical, considering this Section is devoted to authors, composers, designers and couturiers. By and large, they are serious "foodies." Fish and pasta dishes predominate.

The simplest meal is probably the Spaghetti alla Checca from Germaine Greer. A traditional dish from the Tuscany region of Italy, she says she could eat it every day. Another contender for speed is Sir Andrew Lloyd Webber's Potted Shrimps with Mushrooms, a tasty starter he whips up within minutes.

Author Colleen McCullough - still remembered for her superb best selling novel The Thorn Birds - provides a delicious and most unusual recipe for Tahitian Fish, which involves a double marinade, each of different ingredients, and no cooking. Dame Barbara Cartland proffers her chef Nigel Gordon's Salmon Coulibiac, a fine pastry dish guaranteed to keep the salmon moist and appetising.

From the world of fashion, Gianni Versace, who designed our cover photograph, is a keen enthusiast of Pasta with Artichokes. It's deceptively simple to make, but as ever, the secret lies in the sauce - in this case, Bechamel. Another pasta fan is Giorgio Armani, who favours Tortelli alla Piacentina, a home-made pasta and spinach dish his mother used to make. It's time-consuming, but well worth the effort, he says.

Considering the quite atrociously sledgehammer sweet tooths we've encountered elsewhere, particularly among our TV stars and personalities, the desserts offered here are refinement itself. Portait painter Anne Mackintosh offers a rather magnificent hazelnut meringue, while Jeffrey Archer swears by Apple and Cinnamon Slice.

Sci fi author Dr Arthur C. Clarke, from his home in Sri Lanka, offered us the most unusual recipe of all, permission to republish his world-famous short story, Food of the Gods. Unfortunately, the book's format doesn't permit us to take him up on what was a quite incredibly generous offer. What is the doyen of the sci fi world's favourite meal? Welsh Rarebit - made with a special hard cheese. However, he confesses to being not overly interested in food.

His son, Fred, writes: "He lived with me for many years in North London, and drove my wife to despair when he would push away food which she had taken hours to choose and prepare. He told me, when a teenager, that one day we would not need food, and would just live on occasional pills. I hope that day does not come in my lifetime."

And so say all of us!

Salmon Coulibiac

> *"I have seen this dish cooked so often on television, but I think that the way my chef, Nigel Gordon, does it makes the salmon more moist and appetising. Salmon is one of the richest fish there is. The continued belief since Roman times that oysters, fish, especially salmon, raw eggs, raw vegetables, pomegranates and honey lead to increased sexual prowess is right."*

8 oz/225 g fresh salmon, cooked

$^1/_2$ pint/275 ml home-made
  or good quality bought mayonnaise

2 tbsp parsley, chopped (optional)

Salt and freshly ground black pepper

2 eggs, hard-boiled

1 oz/25 g butter

1 onion, finely chopped

4 oz/110 g mushrooms, finely chopped

8 oz/225 g puff pastry

1 egg yolk, beaten with 2 tbsp milk

$^1/_4$ pint/150 ml double cream

Serves: 2

METHOD

Pound the salmon to a paste (you can use a food processor for this) and mix it with half the mayonnaise, then season to taste. Separate the whites of the hard-boiled eggs from the yolks, chop them both finely and set aside. Melt the butter in a pan and saute the onion until soft. Add the mushrooms and continue to cook for 5 minutes, then season.

Roll the pastry out to a 14 x 10 inch/35 x 25 cm rectangle, trim the edges, then cut in half widthways. Brush the edges of one half with a little beaten egg. Arrange the ingredients for the filling on top of it, starting with the salmon mixture, then the mushrooms and onion, and finally the egg yolks and whites, leaving a 1 inch/2.5 cm border. Place the other piece of pastry on top and press the edges together to seal. The coulibiac can be trimmed to resemble a fish, if desired, and decorated with the pastry trimmings. Leave to rest in the fridge for 10 minutes, then brush all over with beaten egg and bake in an oven preheated to 190C/375F/Gas Mark 5, for 25 to 30 minutes, until golden brown. Mix the cream with the remaining mayonnaise and serve separately.

COLLEEN McCULLOUGH

Best selling author

Tahitian Fish

1 lb/450 g thin fish fillets,
such as pompano or pomfret,
extremely finely sliced
8 fl oz/225 ml unsweetened
grapefruit juice
2 tbsp onion, finely chopped
2 tbsp mayonnaise
$\frac{1}{2}$ tsp salt
1 tbsp coconut milk
2 tbsp red pepper, finely chopped
2 tbsp celery, finely chopped

Serves: 4

METHOD

Place the fish in a glass bowl and pour the grapefruit juice over it. Cover with cling film and place in the refrigerator for 48 hours, stirring occasionally. By the time the marinating period is over, all the fish should have turned an opaque white. Drain off the juice and discard.

Place the fish in a clean bowl and stir in the onion, mayonnaise, salt and coconut milk. Cover the bowl and place in the refrigerator for a least 24 hours and up to 48 hours. Before serving, add the red pepper and celery and stir well. Serve on a bed of lettuce.

Kedgeree

CAROLINE CHARLES

Royal designer

METHOD

Put the haddock in a saucepan and add water to cover. Add the parsley, bay leaves, half the lemon juice and the peppercorns. Bring to a simmer and poach gently for 5 minutes. Strain the fish and set aside. Keep the cooking liquid.

Melt 4 oz/110 g of the butter in a pan, add the onion and cook until soft but not brown. Add the rice and stir to coat it with the butter. Pour in enough liquid from cooking the fish to cover the rice by about 1 inch/2.5 cm. Bring to the boil, then lower the heat and simmer for 20 to 30 minutes until the rice is tender.

Skin the fish and remove any bones, then flake the flesh and add to the rice with the eggs, folding them in with a fork. Season with salt, pepper and the remaining lemon juice and stir in the remaining butter, cut into pieces. Cover with buttered paper and put in an oven preheated to 160C/325F/Gas Mark 3 to warm through. Serve with a green salad with lemon dressing.

4 lb/1.75 kg smoked haddock
A few parsley stalks
2 bay leaves
Juice of 1 lemon
A few peppercorns
6 oz/175 g butter
1 onion, finely chopped
1 lb/450 g long grain rice
5 eggs, hard-boiled and chopped
Salt and freshly ground black pepper

Serves: 8 to 10

CAROLINE CHARLES

PORTRAIT: ANNE MACKINTOSH

SIR EDUARDO PAOLOZZI   Polenta

"Polenta is the major dish of Rumania and is eaten with rich butter and garlic sauces. Like many great peasant dishes, it can be eaten hot, cold or reheated. My mother, at a certain point in the preparation, would add spinach, but I have never eaten this since.

Most restaurants in London serve polenta delicately as small, elegant squares. But in my father's village a large pot would be prepared and poured onto a special stone slab outside the stables to be eaten by the hired shepherds as part of their contract.

Polenta is a dish which probably goes back to the Romans - cooked in a large iron pot carried in the baggage cart and sustaining the legionnaires on the long walk from London to Hadrian's Wall. I have eaten polenta once a week ever since I was a child - usually on Fridays, the sauce being baccala with tomatoes.

It couldn't be simpler to cook. Add a quantity from a packet of polenta grains to a large pot of salted boiling water and keep stirring until it thickens (like making porridge). It can be served with a rich sauce which could be garlic, tomatoes, chopped pimentos, mushrooms or a mixture of these."

International sculptor

BRUCE OLDFIELD

Royal designer

Falafel

> *"I can't over-emphasise how important it is to drain the beans, after soaking . . . Dried white broad beans are available from Greek and Middle Eastern delicatessens but you could substitute chick peas for this dish."*

1 lb/450 g dried white broad beans
2 red or Spanish onions, finely chopped
2 large garlic cloves, crushed
A bunch of fresh parsley or coriander
1-2 tsp ground cumin, to taste
1-2 tsp ground coriander, to taste
$^1/_2$ tsp baking powder
Salt and cayenne pepper
Oil, for deep frying

Serves: 6 to 8

METHOD

Soak the beans in water overnight, peel off their skins and drain very thoroughly. Put the beans into a food processor along with all the other ingredients except the oil and process to a paste. Leave the mixture to rest for 1 hour, then form into flat round shapes roughly the size of a walnut. Leave to rest for a further 15 minutes, then deep-fry in batches until golden brown. Serve warm in pitta bread with hummus (a Cypriot and Middle East chick pea and sesame dip).

Dr Germaine Greer

Author and journalist

Spaghetti alla Checca

"This is a spaghetti that Tuscan peasants used to eat in the summer after working since dawn in the fields. From the *orto* by the house they would pick as many large, ripe tomatoes as there were people to be fed. Once indoors, they would put on a large pot of water for the pasta and reserve 200 grams (7 oz) of spaghetti for each person. While the water was heating up, they would set out as many bowls as there were tomatoes and chop a tomato roughly in each bowl, salt the tomato and pour on a dessertspoon or more of good olive oil from the first pressing.

When the water was at a good rolling boil, it would be salted and the pasta thrown in to boil fast for 10 minutes. While the pasta was boiling, a handful of basil would be collected from its pot outside the back door and swiftly chopped and scattered onto the tomatoes in each bowl. Then the pasta would be drained and apportioned to each bowl. Each person would toss the hot pasta in the raw tomato, olive oil and basil mixture and eat."

A Tuscan tale

"In my experience, this is the apotheosis of all three ingredients, pasta, tomato and basil. I could eat it every single day. One unexpected bonus is that if you do eat this pasta every single day, you will lose weight. However, do not even think of making it with store-bought tomatoes."

Tortelli alla Piacentina

GIORGIO ARMANI

Couturier

8 oz/225 g fresh spinach
1 lb/450 g ricotta cheese
1 egg, lightly beaten
4 oz/110 g Parmesan cheese, freshly grated
Salt and freshly ground black pepper, to taste
Butter and freshly grated Parmesan cheese, to serve

For the pasta
1 lb/450 g plain flour
3 eggs
2 tbsp olive oil

"My mother first made this dish for me and it is a favourite recipe. It's a local dish from my home town - a rather long procedure, but it's so good that it's well worth the while."

Serves: 4 to 6

METHOD

Remove the spinach stalks, wash the leaves thoroughly under cold running water, then drain them in a colander and squeeze out all the excess water. Chop the leaves very finely and mix them in a bowl with the ricotta, egg, Parmesan and salt and pepper until well blended. Leave to rest in a cool place.

To make the pasta, mix the flour, eggs and oil to a smooth dough, neither too dry nor too soft, otherwise it will be difficult to shape the tortelli. Add a little tepid water or a little more flour if necessary to achieve the correct consistency. Wrap the dough in a tea-towel to prevent it becoming dry. Pass the dough piece by piece through a pasta machine (or roll it out very thinly by hand with a rolling pin) to obtain the thickness of fettucini. Cut it into diamond shapes about 3 inches/7.5 cm long.

Place a teaspoonful of the filling in the centre of each diamond, then fold up the two opposite sides in order to seal in the filling. Put them into a floured cloth as you make them to prevent them sticking to each other.

Put a large, deep pan of salted water on to boil. When boiling, carefully lower the tortelli into it, without breaking or damaging them. When the tortelli rise to the top, push them down lightly with a slotted spoon (never use a fork or an ordinary spoon) until cooked - about 8 to 10 minutes. Drain the tortelli thoroughly in a colander, then slide them gently back into a casserole dish, adding numerous knobs of butter and some grated cheese. Stir together slowly to coat the tortelli evenly with the butter and cheese. (To obtain a good result, hold the dish by the handles and turn it in a circular fashion back and forth so the tortelli get well dipped in the sauce). Serve immediately.

Pasta with Artichokes

10 baby artichokes
1 small garlic clove, sliced
4 tbsp olive oil
$^{1}/_{2}$ pint/275 ml water
1 tbsp lemon juice
Salt
1 lb/450 g pasta, such as penne or sedani
A little butter
$^{1}/_{2}$ pint/275 ml bechamel sauce (see below)
4 oz/110 g Parmesan cheese, freshly grated

Serves: 4

"If you cannot find baby artichokes, five large artichokes can be used instead. These will need trimming more thoroughly. Remove all the leaves except the tender, pale inner ones and take out the choke."

METHOD

Prepare the artichokes by removing the stalks and the outer leaves and cutting $^{1}/_{2}$ inch/1 cm off the tops of the leaves. Cut the artichokes into quarters and put them in a large pan with the garlic, olive oil, water, lemon juice and a little salt. Bring to the boil, then reduce the heat and simmer, covered, for about 20 minutes, until the artichokes are tender. Remove from the heat, drain and set aside.

While the artichokes are cooking, bring a large pan of salted water to the boil, add the pasta and cook for about 8 to 10 minutes, until al dente. Drain well, then toss with a little butter.

Butter an ovenproof dish, put in a layer of pasta, then arrange some artichokes on top and cover with some bechamel sauce. Sprinkle with Parmesan cheese, then start again with another layer of pasta. Continue until all the ingredients are used up, ending with a layer of Parmesan. Dot with small pieces of butter and bake in an oven preheated to 200C/400F/Gas Mark 6 for about 15 minutes to warm through. Place under a hot grill for 3 to 4 minutes, until lightly browned.

NOTE: *To make bechamel sauce, put $^{1}/_{2}$ pint/275 ml milk in a pan with 1 small piece of onion, peeled, a little diced carrot and celery, 1 bay leaf and 3 peppercorns. Bring slowly to the boil, then remove from the heat, cover and leave to infuse for 15 to 20 minutes. Melt 1 oz/25 g butter in a separate pan, add 3 level tablespoons of plain flour and cook gently for a few minutes. Strain the milk mixture and gradually stir it into the pan. Bring to the boil and simmer for a few minutes until thickened, then season to taste with salt and pepper.*

Risotto Primavera

METHOD

Heat the chicken stock in a large pan until simmering. Heat the olive oil in a separate pan and add all the vegetables except the courgettes, peas and mushrooms. Cook for 2 minutes, add the rice and stir for 1 minute. Add the white wine, then add the simmering stock a ladleful at a time, stirring constantly and only adding more stock when the previous addition has been absorbed. After 10 minutes, add the courgettes and peas. After about 25 minutes, the rice should be al dente and all the stock absorbed. Stir in the tomato sauce shortly before the rice is done. Heat the butter in a small pan and fry the mushrooms until tender, then add them, with their butter, to the rice. Add the Parmesan cheese, whisking the rice to make it fluffy. Finally, season with salt and pepper to taste. Serve immediately, with extra Parmesan on the side.

Serves: 4 to 6

ELIZABETH EMANUEL

Royal designer

3 1b/1.25 kg corn-fed chicken
6 shallots, peeled
1 large bunch of fresh tarragon
$1^{1}/_{2}$ oz/40 g butter
Salt
Freshly ground black pepper
1 tbsp olive oil
$^{1}/_{4}$ pint/150 ml dry white wine
A pinch of coarse salt
2 egg yolks
$^{1}/_{4}$ pint/150 ml double cream
Lemon juice

Serves: 4

VALENTINO

Couturier

$2 - 2^{1}/_{2}$ pints/1.2 - 1.5 litres chicken stock
3 tbsp olive oil
1 large onion & carrot finely chopped
2 celery sticks, finely chopped
$^{1}/_{4}$ leek, finely chopped
1 red pepper, finely chopped
2 oz/50 g French beans
3 oz/75 g asparagus, finely chopped
10 oz/275 g arborio rice
3 tbsp white wine
2 courgettes, finely chopped
3 oz/75 g peas
6 tbsp fresh tomato sauce or passata
$^{3}/_{4}$ oz/20 g butter
4 oz/110 g shiitake mushrooms, sliced
3 oz/75 g Parmesan cheese, freshly grated
Salt and freshly ground black pepper

Tarragon Chicken

METHOD

Put 2 to 3 whole shallots and some stalks of tarragon into the chicken cavity along with $^{1}/_{2}$ oz/15 g of butter, plus salt and pepper. Heat the remaining butter and oil in a casserole dish. Quarter the remaining shallots, add to the pan with the chicken and brown all over. When browned, stir in the wine, then cover and cook on a low heat for 1 hour or transfer to an oven preheated to 190C/375F/Gas Mark 5 for 45 minutes. Baste occasionally. When cooked, transfer to a warmed dish. Drain off the excess fat, leaving the buttery juices. Roughly chop the rest of the tarragon, put it into a bowl with the coarse salt and bruise it with a fork. Add the egg yolks and double cream and mix together well. Off the heat, add this mixture to the juices in the casserole, stirring it in quickly and thoroughly, so that it does not curdle. Return the casserole to a very low heat and cook gently, stirring, for a few minutes (don't allow it to boil or it will curdle). Season and add a squeeze of lemon juice.

Shepherd's Pie

3¹/₂ lb/1.5 kg large potatoes

2 oz/50 g butter

4 tbsp milk

2 tbsp oil

2 lb/900 g lean minced beef

2 onions, finely chopped

2 carrots, sliced

1 celery stalk, sliced

1 tbsp plain flour

2 chicken stock cubes

8 fl oz/225 ml boiling water

2 tsp dried mixed herbs

3 tbsp tomato puree

Salt and freshly ground black pepper

Serves: 4 to 6

METHOD

Boil the potatoes, then drain. Mash them with the butter and milk until fluffy.

Heat the oil in a pan, add the beef and saute until lightly browned. Remove the meat from the pan, add the onions, carrots and celery and fry for 4 to 5 minutes, then return the beef to the pan. Stir in the flour and cook for a few minutes. Crumble the stock cubes into the boiling water and add to the pan. Simmer for 10 minutes, until the sauce has thickened and the vegetables are tender. Add the mixed herbs, tomato puree and seasoning and mix thoroughly, then transfer the mixture to an ovenproof dish. Cover with the mashed potatoes, dot with a little butter, and bake in an oven preheated to 180C/350F/Gas Mark 4 for 35 minutes.

Cottage Pie

Best selling author

2 lb/900 g potatoes
Salt and freshly ground
   black pepper, to taste
3 oz/75 g butter
2 medium onions,
   coarsely chopped
2 lb/900 g minced beef
4 fl oz/110 ml beef stock
2 tbsp Worcestershire sauce
   (optional)

Serves: 6 to 8

METHOD

Cook the potatoes in boiling salted water until tender, then drain. Press the hot potatoes through a coarse sieve to form a puree. Season to taste, add 2 oz/50 g of the butter and mix well. Melt the remaining butter in a large frying pan. Add the onions and saute over a moderately high heat for 5 to 7 minutes, until golden brown. Add the beef and stir until the meat is crumbled and has lost all traces of pink. Stir in the stock and the Worcestershire sauce, if using, season with salt and pepper, and transfer to a buttered shallow 3 pint/1.75 litre ovenproof dish. Spread the potatoes evenly over the meat and press a fork around the edges to make a decorative border. Bake for 25 minutes in an oven preheated to 180C/350F/Gas Mark 4, then increase the temperature to 240C/475F/Gas Mark 9 for the final few minutes to brown the crust.

ANNE MACKINTOSH

Portrait painter

Hazelnut Meringue

> *"Keep an eye on the hazelnuts when browning them as they burn easily."*

4 oz/110 g hazelnuts,
   ground
4 egg whites
8 oz/225 g caster sugar
$^1/_2$ tsp vanilla extract
$^1/_2$ tsp vinegar
$^1/_2$ pint/275 ml whipping
   or double cream
8 oz/225 g raspberries
Icing sugar, for dusting

Serves: 6 to 8

METHOD

Spread the hazelnuts out on a baking sheet and place them in an oven preheated to 190C/375F/Gas Mark 5 for a few minutes until golden brown. Remove from the oven to cool, but leave the oven on. Prepare two 8 inch/20 cm sandwich tins by lightly oiling the sides, then lining the bases with Bakewell paper.

In a bowl, whisk the egg whites until stiff, then gradually whisk in the sugar. When very stiff, add the vanilla and vinegar. Fold in the nuts, spread the mixture evenly into the tins and bake for 30 to 40 minutes, or until they are pale gold.

Remove from the oven and leave to cool. At this stage, the meringues can be frozen, if convenient (do not remove the Bakewell paper from the bottom of the meringues as it makes them easier to handle). To prepare from the freezer, fill the meringues while they are still frozen. Whip the cream and sandwich the meringues together with the cream and raspberries. Dust the top with icing sugar. This dessert tastes better after it has been in the fridge for at least 24 hours.

Apple and Cinnamon Slice

JEFFREY ARCHER

The Lord Archer of Weston-super-Mare
Best selling author

6 oz/175 g self-raising flour
1 tsp baking powder
One pinch of salt
4 oz/110 g caster sugar
4 oz/110 g butter or margarine
1 egg, beaten
6 fl oz/175 ml milk
3 - 4 medium eating apples,
  peeled, cored and thickly sliced
$1/_2$ tsp cinnamon or mixed spice
1 tbsp clear honey

Serves: 8

METHOD

Grease and line an 8 inch/20 cm square cake tin. Sift the flour, baking powder and salt into a bowl. Stir in the caster sugar and rub in the butter or margarine. Combine the beaten egg and milk, pour into the bowl and stir to make a smooth batter. Pour it into the prepared cake tin. Press the apple slices lightly on to the cake and sprinkle over the cinnamon or mixed spice.

Bake in an oven preheated to 200C/400F/Gas Mark 6 for 40 to 45 minutes, or until the sponge is springy and firm to the touch. Using a pastry brush, brush the top of the cake evenly with the honey to glaze the apples. Turn the cake out of the tin while it is still warm. Serve warm or cold.

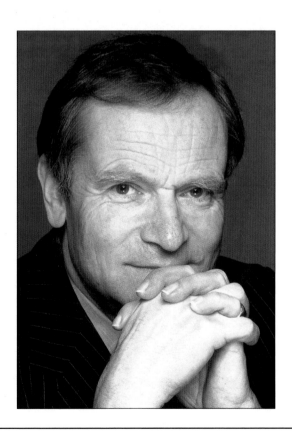

JACK NICKLAUS

Sporting Personalities

THERE ARE CERTAIN SCENARIOS CONCERNING FOOD which just ooze romance. Who among us hasn't dreamed of dining al fresco in our own garden, casually plucking a nearby lemon to flavour a cup of tea, or a lustrous bunch of grapes to brighten up a salad? Somehow, picking shallots or a lettuce from the vegetable plot doesn't quite hold the same allure. Jack Nicklaus therefore had us avocado green with envy with his spicy Guacamole Dip to "use up the avocados from the trees in our yard."

All in all, this is an extremely varied Section, reflecting the international tastes of sports stars. Quite surprising, really. Most of us think of sportsmen and women relying mainly on a high protein diet of steaks to build themselves up. But apart from former Glasgow Rangers football star Derek Johnstone's Steak Diane, there isn't a steak dish in sight.

Boxing champion Lennox Lewis still hankers after his native Jamaica's national dish, Ackee and Saltfish, which he says, as a main course, should be served with sliced avocado, fried plantains, yams, dumplings and roasted breadfruit. Such tropical produce isn't readily available in this country, so you'll need to get advice from a Jamaican expatriate or do a bit of ethnic detective work to track down the items. What is ackee? It's a hard tropical fruit which grows on trees, and requires to be boiled. It also comes in cans.

241

Pork, these days, doesn't enjoy quite as favourable a profile as other meat dishes. Perhaps, rather snobbishly, it is considered a poor folks' choice. In reality, it provides exceptionally tasty meals, provided care is taken in preparation to rid the meat of its fat. Former world racing champion Nigel Manson offers a delicious recipe for Pork Fillet with Port, served on a bed of rice, while Jackie Stewart, another ex-world champion, proffers Deep-fried Pork Balls, which he cooks in a wok. The simplest pork dish of all is Arnold Palmer's sugared bacon strips. Crisped and served hot, they are a wonderful starter. But don't think you can substitute white sugar for brown; it's simply not the same. Good quality Demerara is best. Bacon also gets the vote of world snooker champion Steve Davis. His favourite snack after returning home from tournaments is a bacon and cheese toasted sandwich with Marmite - an acquired taste if ever there was one.

From the world of tennis, three times Wimbledon women's singles champion Chris Evert favours a weight-conscious Chicken and Pineapple Salad which is given a lot of extra zing through ingredients such as mango chutney, lemon juice, curry paste and Greek yogurt or low-fat mayonnaise. US tennis star Jim Courier goes for a labour-saving slow-cooked Pot Roast, with all the vegetables thrown in.

Over-all, our sports stars demonstrate a highly practical approach to food. And there is only sweet course - a Banana Raisin Ring from golfing champion Nick Faldo.

Guacamole Dip

"We have avocado trees in our yard and this is one way we enjoy using them."

2 avocados, peeled and stoned
1 medium onion, chopped
2 green chillies, deseeded and chopped
1 tbsp lemon juice
1 tsp salt
$^1/_2$ tsp black pepper, coarsely ground
4 to 8 tbsp mayonnaise, to taste
2 medium tomatoes, skinned and finely chopped
Tortilla chips, to serve

Serves: 4 to 6

METHOD

Put the avocados, onion, chillies, lemon juice, salt and pepper in a food processor or blender and process until creamy. Add the mayonnaise and process briefly, then turn the mixture into a bowl and stir in the chopped tomatoes. Cover and chill. Serve with tortilla chips.

ARNOLD PALMER

Champion golfer

Sugared Bacon

"This appetiser can be prepared earlier in the day and stored in foil then reheated when required."

8 oz - 1 lb/225 - 450 g bacon rashers,
7 oz/200 g brown sugar
  depending on desired sweetness

Serves: 4 to 8

METHOD

For the best results, have the bacon at room temperature. Roll or pat or shake the bacon in the brown sugar and place it on a baking tray. Bake in an oven preheated to 150C/300F/Gas Mark 2 for about 25 to 30 minutes until dark brown, turning over the rashers halfway through. When the bacon is well done, remove it with tongs and drain it very thoroughly on kitchen paper. As the bacon cools it will get hard and can then be broken into smaller pieces or served whole.

SEVE BALLESTEROS

Minestrone Soup

TOMMY BURNS

Manager, Glasgow Celtic Football club

1 oz/25 g butter

1 lb/450 g carrots, chopped

1 leek, chopped

A small piece of turnip, chopped

1 celery stick, chopped

2 large potatoes, chopped

1 onion, chopped

4 oz/110 g bacon, chopped

3 pints/1.75 litres ham or beef stock

2 x 13 oz/375 g cans of chopped tomatoes

7 oz/200 g pasta, such as spaghetti,
  macaroni or vermicelli

$^1/_2$ small Savoy cabbage, finely shredded

Freshly ground black pepper

Parmesan cheese, freshly grated to serve

Serves: 8

"A spoonful of pesto added to each bowl as it is served is nice."

METHOD

Heat the butter in a pan, add the carrots, leek, turnip, celery, potatoes, onion and bacon and cook slowly until softened. Add the stock and bring to the boil. Simmer for 15 minutes, then add the canned tomatoes. Add the pasta (if you are using spaghetti, break it up into small pieces) and simmer until tender, adding the cabbage for the last 5 minutes. Season with black pepper and serve with grated Parmesan cheese.

Spanish Tortilla

SEVE BALLESTEROS

Champion golfer

METHOD

Heat the oil in a large frying pan, add the diced potatoes, onion and some salt and mix well. Cook gently for about 10 minutes until the vegetables are tender. Taste and add more salt if necessary. Beat the eggs in a bowl with a little salt. Remove the vegetables from the pan with a slotted spoon and drain, then mix with the eggs. Pour the remaining oil out of the frying pan, leaving it just lightly oiled, and put in the potatoes, onion and eggs. Cook over a low heat for a maximum of 4 minutes, then turn out on to a plate and slide back into the pan to cook the other side. Be sure to shake the pan occasionally to prevent the tortilla sticking. Serve hot, warm or cold, cut into wedges.

6 tbsp olive oil

3 medium potatoes,
  diced

1 onion, diced

Salt

4 eggs

Serves: 2 to 3

Boxing champion

8 oz/225 g salt cod

1 oz/25 g butter

4 tbsp olive oil

2 onions, sliced

2 large sprigs of fresh thyme

1 green chilli, chopped

2 tomatoes, chopped

2 x 13 oz/375 g cans of ackee,
 drained

Freshly ground black pepper

Serves: 4

Ackee and Saltfish

METHOD

Put the salt cod in a deep bowl, cover with plenty of cold water and leave overnight. The next day, drain the fish, place it in a pan and cover with fresh water. Bring to the boil and simmer gently for 15 to 20 minutes until tender. Remove from the pan and leave to cool. Remove the skin and bones and break the flesh into large flakes.

Heat the butter and oil in a large frying pan, add the onions, thyme and chilli and cook for 2 to 3 minutes. Add the tomatoes and the prepared fish and cook for a further 3 to 4 minutes, stirring. Add the ackees and cook until heated through, stirring carefully so as not to crush them. Season with plenty of freshly ground black pepper and serve.

"This is Jamaica's national dish. Serve decorated with halved hard-boiled eggs and for a main course, sliced avocado, fried plantains, yams, dumplings and roasted breadfruit."

Attila's Spaghetti

MARK HATELEY

England football internationalist

2 tbsp olive oil

2 large onions, finely chopped

4 garlic cloves, finely chopped

2 x 13 oz/375 g cans of tomatoes

1 tsp tomato puree

1 large glass of dry white wine

1 green chilli, chopped

$1^{1}/_{2}$ vegetable stock cubes

1 tsp fresh basil, chopped

1 tsp fresh rosemary, chopped

1 lb/450 g spaghetti

Parmesan cheese,
 freshly grated to serve

Serves: 4

METHOD

Heat the oil in a saucepan, add the onions and garlic and cook gently until softened. Add the tomatoes, tomato puree, wine, chilli, stock cubes and herbs and stir well, using a potato masher to break up the tomatoes. Cook gently for at least 1 hour. Cook the spaghetti in a large pan of boiling salted water until al dente. Drain thoroughly, then return to the pan and stir in the sauce. Serve with Parmesan cheese.

"The longer you leave the sauce to cook the better."

MARK HATELEY WITH DAUGHTER EMMA

Penne Arrabiatta

WALTER SMITH

Manager, Glasgow Rangers FC

4 tbs olive oil

1 large onion, finely chopped

4 cloves of garlic, crushed

1 red chilli pepper,
  de-seeded and chopped

2 tsp paprika

14 oz/400 g tin of chopped tomatoes

2 tbsp tomato puree

1 lb/450 g fresh tomatoes,
  skinned and chopped

Salt and freshly ground black pepper

12 oz/350 g penne pasta

Parmesan cheese, grated,
  and parsley sprigs, to garnish

Serves: 4

METHOD

For the sauce, heat the oil in a pan and cook the onion and garlic over a gentle heat until the onion is softened, but not browned. Add the chilli and paprika and cook for 1 minute. Stir in the canned tomatoes and bring to the boil. Simmer for about 10 minutes until the mixture is slightly reduced. Stir in the tomato puree and fresh tomatoes and cook for a further 5 minutes, or until the sauce becomes thick and mushy. Season to taste. Meanwhile, cook the pasta in boiling, salted water until al dente. Drain well, pour over the sauce and toss through. Serve immediately, using the grated cheese and a sprig of parsley as garnishing.

Chicken with Cream

Former manager of Glasgow Celtic, Manchester City

4 - 6 chicken quarters

8 oz/225 g packet of frozen broccoli,
  thawed

$^1/_2$ pint/275 ml can of condensed cream of
  chicken soup

4 tbsp mayonnaise

4 tbsp double cream

$^1/_2$ level tsp curry powder or paste

2 oz/50 g Cheddar cheese grated

Serves: 4

METHOD

Arrange the chicken and broccoli in a shallow baking dish. In a bowl, combine the chicken soup with the mayonnaise, cream and curry powder. Spoon the mixture evenly over the chicken and broccoli, then sprinkle with the cheese. Bake in an oven preheated to 190C/375F/Gas Mark 5 for about 40 minutes, until the chicken is cooked through and the cheese is golden brown.

CHRIS EVERT

Former Wimbledon women's singles tennis champion

2 lb/900 g cooked chicken, skinned and chopped

8 oz/225 g pineapple chunks, fresh if possible

5 celery stalks, chopped

5 spring onions, chopped

1½ oz/40 g dry roasted unsalted peanuts

½ tsp salt

2 tbsp mango chutney

2 tbsp lemon juice

Grated zest of half a lemon

½ tsp curry paste

¼ pint/150 ml mayonnaise, low fat if possible,
   or Greek yogurt

Chicken and Pineapple Salad

METHOD

Put all the ingredients in a large bowl and mix together. Taste and adjust the seasoning. Serve on a bed of lettuce.

Serves: 4 to 6

Paad Loog Chin (Deep-Fried Pork Balls)

METHOD

Soak the mushrooms in warm water for 40 minutes. Drain, discard the hard stalks and chop the mushroom caps finely. Mix with the chopped shallots, water chestnuts and bamboo shoots in a bowl and set aside. Put the garlic in a mortar with the coriander, lime juice, sugar, salt and pepper and pound until smooth. Put this spice paste into a large bowl, and add to it the pork and egg, stirring thoroughly. Set aside for 30 minutes. Add the flour and prepared vegetables and mix well. Shape this mixture into 1 inch/2.5 cm balls.

In a wok heat the oil until it is very hot, then reduce to a moderate heat and deep-fry the pork balls for 5 to 10 minutes until cooked right through. Remove from the wok with a slotted spoon and serve with freshly cooked vegetables and steamed rice.

JACKIE STEWART

Former world racing champion

2 dried Chinese black mushrooms

2 shallots, finely chopped

2 canned water chestnuts, finely chopped

3 oz/75 g bamboo shoots, finely chopped

1 garlic clove, finely chopped

½ tsp coriander seeds

2 tsp fresh lime juice

1 tsp sugar

Salt and freshly ground black pepper

1¼ lb/560 g lean minced pork

1 egg, lightly beaten

2 tsp plain flour

Oil for deep frying

Serves: 4

JACKIE STEWART WITH SON PAUL, DAUGHTER-IN-LAW VICTORIA AND FIRST GRANDSON DYLAN

PAUL McSTAY

Scotland football internationalist, Glasgow Celtic captain

Veal Scaloppine a la Creme

4 veal escallopes

1 oz/25 g butter

1 small onion, finely chopped

3 fl oz/75 ml sherry

1 dsp plain flour

$^{1}/_{4}$ pint/150 ml veal or chicken stock

2 oz/50 g button mushrooms,
  thinly sliced

Salt and freshly ground black pepper

2 tbsp double cream

Serves: 4

METHOD

Slice the escallopes horizontally in half to form scaloppine (small escallopes). Heat a saute pan, drop in the butter and when it is foaming put in the pieces of veal in a single layer (cook in two batches if necessary). Fry briskly for 3 to 4 minutes, turning once then remove the meat from the pan. Put the onion into the pan and cook for 1 to 2 minutes then pour in the sherry. Boil until the liquid has reduced a little, then remove from the heat. Sprinkle over the mixture the flour, and mix in well, then stir in the stock. Return the pan to the heat and bring to the boil, stirring constantly. Add the mushrooms and the veal and season to taste. Cover the pan and simmer gently for 8 to 10 minutes. Taste for seasoning, then stir in the cream and reheat gently.

PAUL McSTAY (CENTRE) WITH TEAM MATES

Cheese, Bacon and Marmite Sandwich

STEVE DAVIS

World snooker ace

2 slices of brown or wholemeal bread

Butter

Marmite

Slices of Cheddar cheese, to taste

3 rashers of smoked
  or unsmoked back bacon

Serves: 1

METHOD

Butter both slices of the bread, then spread Marmite on one slice only. Place the cheese slices on the Marmite. Grill or fry the bacon and place the rashers, still sizzling, on top of the cheese. Cover with the other slice of bread and serve immediately.

"Whenever Steve arrives home hungry from his travels, this is his favourite snack."

NIGEL MANSELL

Former world racing champion

Pork Fillet with Port

2 tbsp vegetable oil

2 lb/900 g pork fillet,
  cut into slices $^1/_2$ inch/1 cm thick

1 small onion, sliced

2 tbsp redcurrant jelly

2 tbsp tomato puree

1 tbsp soy sauce

2 level tsp plain flour

$^3/_4$ pint/425 ml chicken stock

$^1/_4$ pint/150 ml port or red wine

Salt and freshly ground black pepper

Serves: 4

METHOD

Heat the oil in a large saucepan and add the meat. Brown it lightly on both sides and then remove it from the pan and keep warm. Add the onion and fry gently for 3 to 4 minutes, then add the redcurrant jelly, tomato puree and soy sauce and cook over a low heat for 2 minutes. Stir in the flour, then remove the pan from the heat and gradually stir in the stock until the mixture is smooth. Return to the heat and simmer until the sauce thickens. Add the port or red wine and season to taste. Return the pork to the sauce and cook over a low heat for 15 to 20 minutes or until the meat is done. Serve immediately with rice and vegetables.

STEPHEN HENDRY

Moussaka

A knob of butter
1 onion, finely chopped
1 lb/450 g steak, minced
13 oz/375 g can of tomatoes, chopped
4 oz/110 g mushrooms, finely chopped
2 small peppers, 1 red, 1 green, deseeded and
  diced
4 oz/110 g baby corn, chopped
1 garlic clove, finely chopped
2 tbsp tomato puree
1 tbsp Worcestershire sauce, to taste
Salt and freshly ground black pepper
2 medium waxy potatoes, peeled and thinly
  sliced
4 oz/110 g Cheddar cheese, grated

Serves: 4

STEPHEN HENDRY

World snooker champion

METHOD

Heat the butter in a large saucepan, add the onion and mince and fry for 10 minutes until browned. Add the tomatoes, mushrooms, peppers and corn, along with the garlic, tomato puree and Worcestershire sauce. Season well and simmer for 45 minutes. Meanwhile, in another pot, cook the potatoes in boiling salted water for 4 minutes. Drain and refresh under cold water. Drain again and pat dry. Put the meat mixture in a 3 pint/1.75 litre casserole dish and arrange the sliced potato neatly over the top. Cover the potatoes with the grated cheese and place the casserole in an oven preheated to 180C/350F/Gas Mark 4 for 30 minutes until the cheese is golden and bubbling.

DEREK JOHNSTONE

Football commentator and former internationalist

METHOD

Heat the olive oil in a pan and fry the onions and garlic until softened. Add the mushrooms and fry for 2 minutes, then add the drained tomatoes and tomato puree. Mix well and pour into an ovenproof dish. In a pan, fry the steaks with the soy sauce until browned on both sides, then place them on top of the vegetable mixture. Sprinkle over the mixed herbs and pepper, then bake in an oven preheated to 190C/375F/Gas Mark 5 for 1 hour, or until the steaks are tender. Take out of the oven and add the cream then return to the oven for 10 minutes. Serve with sauteed potatoes and a mixed salad, washed down with a full-bodied red wine.

Steak Diane

2 tbsp olive oil
2 onions, chopped
1 garlic clove, chopped
4 oz/110 g mushrooms, chopped
13 oz/375 g can of chopped tomatoes,
  drained
2 tbsp tomato puree
4 sirloin steaks
A dash of soy sauce
$1/4$ tsp dried mixed herbs
Freshly ground black pepper
$1/4$ pint/150 ml double cream

Serves: 4

International tennis champion

3 - 4 lb/1.25 - 1.8 kg topside or brisket,
   with all fat removed
Salt and freshly ground black pepper
1 lb/450 g small new potatoes,
   scrubbed and quartered
12 oz/350 g carrots, sliced
1 celery stalk, diced
1 green pepper, diced
1 large onion, cut into chunks
1 garlic clove, finely chopped
1 can of cream of mushroom soup
1 packet of dried onion soup

Mom's Pot Roast

METHOD

Rub the meat with salt and pepper, then put it in a slow cooker with all the remaining ingredients and half a soup can of water. Cook on a low heat all day. Add a fresh salad and bread and you have a great meal.

Serves: 4 to 6

"You will have a wonderful roast with vegetables and gravy, all in one dish."

Banana Raisin Ring

METHOD

Grease and flour an 8 inch/20 cm ring mould. Cream together the butter or margarine and the sugar until light and fluffy. Add the eggs one at a time, beating well after each addition. Stir in the mashed bananas and the raisins. Dissolve the bicarbonate of soda in the milk and vanilla extract. Add it alternately with the sifted flour to the egg mixture and stir well. Pour the mixture into the prepared tin and bake in the centre of an oven preheated to 180C/350F/Gas Mark 4 for 30 to 40 minutes, until well risen and golden brown. When cold, ice with lemon glace icing.

NOTE: *To make lemon glace icing, sift 4 oz/110 g icing sugar into a bowl and gradually stir in 1 tbsp lemon juice to make a smooth, glossy and fairly runny icing. Adjust the consistency with more icing sugar or lemon juice if necessary.*

NICK FALDO

Champion golfer

4 oz/110 g butter or margarine
6 oz/175 g caster sugar
2 eggs, beaten
3 ripe bananas, mashed with a fork
3 oz/75 g raisins, chopped
$1/2$ level tsp bicarbonate of soda
1 tsp vanilla extract
1 tsp milk
6 oz/175 g self-raising flour, sifted

Serves: 4 to 6

"This raisin ring will keep fresh and moist for a long time."

Nick Faldo

One Devonshire Gardens, Glasgow

Grand Hotels & Restaurants

T RAVEL NOT ONLY BROADENS THE MIND - it would broaden the waistline, if you let it. One of the great joys of visiting foreign climes is sampling new and often exotic cuisine. When it is prepared by the hands of a master chef, so much the better. This Section covers many of the world's grand hotels, plus a sprinkling of top restaurants which I have visited, and I am indebted to the many cordon bleu chefs and restaurateurs who have so generously shared with me the secrets of their kitchens.

Actually, I love grand hotels. There is an air of permanence and elegance about them which makes no concessions to the more fleeting values of a fast changing, modern world. From the baroque splendour of the magnificent edifices dotted along the French Riviera and Monaco, with their cathedral-like vaulted rooms and foyers, to their equally stunning, palatial counterparts in the Far East, they embody style, atmosphere and grandeur. Just sitting in their foyers or ornate ante-rooms people-watching, and trying to guess their backgrounds, is a lovely experience. Being me, of course, I like to stay in them, sampling their usually flawless service and superbly presented meals.

In this Section there is a heavy emphasis on seafood and fish, from scallops to red mullet, some fine chicken dishes, and several desserts. Don't expect me to point you in any direction. In the hands of such experts, all these recipes are mouth-wateringly delicious, a fitting finale to this book.

Wild Irish Nettle Soup

12 oz/350 g nettle leaves and young,
   tender stems
3 - 4 oz/75 - 110 g butter
A mixture of leek, onion and celery,
   roughly chopped
   (about 6 oz/175 g total weight)
2$^1/_2$ pints/1.5 litres chicken stock
1$^1/_2$ 1b/675 g potatoes, sliced
$^3/_4$ pint/425 ml single cream
Salt and freshly ground black pepper

Serves: 8

METHOD

Wash the nettles. Melt 3 oz/75 g of the butter in a heavy-based pan and sweat the leek, onion and celery and the nettles for 5 to 6 minutes without browning. Add the chicken stock and bring to the boil, then add the potatoes. Cook over a low heat for about 40 to 50 minutes.

Liquidize the soup to a fine puree, then return it to the pan, and add the cream. Salt and pepper to taste, reheat gently and check the consistency. Some extra butter may be whisked in for a richer, smoother finish. Garnish each serving with a blanched nettle leaf.

Pasta e Fagioli
(Pasta and Bean Soup)

DANIELI HOTEL

Venice, Italy

METHOD

Make a *soffritto* of the onion, garlic, parsley and celery by cooking them gently in 2 to 3 tablespoons of the olive oil in a large pot for 15 minutes, until translucent. Drain the beans, add them to the *soffritto* and fry for 1 minute, stirring well. Add 2$^1/_2$ pints/1.5 litres of water and the ham bone, bring to the boil, then cover and cook gently for about 3 hours or until the beans are very tender, stirring occasionally and topping up with more water if needed. Towards the end, add the remaining olive oil.

When the beans are cooked, remove one-third with a slotted spoon and set aside. Pick the meat off the bone and stir it into the soup. Pass the soup through a food mill or liquidize it in a blender or food processor, then return it to the pot with the reserved whole beans. Check for seasoning, adding salt and pepper to taste and stir in the pasta. Simmer for about 5 to 7 minutes or until the pasta is cooked. Serve with a few drops of olive oil sprinkled over each bowlful and grated Parmesan cheese on the side.

1 onion, finely chopped
2 garlic cloves, halved
2 tbsp fresh parsley, chopped
1 celery stalk, finely chopped
$^1/_4$ pint/150 ml Extra Virgin olive oil
7 oz/200 g dried borlotti beans,
   soaked overnight
1 ham bone
Salt
Freshly ground black pepper
5 oz/150 g macaroni
Freshly grated Parmesan cheese
   and Extra Virgin olive oil, to serve

Serves: 5 to 6

Tortilla Soup

4 tbsp groundnut oil

8 oz/225 g corn tortillas

$\frac{1}{2}$ tsp chilli powder

$\frac{1}{2}$ tsp cayenne pepper

1 tsp paprika

1 tsp ground cumin

1 garlic clove, quartered

2 bay leaves

1 small bunch of fresh coriander, chopped

8 oz/225 g onions, chopped

8 tomatoes, chopped

2 oz/50 g tomato puree

3 pints/1.75 litres chicken stock

Juice of 2 limes

Salt

BEL-AIR HOTEL

Los Angeles, USA

METHOD

Heat the oil in a large saucepan. Add the tortillas, spices, garlic and herbs and cook for about 5 minutes. Add the onions and cook for another 10 minutes. Add the tomatoes, tomato puree and stock, bring to the boil and simmer for about $1\frac{1}{2}$ hours. Strain through a fine strainer, then add the lime juice and salt to taste. Reheat and serve piping hot, with any or a mixture of the suggested accompaniments.

Serves: 6 to 8

"Suggested accompaniments for this dish are tortilla chips, diced avocado, grilled chicken breast strips, chopped fresh coriander or grated Cheddar cheese."

ORIENTAL HOTEL

Bangkok, Thailand

2 inch/5 cm piece of fresh young galungal Siamese ginger, sliced

3 garlic cloves, peeled

3 peppercorns

2 coriander roots (optional)

1 lemongrass stalk, finely sliced

3 shallots, sliced

$1\frac{3}{4}$ pints/1 litre coconut milk

12 oz/350 g boneless chicken breast, sliced

3 - 4 tbsp fish sauce

3 - 4 tbsp lime juice

2 - 3 small chillies, crushed

3 kaffir lime leaves, shredded, to garnish

3 coriander sprigs, chopped, to garnish

Chicken and Herb Soup in Coconut Milk

METHOD

Serves: 4 to 6

Using a pestle and mortar or a food processor, pound half the ginger to a paste along with the garlic, peppercorns, coriander roots, if using, lemongrass and shallots. Bring a quarter of the coconut milk to the boil in a saucepan, then add the paste and stir well.

Add the sliced chicken and keep stirring. Add the rest of the ginger and coconut milk, bring to the boil again and simmer for a few minutes until the chicken is tender. Add the fish sauce, lime juice and crushed chillies to taste. Sprinkle with the shredded kaffir lime leaves and chopped coriander before serving.

"Dark chilli paste (naam prig pow) can be added to this soup to heighten the flavour. If you cannot find galungal, fresh ginger root can be used."

Fish Soup

"This can be served with polenta flavoured with Parmesan cheese and rosemary."

For the fish stock

2 tbsp oil

1 large onion, diced

2 - 3 celery sticks, diced

2 carrots, diced

1 bay leaf

$2^1/_2$ pints/1.5 litres water

Juice of 1 lemon

Salt

A few peppercorns

1- 2 large glasses of dry white wine

2 large fish heads

Serves: 6 to 8

For the soup

2 tbsp olive oil

4 shallots, finely sliced

1 garlic clove, crushed

1 small fennel bulb, finely sliced

1 celery stick, finely sliced

2 x 12 oz/350 g cans of tomatoes

1 large glass of dry white wine

Salt and freshly ground black pepper

Zest of 1 orange or lemon, to taste

For the seafood

12 oz/350 g firm white fish fillets,
    skinned (monkfish or haddock)

2 lb/900 g mussels

10 oz/275 g fresh white crabmeat

METHOD

First make the stock. Heat the oil in a stockpot, add the diced vegetables and cook gently until softened. Add the remaining ingredients, bring to the boil and simmer for 30 minutes. Strain and leave to cool.

To make the soup, heat the olive oil in a pan and saute the shallots, garlic, fennel and celery until softened. Add the fish stock plus the tomatoes, wine, seasoning and orange or lemon zest and simmer for 25 to 30 minutes.

Meanwhile, prepare the seafood. Cut the fish fillets into cubes. Wash and scrub the mussels, removing their beards and discarding any mussels which are not tightly closed. Add the fish and mussels to the soup and simmer for 3 to 4 minutes. Add the crabmeat and simmer for 2 to 3 minutes or until all the mussels are open, then serve.

Souffle d'Oursin
(Sea Urchin Souffle)

For the butter urchin sauce
2 $^1/_4$ oz/60 g unsalted butter, creamed
4 oz/110 g sea urchin roe, pureed
   (use a blender or food processor)
1 $^1/_4$ pint/725 ml double cream
Salt and freshly ground pepper, to taste

For the souffle
1 egg yolk
8 fl oz/225 ml warm Bechamel sauce
4 oz/110 g pureed sea urchin roe
   from 4 sea urchins (reserve shells)
2 egg whites

For the garnish
Seaweed or salad greens
Fresh chervil

METHOD

Serves: 4

For the sauce, beat the butter in a bowl until soft. Beat in the pureed urchin roe, and set aside. Pour the cream into a heavy pan and bring to the boil. Reduce the heat and simmer until it is reduced by $^3/_4$ of its volume. Gradually whisk in the butter and sea urchin mixture, a little at a time, to thicken the sauce. Season to taste, then transfer to a clean bowl. Keep the sauce warm by placing the bowl over a small pan of warm, not boiling, water.

For the souffle, grease 4 ramekins. Beat the egg yolk into the warm Bechamel sauce in a pan. Heat the mixture gently, but do not allow to boil. Remove from the heat. Stir in the pureed sea urchin roe and season to taste. In a bowl, beat the egg whites until they form stiff peaks. Add 1 tsp of the egg whites to the Bechamel sauce mixture, stirring very gently, then lightly fold in the rest, taking care not to over-mix. Fill each prepared ramekin with the mixture, then place the dishes in an oven preheated to 200C/400F/ Gas Mark 6 and bake for 10 minutes. To serve, top each souffle with a little of the butter urchin sauce and garnish with seaweed or salad greens and chervil. Serve any remaining butter urchin sauce in the reserved sea urchin shells. This dish should be served immediately.

NOTE: *Bechamel sauce is a milk-based flavoured white sauce made by the roux method. To make $^1/_2$ pint/ 275 ml, you need: $^1/_2$ pint/275 ml of milk; 1 bay leaf; 6 peppercorns; 1 diced carrot; 1 diced small onion; 1 sprig of chopped fresh parsley; $^3/_4$ oz/20 g butter; $^3/_4$ oz plain flour; a pinch of nutmeg, salt and freshly ground pepper.*
METHOD: *Put the milk in a pan with the peppercorns and bay leaf. Add the diced carrots, onion and parsley. Bring to the boil, then simmer for 3 minutes. Remove from the heat, cover and leave to infuse for a minimum of 30 minutes. Strain off the milk and reserve. Melt the butter in a pan and stir in the flour until well mixed. Gently cook the roux over a low heat until it bubbles but on no account let it brown. Remove from the heat and vigorously whisk in the milk, a little at a time. Return to the heat and whisk until the sauce thickens. Add nutmeg and seasoning, to taste, and allow the sauce to simmer gently over a low heat for 10 minutes, watching constantly to ensure it doesn't stick to the pan. The sauce is now ready for use.*

Lobster Souffle
Plaza Athenee

1 lobster, live

1 tsp butter

1 fl oz/25 g olive oil

1 medium onion, diced

2 shallots, chopped

2 small carrots, diced

2 tomatoes, chopped

1 clove of garlic, crushed

$1/_4$ pint/150 ml white wine

2 fl oz/50 ml cognac

Salt and freshly ground pepper

Cayenne pepper

1 oz/25 g tomato puree

1 bouquet garni

10 tarragon leaves

4 fl oz/110 ml cream, UHT

"This recipe has been served at our hotel for 50 years."

For the souffle

$1 1/_2$ oz/40 g butter

$1 1/_2$ oz/40 g flour

Scant $1/_2$ pint/250 ml milk

4 eggs, separated

Salt and freshly ground pepper

Serves: 2

METHOD

Stun and kill the lobster. Take apart the body and tail, removing the stony pouch. Set aside the creamy parts and the coral. In a heavy pan, melt the oil and butter and over a brisk heat, fry the lobster pieces. Add the chopped onions and shallots and cook for 2 minutes. Add the carrots, tomatoes and garlic. Thin the mixture with the white wine, continue to heat briefly, then add the cognac, salt, pepper and a very small pinch of cayenne pepper. Add the tomato puree, bouquet garni and tarragon leaves. Stir gently, then cook, covered, for 20 minutes. Strain the lobster pieces, shelling the claws and tail, then boil down the strained sauce with the UHT cream. Press through a sieve, then boil down again to obtain a more creamy thickening. Check the seasoning.

To make the souffle, in a bowl, by hand rub together the butter and flour until well mixed. In another pan, boil the milk and add the butter and flour mixture, stirring well. Season, remove from the heat, then beat in the egg yolks to obtain a cream. In a separate bowl, whisk the egg whites until they form stiff peaks, then mix gently into the warm cream sauce. Prepare a floured and buttered souffle mould. Place the lobster pieces in the mould with a little bit of sauce, and cover with the souffle mixture. Place in an oven preheated to 200C/400F/Gas Mark 6 and cook for 20 minutes. Serve immediately with the rest of the sauce.

Lobster Newburg

1 lobster, about 2 lbs/900 g

Butter and oil for frying

2 shallots, chopped

For the sauce

1 tbs Port wine

1 tbs cognac

$^3/_4$ pint/425 ml cream

$^1/_4$ fumet of smoked haddock
   or mackerel, flaked

Serves: 2

METHOD

To prepare the lobster, lay it on its back, and remove the pouch. Cut the tail in sections, and the head and claws into two parts. Keep the coral. Saute the lobster over a brisk heat in a pan containing butter, oil and chopped shallots. Make sure the lobster is well sealed before removing from the pan.

Make a sauce by adding the Port and cognac to the pan juices. Reduce it to $^2/_3$ of its volume, then add the cream and flaked smoked fish. Bring to the boil, add the sealed lobster and simmer for 15 minutes. Remove the lobster and extract its flesh from the shell. Thicken the sauce by adding the coral to the pan, and boiling the mixture for 4 minutes.

Serve the lobster on a bed of pilau rice, garnished with chervil, with the sauce poured over the flesh.

CAMPO DE'FIORI RESTAURANT

Chef Umberto Tinelli   *Western Australia*

Gamberi alla Umberto

4 tbsp good quality olive oil, for cooking

8 anchovy fillets, chopped, or to taste

2 garlic cloves, finely sliced

4 fl oz/110 g ml dry white wine

24 large raw prawns, peeled,
   heads removed and de-veined

10 plum tomatoes, skinned and
   roughly chopped

1 tbsp capers

$^1/_2$ tsp dried chilli flakes

Freshly ground black pepper

2 tbsp fresh parsley, chopped

Serves: 4

METHOD

Heat the olive oil in a heavy-based saucepan and gently saute the anchovies and garlic until the garlic is translucent. Add the wine and stir to deglaze the pan. Boil until the wine is reduced by three-quarters of its original volume. Add the prawns and saute for a few minutes until they are almost cooked, turning from blue to pink. Add the tomatoes and their juice and cook until they reduce and form a fairly thick sauce. Add the capers, chilli flakes and black pepper to taste, then stir in the parsley. Serve very hot over steamed rice or fine capellini pasta.

Tweed Kettle

10 oz/275 g salmon fillet, cubed

Salt and freshly ground pepper

12 queen scallops

12 langoustines

12 mussels

$^1/_2$ oz/15 g shallots

3 oz/75 g butter

$^1/_4$ pint/150 ml Adgestone white wine
(from the Isle of Wight)
or other dry white wine

$^1/_2$ pint/275 ml fish stock (see below)

12 button onions, peeled and blanched

12 pieces of samphire, cut into matchstick
lengths and blanched

2 oz/50 g salsify, cut into matchstick lengths
and blanched

$^1/_2$ oz/15 g chives, chopped

Cayenne pepper

For the fish stock

2 1b/900 g Dover sole bones

1 oz/25 g butter

2 oz/50 g onions, chopped

1 oz/25 g celery, chopped

1 oz/25 g celeriac, chopped

1 oz/25 g fennel, chopped

1 oz/25 g leeks, chopped

$^1/_2$ bay leaf

$^1/_2$ oz/15 g fresh dill

$^1/_2$ oz/15 g fresh chervil

6 white peppercorns

1 tbsp dry white wine

Salt and freshly ground black pepper

2 pints/1.2 litres water

Serves: 4

METHOD

First make the fish stock. Cut up the bones and wash them under cold running water, then dry, ensuring that all the blood has been removed from the bones. Heat the butter in a saucepan and gently cook the bones and vegetables without browning. Add the herbs and peppercorns and then pour in the wine, stirring to deglaze the pan. Season with salt and pepper and pour in the water. Bring to the boil and skim, then simmer gently for 20 minutes. Check the seasoning, then pass through a fine sieve and leave to cool. This quantity makes about $1^3/_4$ pints/1 litre. The surplus can be kept in the refrigerator for a few days or it can be deep frozen for later use.

Season the fish and cook it in a steamer, putting the salmon in first and adding the shellfish 2 to 3 minutes later. Remove and keep warm. Melt 1 oz/25 g of butter in a saucepan and saute the shallots in it without browning. Pour in the wine and stir to deglaze the pan, then boil until reduced by half its original volume. Gradually add the fish stock and boil again until reduced by half. Check the seasoning, then add the onions, samphire and salsify. Fold in the remaining butter (cut into pieces) and the chives. Arrange the seafood in serving bowls, then pour around the sauce. Sprinkle a little cayenne pepper on top and serve immediately.

GLENEAGLES HOTEL

A special taste of Oz . . .
Brook the Butler (above)
with Australian leading
lady Jill Perryman. (Right)
Vera and Gerald Weisfeld
with superstar Barry
Humphries - minus the
glitz of his famous alter ego
Dame Edna.

Risotto with Salt Cod and Squid Ink

"Squid ink can be bought in sachets from good fishmongers. Saffron can be substituted, although this results in a different dish. Salt cod is available in Spanish, Italian and Caribbean food shops."

3 tbsp olive oil

1 onion, finely chopped

1 garlic clove, crushed

2 tomatoes, chopped

1 tbsp tomato puree

$3^1/_2$ fl oz/100 ml dry white wine

$^1/_2$ pint/275 ml water

5 oz/150 g salt cod,
  soaked in water for 24 hours

7 fl oz/200 ml milk

$3^1/_2$ oz/100 g arborio rice

1 tsp squid ink

$^1/_2$ oz/15 g butter

Chopped fresh parsley, to garnish

METHOD

Heat 1 tablespoon of the olive oil in a pan, add the onion and cook over a moderate heat until golden. Add the garlic, tomatoes, tomato puree, wine and water and simmer gently for 20 minutes to make a very simple stock. Meanwhile, drain the salt cod and in another pan poach it in the milk until just tender (it should flake easily).

In a clean pan, sweat the rice in the remaining oil for about 2 minutes, until the outer husk has cracked, then add the hot stock, which should just cover the rice. Cook the rice slowly without stirring. After about 10 minutes, when the rice is half-cooked, add the squid ink. The rice will turn quite black. Continue to cook until the rice is al dente; it should take 20 minutes in all. Finally, stir in the butter. Flake the white salt cod over the black rice and serve garnished with parsley.

Serves: 2

BROOK THE BUTLER

Sheraton Perth Hotel, Western Australia

How to make the Perfect Pot of Tea

METHOD

Fill the kettle with fresh water. Rain water is very soft, perfect for brewing tea, whereas hard water makes the tea cloudy. Switch on the kettle and just before it boils, pour some of the hot water into your teapot, china or earthenware for preference. Heating the teapot ensures that the water stays at boiling point when it hits the tea, encouraging the correct opening of the leaves.

Place one heaped teaspoon of tea leaves per person, and one extra for the pot, into the warmed teapot. As the kettle boils, pour the water over the tea. Allow the tea to brew for five minutes. Give the pot a good stir and pour.

Gentleman's Gentleman

Tartare of Home-cured Salmon with Cucumber and Poached Quail's Eggs

1 1b/450 g fresh salmon fillet,
  with the skin on

$^1/_4$ cucumber, halved lengthways and
  thinly sliced

Olive oil, for brushing

1 tsp caviare

4 quail's eggs, boiled for 4 minutes

For the salt marinade

8 oz/225 g sea salt

6 juniper berries, lightly crushed

6 peppercorns, lightly crushed

1 bay leaf, torn into pieces

1 bunch of fresh thyme, roughly chopped

1 bunch of fresh coriander, roughly torn

For the olive oil marinade

8 fl oz/225 ml olive oil

2 garlic cloves, roughly chopped

2 shallots, roughly chopped

Juice of $^1/_2$ lemon

1 bay leaf

3 tbsp chopped fresh mixed herbs,
  such as dill, parsley and chervil

For the dressing

2 plum tomatoes, skinned and diced

2 tbsp sherry vinegar

Salt and freshly ground black pepper

A pinch of sugar

1 small garlic clove, crushed

2 tbsp water

$^1/_4$ pint/150 ml extra virgin oil

For the mayonnaise

1 egg yolk

1 tsp Dijon mustard

1 oz/25 g anchovy fillets, chopped

1 garlic clove, crushed to a paste

1 tbsp chopped fresh mixed herbs,
  such as chives and basil

1 tbsp sherry vinegar

Juice of $^1/_2$ lime

8 fl oz/225 ml Extra Virgin olive oil

Serves: 4

METHOD

For the salt marinade, mix together all the ingredients. Cover the salmon with it and marinate for 2 hours. Remove the fish from the marinade, washing off any clinging marinade ingredients, then mix together all the ingredients for the olive oil marinade, place the salmon in it and leave overnight. To make the dressing, blend together all the ingredients except the oil, then beat in the oil a little at a time. Pass through a fine sieve. To make the mayonnaise, blend together all the ingredients except the oil in a food processor, then beat in the oil drop by drop. Do not rush this process or it will separate.

Remove the salmon from the marinade, skin it and cut it into $^1/_4$ inch/5 mm cubes. Mix with 4 tablespoons of the mayonnaise (the rest will keep in the fridge for several days) to bind it together. Pack the mixture into four 3 inch/7.5 cm plain metal cutters placed in the middle of serving plates and chill until firm, about 2 minutes. Remove the cutters. (If you do not have 4 metal cutters, line 4 ramekins with cling film, fill with the salmon mixture and chill, then turn out on to serving plates). Brush the sliced cucumber with a little oil and cover each salmon round with overlapping slices, arranged in concentric circles. Place a little caviare in the middle of the cucumber and then place a quail's egg on top of each one. Top the quail's eggs with a little more caviare. Pour the dressing around the salmon tartare and serve.

IS-SOJJIED RESTAURANT

Marsaxlokk, Malta

$^1/_2$ *lemon*

4 lemon sole, weighing about
  1 lb/450 g in total, filleted and skinned

Salt and freshly ground black pepper

4 slices of smoked salmon

1 onion, finely chopped

1 tbsp fresh marjoram, chopped

1 tbsp fresh mint, chopped

$^1/_2$ *pint/275 ml fish stock (see page 266)*

4 cooked prawns in the shell (optional)

For the shrimp sauce

$^1/_2$ *oz/15 g butter*

$^1/_2$ *oz/15 g plain flour*

Salt and cayenne pepper

3 oz/75 g peeled shrimps

Serves: 4

Stuffed Fillet of Fish Ala Sojjied

METHOD

Squeeze the lemon half over the fish and season with salt and pepper. Place a slice of smoked salmon on each fillet. Mix together the onion and herbs and sprinkle on top of the smoked salmon. Roll up the fillets with the salmon and secure with a wooden cocktail stick. Place the fish in an ovenproof dish and pour over the stock. Bake in an oven preheated to 190C/375F/Gas Mark 5 for about 10 minutes, or until the fish is cooked. Remove the fish from the stock, cover and keep warm. Reserve the stock.

To make the sauce, melt the butter in a pan, stir in the flour and cook for a few minutes until foaming. Remove from the heat and whisk in the reserved stock. Return the pan to the heat and whisk constantly until the sauce boils and thickens. Simmer for 5 minutes, skimming off any impurities which rise to the surface. Check the seasoning and pass through a fine strainer, then stir in the shrimps. Arrange the fish on serving plates, pour over the sauce. Garnish with the prawns, if using.

RADISSON OBSERVATION CITY HOTEL

Chef Bert Lozey   *Perth, Western Australia*

Serves: 6   ## Scallop with Salsa

3 ripe tomatoes, skinned,
  deseeded and finely diced

1 red chilli, finely chopped

1 red onion, finely diced

4 tbsp balsamic vinegar

2 tbsp olive oil

1 bunch of fresh chives, finely chopped

Salt and freshly ground black pepper

2 tbsp fresh parsley, finely chopped

20 sprigs of fresh chervil or tarragon,
  finely chopped

10 slices of shredded white bread

1 garlic clove, finely diced

30 fresh scallops in their shells

METHOD

To make the salsa, mix together half the tomatoes with the chilli, onion, half the vinegar, the olive oil, a quarter of the chives and the seasoning. Divide between 6 small bowls and set aside. Mix together the remaining tomatoes and herbs with the breadcrumbs, garlic and seasoning, then set aside. Open the scallop shells with a small, sharp knife, remove the scallops and cut off the connecting muscle. Wash the scallops well, then place them in a bowl, toss them in the remaining vinegar and season. Discard the top half of the shells, clean the bottom halves and place the scallops back in them. Top with the breadcrumb mixture and bake in an oven preheated to 220C/425F/ Gas Mark 7 for 3 to 4 minutes, then brown under a hot grill, being careful not to overcook the scallops. Arrange the scallops, in their shells, on serving plates with the salsa in the middle.

Seafood Chowder

HAYMAN ISLAND RESORT

Great Barrier Reef, Australia

$^{1}/_{2}$ oz/15 g butter

1 onion, finely diced

1 leek, white part only, finely diced

1 celery stick, finely diced

2 garlic cloves, crushed

$^{1}/_{4}$ oz/7 g white peppercorns

2 bay leaves

4 fl oz/110 ml white wine

$1^{1}/_{2}$ pints/875 ml fish stock
  (see page 266)

$^{1}/_{2}$ bunch of fresh thyme

$^{1}/_{2}$ bunch of fresh dill

$^{1}/_{2}$ bunch of fresh chervil

$^{1}/_{2}$ pint/275 ml double cream

8 king prawns, peeled,
  heads removed, de-veined and diced

8 scallops, shelled, cleaned and diced

6 oz/175 g prepared squid

4 oz/110 g firm white fish fillets, diced

1 tsp fresh parsley, chopped

A squeeze of lemon juice

METHOD   **Serves: 4**

Melt the butter in a pan, add the onion, leek, celery and garlic and saute gently, without browning. Add the peppercorns, bay leaves and wine and simmer until most of the liquid has evaporated. Add the fish stock and the stalks from the thyme, dill and chervil. Simmer until the liquid is reduced by half its original volume. Strain through a fine sieve into a clean pan. Bring to the boil and add the cream, then simmer until the liquid is thick. Add the prawns, scallops, squid and white fish. Simmer for a few minutes until tender. Stir in the parsley, lemon juice and a teaspoon each of thyme, dill and chervil. Serve immediately.

Sole Jubilee

Chef Michel Bourdin   *London*

4 small Dover soles, heads and skin removed
  (ask you fishmonger to do this)
$1/_2$ pint/275 ml fish stock
3 fl oz/75 ml dry white wine or vermouth
Salt and freshly ground black pepper
8 oz/250 g puff pastry
1 egg, beaten with a little milk

For the stuffing
2 shallots, finely chopped
2 oz/50 g mixed wild mushrooms,
  finely chopped
  (Ceps, morels, chanterelles)
2 tbsp dry white wine or vermouth
4 tbsp double cream

For the sauce
$1/_4$ pint/150 ml double cream
2 tsp lemon juice
2 tbsp chopped fresh mixed herbs,
  such as chervil, parsley and tarragon

Serves: 2

"This recipe was created in 1977 to celebrate Queen Elizabeth II's Silver Jubilee."

METHOD

Put the Dover sole in a shallow pan with the stock and the wine or vermouth and poach gently for 10 minutes, turning the fish over halfway through. Carefully remove from the stock, draining well. Reserve the stock. Place the fish on a board, remove the fine side bones, separate the top fillets and remove. Carefully take out the main bone. To make the stuffing, put the shallots and mushrooms in a small pan with the wine or vermouth and 2 tablespoons of the stock in which the fish was poached. Simmer for 4 to 5 minutes, until all the liquid has evaporated, then add the double cream and boil rapidly until thickened. Place some stuffing in the centre of each of the 2 bottom fish fillets. Sandwich together with the separated top fillets, seasoning the fish as you do so. Roll out the puff pastry to a 16 inch/40 cm square and cut into quarters. Place each stuffed fish on a square of pastry. Brush the pastry edges with the beaten egg mixture. Cover the fish with the remaining pastry and trim into a fish shape, leaving a $1/_2$ inch/1 cm border of pastry round the fish. Press the edges together to seal, then place on a baking sheet, brush with more beaten egg and bake in an oven preheated to 200C/400F/Gas Mark 6 for 20 to 25 minutes, until the pastry is golden. Meanwhile, make the sauce. Reduce the remaining fish poaching liquid by half to about $1/_4$ pint/150 ml. Stir in the double cream and simmer gently for 10 minutes, until slightly thickened. Season with the lemon juice and salt and pepper then stir in the chopped herbs. Serve the fish accompanied by the sauce.

CARLTON INTER-CONTINENTAL HOTEL

M. Didier Boidin

Red Mullet Fillets

Cannes

4 red mullet, scaled and filleted

3$\frac{1}{2}$ fl oz/100 ml extra virgin olive oil

8 baby white onions, peeled

8 baby carrots, trimmed

8 baby turnips, trimmed

6 oz/175 fine asparagus, trimmed

4 baby artichokes, trimmed

Salt and freshly ground black pepper

Thyme, 2 bay leaves, for seasoning

4 fl oz/110 ml dry white wine

1 white summer truffle (optional)

3 oz/75 g butter, cut into small pieces

Fresh chopped basil

A squeeze of lemon juice

METHOD

Serves: 4

Heat the oil in a pan, then add the vegetables and cook gently until slightly browned. Add the salt, pepper, thyme and bay leaves. Cover the pan and cook for 3 to 4 minutes, then pour in the wine and simmer gently for approximately 10 minutes. Remove the vegetables from the pan with a slotted spoon and arrange on a serving platter. Place them in a very low oven to keep warm. Crush the truffle, if using, and add it to the juices in the pan. Bring to a steady boil and whisk in the butter, a few pieces at a time, until you have a smooth sauce. Continue to whisk until slightly thickened. Add salt and pepper, stir in the basil and lemon juice. Keep warm. Flash-fry the fish fillets on both sides and arrange on the bed of vegetables. Pour the sauce over the fish and vegetables and serve immediately.

Roasted Prawns with Coco Beans

HOTEL DE PARIS

Chef Alain Ducasse   *Monte Carlo*

4$\frac{1}{2}$ 1b/2 kg coco beans, husked

2$\frac{1}{2}$ 1b/1.1 kg onions, diced

3 oz/75 g garlic, finely chopped

3$\frac{1}{2}$ fl oz/100 ml olive oil

1 bouquet garni

15 oz/425 g fresh tomatoes, chopped

$\frac{3}{4}$ oz/20 g fine salt

$\frac{1}{2}$ oz/15 g black pepper

15 oz/425 g fresh tomatoes,
  peeled and deseeded

$\frac{1}{4}$ oz/10 g coarse salt

4 1b/1.75 kg large prawns

8 basil, 8 sage leaves

1 small parsley bag

2 oz/50 g pit black olives

3 tbsp Xeres vinegar

METHOD

In a large pan, cook the beans with the onions, garlic, 3 tbsp of the olive oil, the bouquet garni, the chopped tomatoes, salt and pepper, all covered with water. Put the peeled and deseeded tomatoes in the oven on an oiled baking sheet with a clove of garlic, a little olive oil and coarse salt. Cook for 4 hours at 80C/175F/Gas Mark $\frac{1}{4}$ to turn them into preserved tomatoes. Peel the prawns, leaving the tails on, and set aside. Fry the basil, sage and parsley and set aside. Drain the beans and put them in a saute pan with the preserved tomatoes, black olives, 1 tbsp of crushed parsley, olive oil and the vinegar. Warm the mixture lightly. Cook the prawns in a frying pan with a little oil. Arrange the beans on 4 plates with the prawns and fried herbs on top. Finish off with a sprinkling of freshly ground pepper and an olive oil thread.

Serves: 4

Marinated Jersey Vegetables

ANTON MOSIMANN

French chef and restaurateur
Mosimann's Club, London

3 medium peppers,
  1 red, 1 yellow and 1 green
1 green and 1 yellow courgette
1 medium aubergine
2 heads of chicory
8 shiitake mushrooms
4 red and 4 yellow cherry tomatoes
8 baby sweetcorn
Extra Virgin olive oil
Salt and freshly ground black pepper
$1/_2$ oz/15 g fresh rosemary and thyme,
  finely chopped
$1/_2$ oz/15 g fresh chervil,
  finely chopped
3 tbsp balsamic vinegar

METHOD

Cut the peppers in quarters lengthwise. Cut the courgettes and aubergine into $1/_2$ inch/1 cm slices lengthwise. Trim the chicory and cut it in half lengthwise. Grill or fry all the vegetables in about 3 tablespoons of olive oil until tender, then season to taste and add the rosemary and thyme. Transfer the mixture to a large shallow dish. Mix the chervil with the balsamic vinegar and 3 tablespoons of olive oil and pour this mixture over the vegetables in the dish. Serve warm.

Serves: 4

SHANGRI-LA HOTEL

Singapore

Fresh Goose Liver Pate Salad

METHOD

To make the vinaigrette, vigorously whisk together all the ingredients in a bowl. For the salad, wash and cut the mixed lettuce leaves, and dry on a kitchen towel. Place in a bowl, season and add the walnut vinaigrette. Toss well and place on a serving plate.

Pan fry the goose liver in a little heated oil until both sides are brown, but do not overcook. Remove from the heat, add the butter, Port and honey, ensuring the goose liver is well coated with the mixture. Place the liver on the tossed salad, and pour over the rest of the mixture. The dish is ready to serve.

Mixed fresh lettuce, for one person
  (Butter lettuce, red Frissee, Endive,
  Frissee, Red Chicory)
1 fl oz/25 ml walnut vinaigrette
3 oz/75 g fresh goose liver, sliced
Some good olive oil
$1/_2$ tsp butter
1 tbs Port wine
1 tsp honey
Salt and freshly ground pepper, to taste

For the walnut vinaigrette
2 fl oz/50 ml raspberry vinegar
4 fl oz/110 ml walnut oil
1 tsp French mustard
Salt and freshly ground pepper, to taste

Serves: 1

PALACE HOTEL

Chef Gaetano Ascione   *Bophuthatswana*

$^3/_4$ *oz/20 g butter*

1 sprig of rosemary

2 1b/900 g baking potatoes

$3^1/_2$ *oz/100 g Parmesan cheese,*
  freshly grated

2 eggs

8 oz/225 g plain flour

$3^1/_2$ *oz/100 g semolina*

Butter and freshly grated

Parmesan cheese, to serve

Serves: 4 to 6

*"You can serve
this with a
sauce instead
of cheese."*

Potato Gnocchi

METHOD

Melt the butter in a small pan, add the rosemary, then remove from the heat and leave to infuse. Bake the potatoes until tender in an oven preheated to 200C/400F/Gas Mark 6. When they are cool enough to handle, peel them and put them through a fine sieve, together with the cheese. Put the potato mixture on a work surface, make a well in the centre and add the eggs, flour, semolina and melted butter. Knead together for a few minutes until you have a soft, smooth, slightly delicate dough.

Divide the dough into 4 and form each piece into a long baton about $^3/_4$ inch/2 cm thick. Cut into $^5/_8$ inch/15 mm lengths, then roll them off the prongs of a fork, pressing gently with your finger to form a gnocchi shape (small dumplings).

Bring a large pan of salted water to the boil and add a few gnocchi. When they rise to the top, lift them out with a slotted spoon and keep them warm in a buttered serving dish while you cook the remaining gnocchi. Serve with butter and grated Parmesan cheese or with a sauce of your choice.

Summer Pasta

1 1b/450 g pasta

1 tbsp olive oil

2 tbsp garlic, chopped

1 bunch of fresh basil, chopped

4 large ripe tomatoes
  (preferably vine-ripened),
  skinned, deseeded and chopped

Salt and freshly ground black pepper

Freshly grated Parmesan cheese, to serve

Serves: 4

RITZ-CARLTON HOTEL

Sydney, Australia

METHOD

Cook the pasta in a large pan of boiling salted water until al dente. Meanwhile, heat the oil in a frying pan, throw in the garlic, half the basil and the tomatoes and saute briefly. Add the sauce, then serve sprinkled with lots of cheese and garnished with the remaining basil.

*"This is a wonderfully refreshing
summer pasta dish."*

THE MANDARIN

Singapore

1 roasting chicken, about 4lbs/1.8 kg

3 $\frac{1}{2}$ oz/90 g butter

1 tbs oil

2 onions, sliced

1 carrot, sliced

2 cloves of garlic, chopped

Bouquet garni (1 bay leaf,
  1 thyme sprig, 3 parsley sprigs)

$\frac{1}{2}$ pint/275 ml Riesling wine

1 tbs flour

8 oz/225 g button mushrooms

9 fl oz/250 ml double cream

Salt and freshly ground white pepper

Serves: 4

Coq au Riesling

METHOD

Quarter the chicken. Melt $\frac{2}{3}$ of the butter and all the oil in a large saucepan. Add the chicken and lightly brown all over. Add the onions, carrot, garlic, bouquet garni and flour. Mix well and cook for several minutes. Pour in the wine, bring to a boil, then reduce the heat. Cover and simmer for 35 minutes, or until the chicken is cooked.

Meanwhile, cut the mushroom stalks level with their caps and fry the heads over a low heat in the last of the butter.

When the chicken pieces are cooked, remove them to a serving platter and keep warm. Strain the cooking juices into another saucepan, add the double cream and over a high heat reduce the mixture to half its volume. Add the mushrooms and stir over a very low heat until the sauce begins to thicken. Season to taste. Spoon a little of the sauce over the chicken when serving, and surround the pieces with mushrooms. Serve the remaining sauce separately.

"This is a traditional recipe from Alsace in France. A special tip, serve with fresh noodles."

STEAK FORSYTH

(From the Wig & Pen Club, London)

METHOD

Grill one sirloin steak until almost cooked. Spread one side of the steak generously with mustard. Sprinkle on demerara sugar, completely covering the mustard. Return to the grill and cook until the sugar caramelizes. Serve immediately.

Serves: 1

Fatted Chicken from Bresse

> *"If wished,
> you may add
> 2 oz/50 g
> of truffles
> and foie-gras
> cut into cubes
> like chicken liver."*

Pig's bladder, soaked in water
  and seasoned with salt, vinegar
Fatted chicken from Bresse, about 4lbs/1.8 kg
8 good strips of truffle
White part of 1 leek
7 oz/200 g veal mousse
Butter, to sautee
2 tsp Madeira wine
Salt and freshly ground pepper, to taste
2 oz/50 g each of diced carrots, turnip and celery
2 oz/50 g petit pois
2 oz/50 g green beans, cut into thin strips
Approx. 8 ³/₄ pints/5 litres chicken stock

Serves: 4

METHOD

Carefully gut and clean the fowl. Bone it along its back, leaving in the wing and leg bones. Place under the skin the strips of truffle so that the fowl is garnished with them on the breast and wings. Place the leek in the chicken cavity.

In a pan, sautee all the other vegetables in butter until cooked. Season to taste, then mix with the veal mousse. Stuff the cavity with the mixture, around the leek which should be in the centre. Sew up the aperture then truss the bird to restore it to its original shape.

Turn the seasoned pig's bladder inside out and place the fowl inside, adding a pinch of salt, pepper and 2 tsp of wine. Close up the bladder, knotting the open end twice with a piece of string.

Place the bladder-covered fowl in a large cooking pot containing the chicken stock. This should have been previously prepared from the chicken giblets and fowl bones. Don't boil the fowl, but simmer in the stock for approximately 1 ¹/₂ hours.

Present the chicken on a plate, removing it from the bladder in front of the dinner guests before carving. Serve with its delicious stuffing, and vegetables of your choice.

NOTE: *To make the veal mousse, in a mixer blend 4 oz/110 g fillet mignon veal, seasoned with salt and pepper. Place the blended meat in a bowl, then chill by putting the bowl on ice. Using a spatula mix in 3 fl oz/75 ml double cream and adjust the seasoning.*

Chicken with Almond and Champagne Sauce

1 medium onion, very thinly sliced
2 garlic cloves, very thinly sliced
4 oz/110 g mushrooms, very thinly sliced
6 tbsp olive oil
1 small bunch of fresh thyme
1 small bunch of fresh parsley
1 tsp grainy mustard
Juice of $^1/_2$ lemon
4 oz/110 g flaked almonds, toasted
$^1/_2$ bottle of champagne
6 skinless, boneless chicken breasts
Salt and freshly ground pepper

For the stock
$1^1/_2$ lb/675 g chicken pieces
2 medium carrots, chopped
1 large onion, chopped
1 celery stick, chopped
1 medium potato, chopped
$3^1/_2$ pints/2 litres water
Salt
Freshly ground black pepper

Serves: 6

"This is a superb dish, with a light , distinctive flavour which will grace any occasion."

METHOD

To make the stock, put all the ingredients in a large pan, season, and slowly bring to the boil, then simmer for about $1^1/_2$ hours, until reduced to half its original volume. Strain and set aside.

Saute the onion, garlic and mushrooms in 2 tablespoons of the oil until brown. Finely chop half the thyme and parsley and add to the pan with the mustard, lemon juice, almonds, champagne and 1 pint/ 575 ml of the stock. Simmer for 20 minutes, or until the mixture is reduced by half, then puree in a blender.

Season the chicken breasts with salt, pepper and some of the remaining thyme and parsley. Heat the remaining oil in a frying pan and saute the chicken until brown. Transfer the chicken breasts to an ovenproof casserole dish, pour over the sauce and bake in an oven preheated to 190C/375F/Gas Mark 5 for 15 minutes, or until the chicken is completely cooked. Sprinkle with the remaining parsley and garnish with sprigs of thyme on the side

MARINA MANDARIN HOTEL

Singapore

Spiced Chicken in Coconut Milk

2 shallots, chopped

2 garlic cloves, chopped

1 inch/2.5 cm piece of lemongrass, chopped

3 tbsp red turmeric

1 tbsp fresh chilli, chopped

1 tbsp chilli paste (harissa)

1 inch/2.5 cm piece of fresh ginger root, chopped

4 tbsp corn oil

4 skinless, boneless chicken breasts, cut in half

1 inch/2.5 cm cube of tamarind paste

1 kaffir lime leaf

14 fl oz/400 ml coconut milk

METHOD

In a food processor, blend the shallots, garlic, lemongrass, turmeric, chilli, chilli paste and ginger to a smooth paste and set aside. Heat the corn oil in a large pan, add the prepared spice paste and stir-fry for $^1/_2$ minute. Add the chicken pieces and stir-fry for about 15 minutes, until the chicken is tender. Add the tamarind paste, lime leaf and coconut milk and simmer until the sauce has thickened, then take out the lime leaf. Serve hot.

Serves: 4

Devil Curry

THE ORIENTAL HOTEL

Singapore

20 small shallots, chopped

4 slices of galungal (Siamese ginger), chopped

1 inch/2.5 cm piece of fresh ginger root, chopped

20 dried chillies or 2 tbsp chilli powder

3 tbsp oil

1 roasted chicken, cut into pieces

10 oz/275 g roast pork, cut into cubes

3 Chinese sausages, each cut into 3

$^1/_2$ small cabbage, shredded

1 cucumber, deseeded and cut into broad strips

$^1/_2$ tbsp mustard powder

1 tsp sugar

3 tbsp rice wine (or white wine) vinegar

3 potatoes, boiled and sliced

Salt

METHOD

Put the shallots, galungal, ginger and chillies or chilli powder in a food processor and process until very finely chopped. Heat the oil in a large pan or wok and fry the prepared spice paste for a few minutes. Add the chicken and any juices from it, together with the roast pork, sausages, cabbage and cucumber. Stir-fry over a moderately high heat for 3 to 4 minutes until the vegetables are half-cooked. Dissolve the mustard and sugar in the vinegar and add to the pan, then stir in the potatoes and salt to taste. To make the garnish, heat the oil in a large frying pan and stir-fry the onions and ginger until brown and crisp. Sprinkle over the curry along with the chillies and serve with boiled rice

For the garnish

3 tbsp oil

2 large onions, thinly sliced

1 inch/2.5 cm piece of fresh ginger root, cut into slivers

2 red chillies, deseeded and thinly sliced

Serves: 8

Calf's Liver and Onions
Chef Lugio Zanon

"There is only one Harry's Bar. Located on Venice's Calle Vallaresso, near the Piazza San Marco, this legendary restaurant has been, for five decades, the meeting place for artists, writers, royalty, maestros, divas, celebrities, the very rich and lots of ordinary . . . but very wise . . . Americans and Europeans. Everyone from the Windsors and the Onassises and the Burtons to Cole Porter, Ernest Hemingway and Joan Crawford has come here for great food, fine drinks and the incomparable ambience."

2 lb/900 g calf's liver, sliced thinly
6 tbsp olive oil
3 large onions, sliced thinly
Salt and freshly ground black pepper
3 tbsp butter, unsalted
3 tbsp flat leaf parsley, finely chopped

Serves:4

METHOD

Have the butcher trim the liver for you, removing the surface tissue and any large gristly tubes. Cut the liver into 4 pieces and then with a razor sharp knife slice it really thinly.

Heat 4 tbsp of the oil in your largest skillet over a medium heat, then add the onions and cook, stirring frequently, until they are limp and nicely browned, about 25 minutes. Remove the onions with a slotted spoon and set aside.

Increase the heat to high and add the rest of the oil. When the oil is sizzling hot, add the liver and cook until it loses its raw colour and becomes nearly crisp, no longer than 5 minutes, tossing it constantly with a spatula. Add a large pinch of salt and pepper and add the onions to the skillet. Mix the liver and onions vigorously and allow them to cook together for a couple of minutes. Transfer the liver and onions to a serving dish and keep warm.

Add the butter to the skillet and melt it, scraping up any browned bits from the bottom of the pan. Take the pan off the heat and stir in the parsley. Spoon the sauce over the liver. Serve immediately.

Lamb Cutlets
a la Reforme

12 small lamb cutlets (chops), about 1¹/₂ lb/675 g

Salt and freshly ground black pepper

2 oz/50 g butter, clarified

5 oz/150 g breadcrumbs

5 oz/150 g raw ham, chopped

3 oz/75 g hard-boiled egg white, chopped

Chopped fresh parsley, to decorate

Serves: 4

For the mirepoix of vegetables

3 oz/75 g butter

1 oz/25 g carrots, finely chopped

1 oz/25 g shallots, finely chopped

¹/₄ oz/7 g garlic, finely chopped

1 bay leaf

A dash of powdered thyme

3 tbsp white wine vinegar

¹/₄ pint/150 ml dry white wine

¹/₂ pint/275 ml demi-glace

1 oz/25 g peppercorns

4 oz/110 g straw mushrooms, sliced

2 oz/50 g ox tongue, cut into fine strips

2 oz/50 g gherkins, cut into fine strips

METHOD

Season the cutlets and dip them in clarified butter, then coat them in a mixture of breadcrumbs and raw ham. Saute the cutlets in a large pan with clarified butter for 2 to 3 minutes each side, then set aside and keep warm.

Saute the mirepoix of vegetables in butter, along with the garlic, bay leaf and thyme, then deglace the pan with wine and vinegar. Add the peppercorns and reduce for 2 minutes. Add the demi-glace and cook for another 3 minutes.

Remove from the heat and pour the sauce through a sieve, then add the mushrooms, ox tongue and gherkins. Place the cutlets in an oval serving dish and pour over the sauce with the garniture on top. Add the egg white and decorate with chopped parsley.

"This recipe for a traditional English dish brings out the flavour of the meat and is well complemented by the vegetables."

Cappuccino Brulee

Glasgow, Scotland
Proprietor Ken McCulloch

18 fl oz/500 ml double cream
1 vanilla pod
8 egg yolks
4 oz/110 g caster sugar
3 fl oz/75 ml strong espresso coffee
$^{1}/_{4}$ pint/150 ml whipping cream
Icing sugar, to taste

Serves: 6 to 8

METHOD

Put the double cream in a saucepan with the vanilla pod, bring slowly to the boil and then set aside. Whisk the egg yolks and sugar together in a bowl set over a pan of hot, but not boiling, water until the mixture is very thick, pale and creamy. Fold in the cream and vanilla pod, together with the coffee. Stir very gently over the heat for 2 minutes; the mixture should be thick enough to coat the back of a spoon. Pour it into coffee cups or large ramekins, leave to cool, then put them in the fridge for 2 to 3 hours. Skim off the bubbles that rise to the top, then place the coffee cups or ramekins in an ovenproof dish, pour in water to come half way up the sides of the cups and bake in an oven preheated to 170C/325F/Gas Mark 3 for 50 to 60 minutes, until firm to the touch. Leave to cool for 4 hours. Before serving, whip the cream and sweeten to taste with icing sugar. Spoon it over the cappuccino cups or ramekins.

THE DORCHESTER HOTEL

Chef Willi Elsener   *London*

Fresh Apple Compote

Serves: 2

1 oz/25 g butter
3 apples, peeled, cored and cut into
   1 inch/2.5 cm cubes
$3^{1}/_{2}$ fl oz/90 ml white wine
A pinch of cinnamon
A piece of lemongrass,
   1 inch/2.5 cm long
1 oz/25 g caster sugar
4 fl oz/110 ml single cream
A dash of brandy

METHOD

Heat the butter in a pan, add the apples and cook gently for 1 minute without colouring. Add the white wine, cinnamon and lemongrass, cover and cook over a medium heat until the apples are tender. Add the sugar and cream and bring to the boil. Remove the lemongrass and puree the mixture in a blender or food processor. Return to the pan and bring back to the boil. Stir in the brandy and serve hot.

RAYMOND BLANC

French chef
TV personality and proprietor of Le Manoir aux Quat' Saisons Great Milton, Oxford

Tartes Fines aux Pommes

14 oz/400 g puff pastry, made with butter

1 egg, beaten

For the topping
6 Granny Smith apples, peeled cored and quartered

3¹/₂ oz/90 g butter, unsalted

1 tsp lemon juice

3 tbsp caster sugar

1 tbsp Calvados (optional)

Serves: 4

"This is one of the best apple tarts I know. The delicious texture and taste of the soft caramelized apple with the thin crust of puff pastry make this simple dessert a very special one. I find Granny Smith apples to be the best type for this dish. You could replace them with ripe William or Comice pears, in which case, omit the Calvados."

METHOD

Allow the pastry to come to room temperature, then roll it out on a lightly floured work surface until it is no more than 1/16 inch/1 mm thick. Place the pastry on a floured tray and refrigerate for 10 minutes, then remove from the refrigerator. With an upturned 5 inch/13 cm plate, cut out 4 rounds. Place these on a dampened 12 x 16 inches/30 x 40 cm baking sheet and place in the fridge. Press the pastry trimmings together and roll out into a strip 12 inch/30 cm long and ¹/₄ inch/5 mm thick. Place the strip in the freezer for 10 minutes so that the pastry firms up and will be easy to cut. Remove after chilling and cut it into 4 bands, each 12 inches/ 30 cm long. Remove the pastry rounds from the fridge, moisten the edges with a little egg and stick the bands of pastry around each. Reserve.

Preheat the oven to 230C/450F/Gas Mark 8. Cut the quartered apples into segments about ¹/₄ inch/5 mm thick. Place them in 2 concentric circles, overlapping, inside the banded rim of the pastry rounds.

Melt the butter, add the lemon juice, 2 tablespoons of sugar and the Calvados, if using, then brush all over the apples to glaze (you won't use all of this mixture). Bake the tarts in the oven for 20 to 25 minutes. Remove, brush with the remaining butter mixture and sprinkle with the remaining sugar, then carefully slide on to plates and serve.

Perth, Western Australia

Auntie Vera's Irish Soda Bread

*14 oz/400 g self-raising flour,
  white or wholemeal*

$^1/_2$ tsp salt

$^1/_2$ tsp bicarbonate of soda

1 oz/25 g butter or margarine

$^1/_2$ pint/275 ml skimmed milk

Serves: 6 to 8

METHOD

Mix all the dry ingredients together in a bowl and rub in the butter or margarine. Add the milk and mix to a wet dough. Turn onto a floured board and shape into a round. Transfer to a greased baking sheet, cut a large cross on the top and bake in an oven preheated to 200°C/400°F/ Gas Mark 6 for 40 to 45 minutes, until the loaf is well risen and brown and sounds hollow when tapped underneath. Cool on a wire rack.

TABLE SETTING: VERSACE

Theme Menus

T HE BEST MEALS PROVIDE MORE THAN JUST GOOD FOOD. They provide fellowship and a sense of occasion. In their own way they are a little bit of theatre. How the meal is presented has a great deal to do with the sense of well-being it induces in the guests. It is the reason that hosts and hostesses go to such lengths to ensure that everything, from the gleaming cutlery and sparkling wine glasses to the beautifully served dishes is just right.

In this Section we suggest another element of theatre for your dinner party, theme menus. Drawing recipes from the celebrity dishes it is possible, with a little imagination, to create for your guests special nights commemorating special occasions such as important national anniversaries or major sporting or showbusiness events. The choice of theme is very much one of personal taste, but one thing is certain: it will make your special night go with extra zing. To help you on your way, over-leaf are a number of theme menus you might consider.

Her Majesty The Queen's Royal Birthday
17h June

Watercress Soup
(Princess Diana)

Circassian Chicken
(Prince Sadruddin Aga Khan)
with
Wild Rice & Vegetables

Chocolate Roulade

with
Hokie-Pokie Filling
(Duchess of York)

Coffee & Mints

Recipes for the above menu are in the Royalty Section: Watercress Soup, page 27; Circassian Chicken, page 35; Chocolate Roulade with Hokie-Pokie Filling, page 29.

Opening of Parliament

Onion Soup
(John Major, MP)

Tuna Fish Pie
(Paddy Ashdown, MP)

Macaroons
(Lord Callaghan)

House of Commons Whisky
&
Cheeseboard

Recipes for the above menu are in the Church & State Section: Onion Soup, page 46; Tuna Fish Pie, page 53;Macaroons, page 67.

St Andrew's Day
30th November

Cullen Skink
(Alex Salmond, MP)

Chicken Stuffed with Haggis
(Jimmy Logan)

Clootie Dumpling
(Hugh and Jean Adam)

Whisky & Oatcakes

Recipes for the above menu are in the Church & State and Scotland sections: Cullen Skink, page 46; Chicken Stuffed with Haggis, page 143; Clootie Dumpling, page 149.

Oscar Night

Walnut & Cucumber Soup
(Jenny Agutter)

Chicken Vindaloo
(Sir Anthony Hopkins)
with
Spiced Basmati Rice
(Julie Christie)

Creamy Cheese Cake
(Tom Hanks)

Bloody Mary
(Michael Grade)

Recipes for the above menu are in the World Showbusiness Section: Walnut and Cucumber Soup, page 164; Chicken Vindaloo, page 185; Spiced Basmati Rice, page 180; Creamy Cheesecake, page 188; Bloody Mary, page 189.

The British Open

Guacamole Dip

with

Tortilla Chips

(Jack Nicklaus)

Fresh Tagliatelle

with

Bacon & Pesto

(Archie McPherson)

Banana Raisin Ring

(Nick Faldo)

Brandy & Cigars

Recipes for the above menu are in the Sporting Personalities and Scotland sections: Guacamole Dip with Tortilla Chips, page 243; Fresh Tagliatelle with Bacon and Pesto, page 137; Banana Raisin Ring, page 256.

International Women's Day
8th March

Hot Avocado Parcels
(Honor Blackman)

Pasta
with
Pork & Basil
(Lady Thatcher)
with
Susan's Salad
(Susan Hampshire)

Lemon Syllabub
(Mrs Arline Woutersz)

Recipes for the above menu are in the World Showbusiness, Church & State and Business Sections:Hot Potato Parcels, page 169; Pasta with Pork and Basil, page 57; Susan's Salad, page 166: Lemon Syllabub, page 126.

Eurovision Song Contest

Baked Potato

with

Avocado & Broccoli

(Lulu)

Chicken & Asparagus Casserole

(Terry Wogan)

Transkei Mud

(Sir Cliff Richard)

Liqueurs & Coffee

Recipes for the above menu are in the A Taste of Music and TV and Stage Sections: Baked Potato with Avocado and Broccoli, page 215; Chicken and Asparagus Casserole, page 200; Transkei Mud, page 223.

St Patrick's Day Dinner
17th March

Wild Irish Nettle Soup
(Ashford Castle Hotel)

Glens of Antrim Irish Stew
(Liam Neeson)
with
Irish Colcannon
(Helen Mirren)

World's Finest Chocolate Gateau
with
Double Cream
(Michael J. Sullivan)

Irish Coffee

Recipes for the above menu are in the Grand Hotels and Restaurants, International Showbusiness and US Politics Sections: Wild Irish Nettle Soup, page 260; Glens of Antrim Irish Stew, page 187; Irish Colcannon, page 175; World's Finest Chocolate Gateau, page 104.

The American Superbowl

A NEW KIND OF MIDNIGHT "GOURMET" IS EMERGING IN BRITAIN, the American football addict. The biggest day in the calendar is the American Superbowl where the titans of the turf compete in a play-off for the supreme sporting prize. To the uninitiated it's a puzzling four-hour TV spectacle with innumerable interruptions and time-outs. Believe it or not, tens of thousands of otherwise sane sports fans sit up through the night in Britain to watch the drama unfold. The long pauses in the action on the field afford plenty of opportunities for the armchair enthusiasts to take a little sustenance. In fact it tends to be a four-hour munch-in. So here are a few suggestions for the big night - while the rest of us are sensibly fast asleep. These can be served with a selection of cold drinks and milk shakes.

New York Diner French Toast
(Robbie Coltrane)

Sugared Bacon
(Arnold Palmer)

Mount Diablo Dip
(Stephen Merrill)
Chip Dip
(E Benjamin Nelson)
with
A selection of chopped vegetables and Tortilla chips

Chilli
(Johhny Cash)

Chocolate Pecan Cookies
(David Beasley)
Indiana Mint Brownies
(Evan Bayh)
Mississippi Mud Cake
(Kirk Fordice)

Recipes for the above menu are in the US Politics, TV and Stage, Sports and A Taste of Music Sections: New York Diner Toast, page 192; Sugared Bacon, page 243; Diablo Dip, page 77; Chip Dip, page 74; Chilli, page 222; Chocolate Pecan Cookies, page 100; Indiana Mint Brownies, page 95; Mississippi Mud Cake, page 98.

Contributors' Index

A

B

D

E

F

G

H

I

J

K

L

M

N

O

P

Q

R

S

SHIELDS, BROOKE - Vegetable health soup, 163
SIM, ANDREW - Haddy Monte Carlo, 153
SMILLIE, CAROLE - Mum's bread and butter pudding, 208
SMITH, ELAINE - Tropical chicken kebabs, 202
SMITH, JOHN - Poached salmon, 50
SMITH, WALTER - Penne Arrabiatta, 248
STATT, DEREK - Tuna noodle casserole, 112
STEWART, ALLAN - Pasta Stewartoto, 199
STEWART, JACKIE - Deep fried pork balls, 250
STEWART, ROD - Roast chicken, 220
STORRIE, MAY & DONALD - Chicken in cider, 116
SULLIVAN, MICHAEL - World's finest chocolate gateau, 104
SUNDQUIST, DON - Poppy seed chicken casserole, 84
SYMINGTON, FIFE - Turkey sopa, 86

T

TAYLOR, ELIZABETH - Spicy chicken, 182
THATCHER, LADY MARGARET - Pasta with pork and basil, 57
THOMPSON, TOMMY - Broccoli and cheese quiche, 75
TOPOL - Gefilteh fish, 175
TRUMP, DONALD - Manhattan clam chowder, 112
TUCKER, JIM GUY - Chocolate soured cream cake, 96

V

VALENTINO - Risotto primavera, 235
VALLANCE,
  SIR IAN & LADY - Prawns with mushrooms, 114
VOINOVICH, GEORGE - Pork chops with apples, 87
VERSACE, GIANNI - Pasta with artichokes, 234
VICTORIA, LADY WHITE - Carrot souffle, 36

W

WAIHEE, JOHN - Ono banana bread, 103
WALTERS, BARBARA - Mother's stuffed cabbage rolls, 204

WALTERS, DAVID - Marinated chicken breasts, 85
WATERSTONE, TIM - Bacon risotto, 111
WATT, IRENE - Cream of Christmas soup, 151
WEBBER, SIR ANDREW LLOYD - Potted shrimps, 215
WEINSTOCK, LORD - Chicken soup, 108
WEISFELD, VERA - African stew, 154
WELD, BILL -Eggs a la Bill, 76
WHITE, LORD - Steak and kidney pie, 41
WHITESON, DR ADRIAN & MYRNA - Honey cake, 157
WHITMAN, CHRISTINE TODD - Raspberry chicken, 84
WIG & PEN CLUB - Steak Forsyth, 277
WILMOT, GARY - Ginger surprise, 207
WILSON, PETE - Barbecued chicken, 85
WILSON, RICHARD, Cullen Skink, 193
WINNER, MICHAEL - Scrambled eggs, 171
WOGAN, TERRY - Chicken and asparagus casserole, 200
WOLFSON, LESLIE & ALMA - Heavenly chicken, 140
WOOD, PETER - Fettucini al filetto, 120
WOUTERSZ, ARLINE - Lemon syllabub, 126

Y

YORK, SUSANNAH - Pasta Cosa Nostra, 179
YOUNG, JIMMY - Alicia's crunchy peach crumble, 205
YOUNGER, LORD GEORGE - Apricot and orange mousse, 122

Dishes

Vegetables

Fish & Seafood

Chicken and other Fowl

Baking Miscellany

Conversion Charts

Metric and imperial measures do not convert exactly to easy to manage quantities, so recipe books round up or down conversions. To maintain correct proportions of ingredients, we advise using either the metric system or imperial throughout a recipe. Don't mix them. Below are the conversion charts used in this book:

WEIGHT

Ounces	Grams (Approx)
1	25
2	50
3	75
4	110
5	150
6	175
7	200
8	225
9	250
10	275
11	300
12	350
13	375
14	400
15	425
16	450

LIQUID

Fluid Ounces		Millilitres (Approx)
	1	25
	2	50
	3	75
	4	110
	5	150
	6	175
	7	200
	8	225
	9	250
($^1/_2$ pint)	10	275
	11	300
	12	350
	13	375
	14	400
	15	425
	16	450
	17	475
	18	500
	19	550
(1 pint)	20	575

OVEN TEMPERATURES

Fahrenheit	225	250	275	300	325	350	375	400	425	450	475
Centigrade	110	130	140	150	170	180	190	200	220	230	240
Gas Mark	$^1/_4$	$^1/_2$	1	2	3	4	5	6	7	8	9

Fame . . .

BEN KINGSLEY

BOB HOSKINS

Feasting . . .

Forgotten . . ?

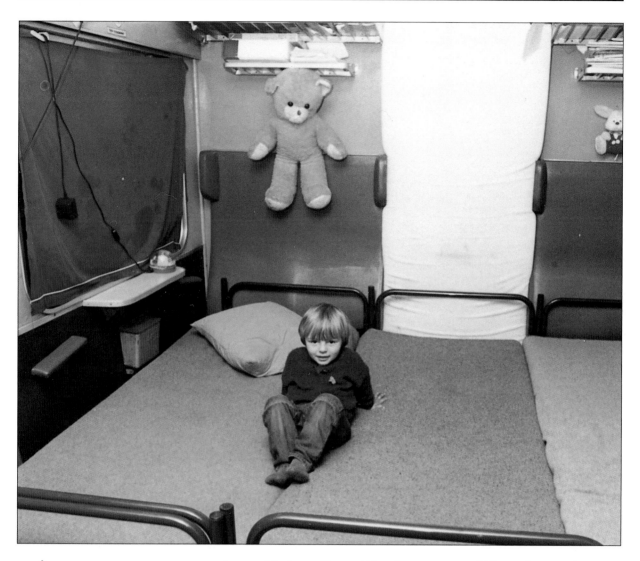

ALL HE OWNS IN THE WORLD is a teddy bear. Doesn't he deserve more? If you have enjoyed this book, why not buy another copy for a friend? Every penny the Weisfeld Foundation receives from book sales goes to help children and others in need secure happier and more fulfilling lives.

Order your copies direct from:

Recipes for Life, The Weisfeld Foundation, 21 Candleriggs, Glasgow G1 1LD Scotland.

● *£19.99, plus £1.50 packaging and postage.*

Kitchen Notes

Kitchen Notes

Kitchen Notes